H. M. Feldman

April, 1967

CROSSCURRENTS *Modern Critiques*

CROSSCURRENTS *Modern Critiques*
Harry T. Moore, *General Editor*

John J. Enck

Wallace Stevens

IMAGES AND JUDGMENTS

WITH A PREFACE BY
Harry T. Moore

Carbondale

SOUTHERN ILLINOIS UNIVERSITY PRESS

To My Mother

Copyright © 1964 by Southern Illinois University Press
All rights reserved
Library of Congress Catalog Card Number 64–11169
Printed in the United States of America
Designed by Andor Braun

JOHN J. ENCK POINTS OUT, in the pages which follow, that in the little we know of Wallace Stevens' life, one fact invariably conditions a reader's response to his poetry: Stevens was vice president of a Hartford insurance company. I can't find any reference to this in Yeats, who might have found it an adaptation of the anti-self. Stevens himself tried to play down his "double life" and once said, "I prefer to think I'm just a man, not a poet part time, businessman the rest." Apparently he succeeded in keeping his two worlds separate, for he didn't mix his poetic friends with his business friends; it seems that the latter knew very little about Stevens' literary career, or at least didn't realize how seriously he was taken in his other world. Such matters will certainly be cleared up in the critical biography on which Samuel French Morse has been working for some years; Mr. Morse knew Stevens and his family and has access to the necessary papers. There will probably be no earth-shaking revelations, but Mr. Morse will undoubtedly define the boundaries between Stevens' two lives.

Just now, it is amusing to note how smoothly Stevens' political ideas fitted in with those of the stereotype of a high-ranking executive. William York Tindall tells us that "Stevens was a Republican, a Taft Republican, who thought Eisenhower a dangerous radical." But if there was a split between Stevens the businessman and Stevens the avant-garde poet (or just being a poet at all), it didn't

seem to pull him apart. The pictures of him in his seven-
ties show a healthy-looking individual. He went on working with the insurance company beyond retirement age
until, in 1955, he died at seventy-five. He left behind him
an impressive body of poetry, as the present book amply
demonstrates.

Mr. Enck is right in saying that Stevens' "renown
derives not from his whole output but random segments."
The reason for this is that Stevens is copiously antholo-
gized: every reader of modern poetry is familiar with
"Sunday Morning," "Peter Quince at the Clavier," and
several other pieces which invariably attract editors of
collections. But those poems are at the top of modern
literature, and an editor could hardly omit them. Ideally,
however, readers interested in the subject should be familiar with two books published by Knopf: The Collected
Poems of Wallace Stevens (1955), and Opus Posthumous
(1957), the latter a collection by Samuel French Morse,
including a number of poems either omitted from the
Collected edition or never previously published, as well as
some plays and prose commentaries. For those who wish
to go still further, another book also on the Knopf list
will prove useful: The Necessary Angel: Essays on Reality
and the Imagination (1951).

Besides the double life of Stevens, one other biographical fact seems to me to stand out. As Mr. Tindall notes,
"To remain in America is what one expects of an American poet; but it may seem strange that one who was also
the poet of lions in Sweden never visited Europe." Strange
indeed, one of the strangest things in modern literature.
Unlike Franz Kafka turning out a novel about an unreal
America, Stevens often wrote of what seems to be a
Europe very real both in spirit and decoration. American
as Stevens' vision might have been, it was conditioned by
European ideas and images; yet it is remarkable that he
never saw Europe itself, never felt the place as it can be
felt only in its countryside, streets, and mountains. Stevens
in his time made many statements about what we speak
of as reality, one of them appropriate in the light of the

foregoing; in one of his notebooks, quoted by Mr. Morse in Opus Posthumous, Stevens said that "the thing that is incessantly overlooked" is "the artist, the presence of the determining personality. Without that reality no amount of other things matters much." And among the "Adagia" aphorisms, also in Opus Posthumous, Stevens noted: "Realism is a corruption of reality."

One of the ways in which Europe penetrated his consciousness was through the painting of our time, whose techniques seem to have much in common with his poetry. In both verse and prose, Stevens frequently refers to modern painters, from Cézanne on. Mr. Enck, in the last chapter of the present book, refers to the similarities between the poetry of Stevens and the paintings of Paul Klee, as noted by Clement Greenberg and other critics. "Drawing analogies between the arts still proves hazardous," Mr. Enck says; "the measure, at best, remains subjective; it quickly reaches limits beyond which speculation sounds like nonsense or improvisation." This is a twentieth-century variation of an attitude often attributed to Lessing; yet, as Jean Hagstrum has pointed out in The Sister Arts (1958), "it is possible to read the Laokoön as an attack upon the abuses of pictorialism that nevertheless manages to recognize its legitimate values." Mr. Enck points out that, although Stevens was fascinated by the subject, "his essay 'The Relationship between Poetry and Painting' establishes only tangential bonds." Mr. Enck admits, however, that "for incidental insights a comparison might have a value." He himself, in his fourth chapter, says of Stevens' later poems: "One might compare them with Klee's last canvases, such as Paukenspieler, where a slowly evolved technique revels in a strength, indeed brutality, hitherto unavailable." Likewise, in his first chapter, Mr. Enck makes an explicit comparison when he speaks of some of Stevens' stanzas jangling "in overtly clipped accents, like Klee's painting Die Zwitscherma-schine." The jangle and the clipped quality, as well as ellipsis, intense image, and zigzag of color in Stevens' poems all suggest modern painting. Consider the opening lines of one of Stevens' greatest achievements, which is also one of the greatest poetic achievements of our time, "Sunday Morning":

> Complacencies of the peignoir, and late
> Coffee and oranges in a sunny chair,
> And the green freedom of a cockatoo
> Upon a rug mingle to dissipate
> The holy hush of ancient sacrifice. . . .

Does not this poem of 1923 resemble some of the paintings of the earlier Fauviste movement, particularly of Matisse? Framed between the first and last phrase here, from Complacencies to sacrifice, with the wonderful contrast of those phrases and even of the two key words quoted, we have the sunshine on a chair, color unknown, and on coffee and oranges and, in that adroit combination of abstract and concrete, on "the green freedom of a cockatoo." It looks like Matisse, or the German, Macke, or Stevens' admired Dufy. But, in the way poetry can, the piece moves on to become one of the finest modern dramatized discussions of religion. From its striking pictorial setting, the poem draws upon other energies of the medium, including of course its blank-verse cadences, at once conversational and exalted.

"Sunday Morning" is both European and American, and part of its European tinge comes from the correspondence of the poem to modern European art. In Samuel French Morse's essay on Stevens, "The Native Element," he quotes Stevens' comments on a Tal Coat painting and explains that it was sent to the poet by his Paris bookseller, who doubled as a purchaser of modern paintings for him. And yet Stevens never got to Paris!

In the present book, Mr. Enck at one point compares the reactions of Wallace Stevens and Henry James to the famous equestrian statue of Colleoni, by Verrocchio, and makes an interesting assessment of their responses. He notes, after accounting for the differences in style, that Stevens and James both feel the force of the statue. James's evocation of the Colleoni provides an important

moment in The Aspern Papers, when sight of the equestrian statue motivates the literary condottiere into action;
Stevens' description is from an essay in The Necessary
Angel. James of course was well acquainted with Venice
and with that statue rising near the Church of S. Giovanni
e Paolo; Stevens could only have seen a picture of the
Verrocchio, or perhaps a life-size replica such as the one
that is, or at least used to be, in the Art Institute of
Chicago. Yet Stevens, in the passage Mr. Enck quotes,
writes of the statue with authority, as if he knew the
original. That he was able to do this helps provide one
explanation of his power: his ability to assimilate so much
and to make so much of what he took seem indelibly his
own.

What Mr. Enck calls the "invented world" of Wallace
Stevens he investigates faithfully and valuably. As an opponent of the fragmentary approach necessitated by anthologies, Mr. Enck works inward from without, gradually
putting his conception of Stevens together and at the same
time providing us with a coherent account of the man's
writings. He has given Stevens studies an important
impetus.

                              HARRY T. MOORE
Southern Illinois University
October 12, 1963

ACKNOWLEDGMENTS

AN INITIAL NOTE about the origins of this book may help explain the acknowledgments. Twenty years ago, an undergraduate and about to be drafted into the army, I bought the four volumes which Stevens had published to that time and read them as preferable to assignments or war, neither of which could I quite ignore. Since then, returning to his poems unofficially has continued to give me more pleasure than that provided by any contemporary writer. Inevitably, no commentary on him struck me as entirely satisfactory, so I began noting my responses: the manuscript grew haphazardly. Believing that systematic attempts to extract a rigorous philosophy out of his poems or, more damaging, to press a thesis down upon them guarantee misunderstandings, I favored from the outset a loosely chronological arrangement which lets points emerge casually. In the conclusion, a bit against my better judgment, I set forth a general statement but do not pretend that it achieves completeness. If my chapters succeed at all, they will say a few first but no final words.

With so informal a method I must along the way have picked up others' concepts, which I have come to consider my own. While preparing this version, I reviewed or dutifully consulted most criticism about him. One reader has described my attitude toward these pieces as uncharitable, a term I object to as unduly harsh. Trying to arrive at a statement about many of his topics does demand the greatest ingenuity from anyone, although the effort in the very process produces its unique, generous rewards. I sometimes quote others to concede that alternate interpretations have their advocates; toward some of these I admit a labile impatience. (Here I should mention specifically an article with which I agree: Robert W. Buttel, "Wallace Stevens at Harvard: Some Origins of His Theme and Style," *ELH*, XIX [March, 1962], 90–119; I had gone through Stevens' collegiate work and arrived independently at the conclusions which occur throughout these pages. Obviously, at points I echo his findings.) Because full bibliographies of both Stevens' own publications and the opinions about them have appeared, I saw no reason to tack on an edited version. Having persisted in a somewhat unprofessional approach, I shirked no details for the accuracy and the thoroughness which research requires.

Some specific debts to individuals happily remain with me. Since the first time I mentioned writing on this topic, Harry Levin, as before, has offered various kinds of encouragement. Jonas A. Barish read some chapters in a rough draft, but whatever appears in the final one cannot be blamed on him. Among colleagues at the University of Wisconsin the late Ruth Wallerstein discussed this project with me, and, like so many others, I profited from her insights into poetics. An invitation from Samuel French Morse to present for the English Institute, meeting at Columbia University in September, 1957, a paper on Stevens permitted me to try out, as "The Graded Exercises of *Harmonium*," views which occur in the second chapter. His patient answers to my enquiries have since greatly aided and reassured me; nothing I include here, however, carries his official sanction as reader.

A portion of the second chapter was published, in a different form, by *The University of Texas Studies in Literature and Language*, as "Stevens' Crispin as the Clown," and I am grateful for permission to reprint it. The Houghton Library, Harvard University, permitted me to quote from a letter in manuscript by Stevens. Finally, I wish to thank Alfred A. Knopf, Incorporated, for generously allowing me to quote from the books by Wallace Stevens on which they hold the copyright and for supplying the portrait of him for the jacket. Time for bringing this study to completion became available through the grant of a Fellowship by the John Simon Guggenheim Memorial Foundation in 1957–58 and two leaves, in 1957–58 and 1961–62, made possible through the Research Committee of the Graduate School of the University of Wisconsin. Yet, I received these awards for another study, and so, again, my research was not quite official.

Stevens has sometimes been called a holiday poet, a term of limited validity. Were I rash enough to invite a remote comparison, I might refer to this book as holiday scholarship. Considering its wayward growth, I think it most agreeable and appropriate to dedicate it to someone who has always encouraged me to take vacations and frequently made them possible.

JOHN J. ENCK

Lititz, Pennsylvania
15 July 1963

CONTENTS

PREFACE   *v*

ACKNOWLEDGMENTS   *x*

1 Images   3

2 On the Harmonium   43

3 On a Blue Guitar   94

4 On Old Lutheran Bells   145

5 And Judgments   198

NOTES   246

INDEX   253

Wallace Stevens

IMAGES AND JUDGMENTS

1   IMAGES

Realism is a corruption of reality.

WALLACE STEVENS [1]

L'histoire littéraire est tissue comme l'autre de légendes
diversement dorées. Les plus fallacieuses sont nécessaire-
ment dues aux témoins les plus fidèles. Quoi de plus
trompeur que ces hommes véridiques qui se réduisent à
nous dire ce qu'ils ont vu, comme nous l'eussions vu nous-
mêmes? Mais que me fait ce qui se voit? . . . Tout ce
qui compte est bien voilé; les témoins et les documents
l'obscurcissent; les actes et les oeuvres sont faits expressé-
ment pour le travestir.

PAUL VALÉRY [2]

BEGIN, EPHEBE, by perceiving the idea | Of this inven-
tion," Wallace Stevens at one point recommends, then
tantalizingly reverses the paradox, "this invented world, |
The inconceivable idea of the sun." [380a] Anyone who,
in turn, tries to look directly at Stevens' own poetry may
discover that three obstacles, quite apart from its inherent
brilliance, interpose themselves before, and partially
eclipse, it. One problem, persistent for all literature, assumes a special aspect with him: biography. Except for
meager publicized data, his life remains independent from
his books, and, although one might ordinarily rejoice at
not having to trim away extraneous frills, the few items [3]
bulk beyond their transparent significance. Secondly, he
perhaps belongs to what literary history, bent on tagging
influences and trends, has already enshrined as a seminal

movement. Yet, among those writers who in the first quarter of the twentieth century supposedly swore themselves to an insidious coterie, then during the second won deserved praise and authority, and with the third rightly stand as masters by whom to judge others, he exemplifies few traits. Finally, explicators have hammered away so doggedly at a handful of his poems—the jar in Tennessee, the Emperor of Ice-Cream—that anyone puzzled by the minutiae searches in vain for enlightenment. Consequently, to enumerate backwards, his renown derives not from his whole output but random segments, not from his unique style but whom he superficially resembles, not, the crowning irony, from a sustained faith in pure poetry but a fear of actuality. Before inaugurating a study of his invented world to approach eventually its idea, one must, perforce, examine first what passes for essentials, if only to dismiss them. The initial topics may resemble images, neither fully documented nor aspiring to theory, since what they oppose derives from less than absolute fact.

i

The sole biographical detail which distinguishes Stevens does not, patently, pertain directly to his writings, but obliquely it has served for inevitable contrasts: he became the vice-president of an insurance company. Despite adequate evidence against the fallacy, almost everybody still subscribes to the Victorian whim of viewing poets as mad, ineffectual angels, or a similar caricature, and gasps with naïve awe at an orderly one. Scholars, poetasters, historians, and critics, whether partisans of Taine, Freud, Parrington, or Marx, maintain that the bourgeois exiles its artists, who subsequently send their heads spinning off among the clouds. Or, they insist, at the very least, that the executive-poet must wear a mask; one sketch terms Stevens "Verlaine in Hartford." The surprise harks back a number of years; as early as 1919 William Carlos Williams made him "a fine gentleman whom Cannell likened to a Pennsylvania Dutchman who has suddenly become aware of his habits and taken to 'society' in self-defense. He is always immaculately dressed." [4] If one single truism holds good about writers, it acknowledges the folly of predicting where the muse will choose to bestow gifts. Arguments to credit an author slightly less anonymous with Shakespeare's plays have raged over centuries, and no relief from the fierce manias of those detectives who insist on tracking down the motives for art in biography appears imminent. Confronting such stubbornness, one can but wearily observe again that a minority of poets, at best, composed to the exclusion of all other pursuits. Allied arts have not had to put up with this journalistic reductio ad absurdum; Charles Ives, among the experimenters in music and likewise an insurance executive, has not become an equally victimized symbol. Stevens himself said, "I have not tried to make a living by writing. However, the fact that writers commonly take advantage of 'such crutches as teaching and editorial work' is nothing that entitles writers to indulge themselves in spasms of self-pity. Most people avail themselves of crutches of one sort or another: lawyers promote business enterprises; doctors marry rich women and buy and sell securities." [5]

Nevertheless, lacking an obsessive attachment which very few have affected toward poetry, Stevens becomes a self-conscious clown trapped in a gray flannel suit, an uneasy apologist for his capitalistic values, a holiday littérateur dangling contrived snippets, a provincial who relieves tedium through exotic phantasies, or an amateur of five-finger exercises: so run the common complaints. Transformed to partial praise, the poses establish him as dandy, hedonist, aesthete, connoisseur, or virtuoso: none quite evades pejorative undercurrents. The example of the really haunted writer in the United States, Sherwood Anderson, walking out from his factory one day and into literature, has served well as propaganda, but as truth it needs closer scrutiny. How does one evaluate a talent which rhapsodizes on a realistic, albeit depraved, Ohio community without an inhabitant steady enough to keep municipal services functioning a week and populated solely by grotesques so driven that they substantiate Bergson's theory of the mechanical as ludicrous? Citing the extensive list of twentieth-century poets who have supported themselves by varied, responsible jobs would serve no purpose. Even those who deplore Amy Lowell, one who, incidentally, did live wholly within her craft, share her bouncing verdict, delivered by 1922.

> *He has published no book and adopts this as pose,*
> *But it's rather more likely, I think, to suppose*
> *The particular gift he's received from the Muses*
> *Is a tufted green field under whose grass there oozes*
> *A seeping of poetry, like wind through a cloister;*
> *On occasion it rises, and then the field's moister*
> *And he has a poem if he'll trouble to bale it,*
> *Address it to 'Poetry,' and afterwards mail it.*
> *His name, though the odds overbalance the evens*
> *Of those who don't know it as yet's Wallace Stevens,*
> *But it might be John Doe for all he seems to care—*
> *A little fine work scattered into the air*
> *By the wind, it appears, and he quite unaware*
> *Of the fact, since his motto's a cool 'laisser-faire.'* [6]

Were such smugness not enough, commentators take for granted that Stevens himself either could not define his dilemma or escape from it. Ironically in 1899 he already presented a more succinct analysis of this aspect than anyone had contrived by 1919, 1922, or since. A short story, "Part of His Education," published in the *Harvard Advocate* during his freshman year, wryly predicts his later role. It opens as Geoffrey and Bill, two proper college students, experiment with lower class life in a beer hall. Geoffrey, the more sheltered, feels embarrassed when their crème de menthe draws derisive notice. His subsequent public chagrin heightens an antagonism between him and the group. In exasperation he lectures the room on Duty.

"I say I despise you, yes everyone of you. This grime and foulness are the elements in which you seek relaxation from your day's work—if any of you are honest enough to work by day. Here in this glare you lose sight of all that is

best in life, you pervert your emotions, you become pigs—
pigs." The waiter whistled and the crowd began to take a
delight in goading Geoffrey further on in his harangue. He
lifted up his creme de menthe to make a gesture and
the liquor flew out of the glass in a bright, iridescent spray.

"Oh, rainbows, rainbows," cried the professor [pianist]
from his platform.

"Yes, rainbows," answered Geoffrey, all restraint leaving
him, his face furious with anger, "rainbows, all of you,
jewels and pearls."

The crowd jeered him as though he were a child. Then
he took the empty glass in his hand and raising it above
his head he hurled it to the floor with a crash.

"Oh, come on banjy," said the professor to his com-
panion, "let the fool be bounced. He's a crazy blubberer.
Let's strike up." [7]

The general image of Stevens remains a businessman who
worked efficiently in his office but who, now and then,
stole away from it for a mildly disreputable binge with
bohemians. If he rarely chided them, he continued creating
rainbows—"A little fine work scattered into the air"—and
rejoicing in delicate sounds—"the ear is glass, in which the
noises pelt." [252a] Geoffrey has uneasily reconciled himself with the crowd by the end of the story, but Stevens
kept aloof. In one way he is a connoisseur, an awareness of
which, with present facts about the artist and psychology,
cannot unlock his books; "It is the word *pejorative* that
hurts" [120a], as the first poem in the limited Alcestis
Press edition of *Ideas of Order* begins. Although his poems
often celebrate their subjects, his sensitivities did not des-
perately seek just the recherché for nourishment. His voice
did not sing ditties in a financier's retreat while intransi-
gents protested with genuine despair against all the execu-
tives who had undone them and culture.

ii

An unfaltering elegance has served to set him off
from others of his generation in England and the United
States. The point for the start of their style, Imagism,
nevertheless, claims him, and irresponsible historians have

drawn few lines between him and the rest. Recently one of the less pedantic commentators on modern literature de- limited an era: "Ezra Pound had finished *Hugh Selwyn Mauberly* and some of his most characteristic *Cantos* in 1921: the artist as hero *manqué*. Wallace Stevens' *Har- monium* appeared in 1923; a dandy finding an old chaos in the sun. . . . we have only to remember that Eliot's *Wasteland* and Joyce's *Ulysses* appeared in 1922, and that around that year hovers Yeats' most powerful work." [8] Thirty years earlier two perceptively skeptical collabo- rators quoted four unidentified passages and deduced: "Richard Aldington, William Carlos Williams, Ezra Pound and Wallace Stevens are the so-called authors of these poems. These might pass as legitimate instances of correspondence and not be suspect as parasitical inter- imitativeness, were any of the poems in themselves of separate poetic importance; were not all of these poems, and many more like them, closely dependent on one another—were they private individuals and not members of an institution; and were not the Imagist school, to which all of these poets at one time or another belonged, a notoriously self-advertising institution." [9] Broadly speak- ing, the Imagists obeyed dicta almost as clear-cut as the tropes they desired in verse; about subtleties the school soon broke up into petulant bickering. [10] Whether Ezra Pound, in the pun he employs to crush Miss Lowell, would term Stevens an Imagist or amygist does not alter the binding traits. Stevens summed up his ties with the mod- erns as, "Unquestionably and notwithstanding the fact that I indulge in a good deal of abstraction, I do not regard my poems as mainly an expression of myself, nor as mod- ern in the sense in which that unpleasant commonplace is so frequently used. Still, some time ago, when I sent out one of my books to an honest man in England, he wrote to me saying that he found it personal and modern, and that these qualities were not his dish of tea." [11]

Whomever the Imagistic movement embraced, what it derived from the French symbolists, how many affinities it shared with Rilke's Dinggedicht, whether it copied the

Japanese hokku, it sought by offering the unaccommo-
dated, bare object transcendent overtones through com-
pressed metaphors. An example, which, although not by a
member of the founding group, shows the method in full
simplicity, goes: "Her ears | Two little slippers | For the
feet of my voice." [12] Once under way this manner can run
on almost indefinitely. Just where one "poem" stops often
bemuses a reader for, while stressing the integrity of the
separate subjects, the Imagists frequently hoarded contin-
gent aspects. Harry Crosby's three lines appear under a II;
the over-all title is "Little Poems," and I is: "Two dark
little doors | (Her eyes)." In spite of their apparent geneal-
ogy, these exercises may not derive from the same impetus
as Imagism. For anyone not sharing a literary historian's
Olympian perch, T. S. Eliot's introduction to *Transit of
Venus* defines succinctly the risks of isolating "influences."
"I doubt whether anyone himself engaged in the pursuit of
poetry can 'like,' any more than he can 'understand,' the
work of his contemporaries; if it is wholly unrelated to
one's own efforts it is irrelevant, and if it has some relation
it is merely disturbing." Wherever it began or ended, for it
still eludes a full analysis, Imagism did not long content
itself with the single, direct impact.

Had the Imagists, using that term quite loosely, limited
their "things" to ears as slippers, the results might sound
deliberately simple but hardly shocking. Had they
restricted themselves to lists, they might have bogged
down in the donnish delights of ingenuity at versified
riddles: how many ways does the Church resemble a
hippopotamus? Stevens never abandoned this technique
from the early "Thirteen Ways of Looking at a Blackbird"
to the late "Someone Puts a Pineapple Together." [83–
87c] Between "These lozenges are nailed-up lattices" and
"An uncivil shape like a gigantic haw" stands the identify-
ing pineapple. On the whole unfortunately, one must admit, many Imagists had soaked up a heady academic atmosphere: H. D.'s classical training, T. S. Eliot with
courses at Harvard, the Sorbonne, and Oxford, Marianne
Moore's period in a public library, Ezra Pound as the ama-

teur linguist, et cetera. Presumably anyone might begin at the unexceptionable "doors [are] eyes" and take in stride the fanciful "haw [is] pineapple"; when the poet resurrects his unnamed reference from a Koine text translated into medieval Latin which he has unintentionally misread, this blurring may quickly shrivel imaginative freshness. Poets' pilfering for centuries shocked no one, but the Imagists' agility at leaping from one elliptic association to another without visible links, not even blackbirds, pineapples, hippopotami, or forms of *to be* caused Edwardian readers to reel in vertigo. At first charges of lunacy, clannishness, hoaxes, and downright anti-Americanism issued from provincial newspapers and campuses. Hints soon escaped, however, and the game of explication became a popular indoor pastime.

In the long run scholarship always annexes an allusion or annihilates it. Granted that as a tour de force it transcends Imagism, not a line from *The Waste Land* remains which someone has not tied together in terms of Ovid, the Tarot pack, *The Golden Bough*, or a more recondite source. Long before *The Cantos* neared their poetic end, busy excavators bared the labyrinthine foundations sunk down in three thousand years of prose. Often during the process of being documented, the basic text withers or perishes. When a glance at any line flips all its ponderous glosses before a reader, the pliability sought through fluid contrasts hardens into a rigid framework. One need not emphasize the irony that rage against a static monumentality incited the Imagists to their initial revolt, another disquieting example of the theory that the very drive to realize a perfect pattern ultimately creates its opposite. The epidemic of solving nonexistent poetic puzzles through sources has disturbed T. S. Eliot, who apologized for annotating *The Waste Land*. "No, it is not because of my bad example to other poets that I am penitent: it is because my notes stimulated the wrong kind of interest among the seekers of sources. It was just, no doubt, that I should pay my tribute to the work of Miss Jessie Weston; but I regret having sent so many enquirers off on a wild goose chase after Tarot cards and the Holy Grail." [13]

Although developing his own brand of Imagism, Stevens unquestionably belongs to his era, as any memorable artist does, if only because he rejects his immediate predecessors' clichés. "What a modern poet desires, above everything else, is to be nothing more than a poet of the present time. I think it may be said that he considers his function to be this: to find, by means of his own thought and feeling, what seems to him to be the poetry of his time as differentiated from the poetry of the time of Sir Walter Scott, or the poetry of any other time, and to state it in a manner that effectively discloses it to his readers." [244b] Conversely, he shuns specious novelties, whether of typography or form, subject or knowledge, which lured others who feared to forego any gimmick: "One cannot spend one's time in being modern when there are so many more important things to be." [175b] About Imagism itself he expressed differing views: "Not all objects are equal. The vice of imagism was that it did not recognize this." [161b] If things of this world exist in a hierarchy, the individual poet must eliminate some, then order the rest by his own insights. "A grandiose subject is not an assurance of a grandiose effect but, most likely, of the opposite." [159b] When the humble blackbird assumes thirteen poses, the number, chosen for its arbitrariness, says that it may contain further poems, four-and-twenty, or more. The bird, or any other subject, need not by itself belong to an enshrined poetic category. Viewing a scene through a candid eye and presenting it with dispatch comprise the prerequisites for Imagism, which Stevens incorporates as part of his equipment, and which "is not something superficial. It obeys an instinct. Moreover, imagism is an ancient phase of poetry. It is something permanent." [258b] One technique does not constitute the whole of poetry, but he continually elaborates upon it and returns.

On the basis of these notes one might posit that, contrary to the first among the three prevalent opinions mentioned at the outset, Stevens differs little from other contemporary poets by having entered seriously into business.

His achievements there, if more impressive and more
closely tied with commercial life than theirs, need not,
ipso facto, stamp any special brand upon his volumes. For
the second error: assuming that as a writer he subscribes to
a vogue seized by the avant-garde and that he then constructs his verse upon it derives from an opposite extreme
which denies him his true originality. His sharing aspects
of a manner does not limit him in either expression or
outlook. Whereas most poets of this period have drastically
overhauled their beliefs and idioms, he shifts his tone
erratically, his ideas by degrees, and his subjects seldom.
None of these, however, remains quite static, while the
style itself exploits a nearly identical range for forty years.
At least, one can discern abiding traits which run through
all his books no matter what the tone, ideas, and subjects.
Countering, finally, the third mistake, that of letting a few
poems represent all, one should review his formal predilections now so that later chapters will not have to backtrack
awkwardly. This topic involves more complexities than the
other two have and will require a number of separate
rubrics.

iii

The weaker Imagistic experiments abundantly
prove that objects, by themselves exotic or trite, cannot
long endure isolated on the page; with the years they
wither like the chic of fashion photographs or a red wheel-
barrow washed by too many rains. What formerly stunned
as daringly modern soon ages embarrassingly; in an apt
epigram, "Mlle Chanel disait que *la mode crée du beau
qui deviendra laid et l'art du laid qui deviendra beau.*'" [14]
Compiling lists of novel pleasures bewitches an adolescent
in his idle moments. To capture these fancies through a
vocabulary which heightens without distorting them tests
a poet's assurance. Because of his distinctive style, Stevens'
reputation, which dates from his debut in national magazines, still rests pejoratively on idiosyncratic syllables. Supposedly he so revels in sound effects that whimsey determines onomatopoetic words and coinages. Critics, after

compiling lists of their favorites, conclude unanimously
that seldom would a synonym serve. Each word, no matter
how polyglot its phonemes, becomes part of the design:
for example, the nearly infamous, "Chieftain Iffucan of
Azcan in caftan | Of tan with henna hackles, halt!" [75a]
The sun serves as a blackamoor to bear the blazing tail of
this bantam, a crowing egoist. Pine-woods and bird glow
resplendently in the jovial syllables and precise phrases,
which chide pomposity. The poetic context justifies what,
by itself, may tinkle. When the stanzas jangle in overly
clipped accents, like Klee's painting *Die Zwitschermas-
chine*, the result does not contain a blueprint of how to
reproduce birds' songs. Now and then twitter they undeniably do; it takes a dedicated reader not to boggle at "oh
beau caboose." [347a] The occasional slang phrases have
not aged well, but a few "thing-a-ma-jigs" [218a] and
"shebangs" [37a] cause as slight disturbances as the foreign
words, which either blend or contrast with the dominant
idiom.

In letters to Renato Poggioli, who translated a selection
into Italian, Stevens confides sources which only a reckless
critic would have dared suggest. One explains a stanza in
"The Man with the Blue Guitar" [178a], where the musician experiences an exalted control:

> He held the world upon his nose
> And this-a-way he gave a fling.
>
> His robes and symbols, ai-yi-yi—
> And that-a-way he twirled the thing.

His comment is "This-a-way and that-a-way and ai-yi-yi are
colloquialisms, at least in Pennsylvania and elsewhere, for
that matter. People think of ai-yi-yi as Spanish but it is
equally Pennsylvania Dutch. . . . A man who is master
of the world balances it on his nose this way and that way
and the spectators cry ai-yi-yi." [180d] The Pennsylvania-
Germans, with their broad, emphatic speech, resort frequently to ai-yi-yi; whether connoting delight or shock, it
signifies the unexpected. Being unaware of its origins,
mistaking it for Spanish, one could arrive at the correct

reading. Far from willful perversities, the style defines the subjects in the only way possible. While one need not rejoice in each stroke, neither should one strain at iotas, when the trick of "The A B C of being" [288a] stretches into "It is the infant A standing on infant legs, | Not twisted, stooping, polymathic Z." [469a] Principally, those who, like Bluebeard's wives, overindulge their curiosities stumble upon unnecessary troubles, e.g., " 'Flotillas' suggests a 'fleet of flowers,' an image which a child's fancy would evoke. Another, the naval, use of the word is in this instance irrelevant and distracting. When once I asked Mr. Stevens about the value to give this connotation, he wrote: 'You are in much too close focus. As I use the word, it means merely floating things.' I cannot see how the word, with its past history, can mean *merely* that in the present context. Another word might have been better." [15]

A single word indicates his nice control without pyrotechnics. In describing a visit to the region of Pennsylvania where he was born, "The man told me that last spring a scovy duck had built her nest in the chimney of the church. When, finally, her brood was hatched, the ducklings came out of a stove in one of the rooms in the basement of the church. There were six of them and they are alive today on the sexton's farm." [100c] Few standard dictionaries list *scovy*. Self-evidently an abbreviated term for muscovy duck, it has become an accepted usage among the Pennsylvania-Germans. To have remembered the localism scarcely surpasses a competent reporter's equipment, but to command both a respect for the specific and a true style which will bear a homely word without apologetic inverted commas distinguishes an imaginative literalist. The account of the trip continues with a bleak graveyard and concludes at an exhibition in the Morgan Library. "The brilliant pages from Poland, France, Finland and so on, books of tales, of poetry, of folk-lore, were as if the barren reality that I had just experienced had suddenly taken color, become alive and from a single thing become many things and people, vivid, active, intently trying out a thousand characters and illuminations." [102c] The easy movement from rustic to urban, colloquial to formal, drably seen to vividly invented, transitory to permanent puts people off. Obviously, the theory runs, not only does he praise too much but he even makes the world a museum which houses a Pennsylvania scovy duck next to the Morgan Library in New York. Moreover, when one remembers that this vignette forms a digression in a lengthy reading of Marianne Moore's "He 'Digesteth Harde Yron,'" both places seem unlikely. The belief thus becomes reinforced: the very freedom from official attitudes, which opens expanses of sound and metaphors denied others, locks him in a private estate.

Were the extravagant language merely purple patches, the strictures might hold good, but every part reinforces the uniform fabric capable of a wide range without jarring transitions. Moreover, rather than distorting by a parroted realism, this vocabulary becomes a genuinely American idiom. His knowledge of French culture notwithstanding, Stevens never traveled in Europe. So assured of native and foreign arts that he lightly steps from a farm to a library, he can steer between a boastful provinciality and an academic cosmopolitanism. In two complementary jottings: "Nothing could be more inappropriate to American literature than its English source since the Americans are not British in sensibility" [176b], and "I have never been able to see why what is called Anglo-Saxon should have the right to higgle and haggle all over the page, contesting the right of other words. If a poem seems to require a hierophantic phrase, that phrase should pass. This is a way of saying that one of the consequences of the ordination of style is not to limit it, but to enlarge it, not to impoverish it, but to enrich and liberate it." [205b] Finally, if any uncertainty remains, in answer to the question, "Are you sympathetic to the current tendency toward what may be called 'literary nationalism'—a renewed emphasis, largely uncritical, on the specifically 'American' elements in our culture?" he replied, "I don't believe in factitious Americanism. An American has to be an American because there is nothing else for him to be and also, I hope, because it would not matter if there was. Even so, I believe in forgetting about it except as a quality, a savor." [16] Stevens' poetic idiom claims its freedoms as a uniquely American privilege. The passages from his prose already cited in these pages—and those to follow—prove that his statements embody the wit and directness of epigrams, as, indeed, do many lines throughout the poems themselves. Although widely scattered among his books, his opinions on any topic cohere around persistent themes, which do not become the philosophic systems sometimes extracted from them by critics. Despite a tendency toward the hermetic, he serves as his own best commentator. The point about his style need not be labored further; the correct verdict appeared a number of years back. "Apparently he can absorb the extremes of *patois* and archaism without the slightest effort. Imperturbably he ranges so far afield that he finally leaves us not with a strange collection of curiosities, but with a quizzically familiar point of view." [17]

iv

Techniques for containing the diction move from unabashed vers libre through a few exercises in strict stanzas to his favorite, a supplely modulated blank verse. Standard metrical patterns frequently fail to quite define the limits of his poems because analogy and resemblance proliferate ad infinitum. No regular versification wholly suffices.

> *Twenty men crossing a bridge,*
> *Into a village,*
> *Are twenty men crossing twenty bridges,*
> *Into twenty villages,*
> *Or one man*
> *Crossing a single bridge into a village.*
>
> *This is old song*
> *That will not declare itself . . .*
>
> *Twenty men crossing a bridge,*
> *Into a village,*

Are
Twenty men crossing a bridge
Into a village.

This will not declare itself
Yet is certain as meaning . . .

The boots of the men clump
On the boards of the bridge.
The first white wall of the village
Rises through fruit-trees.
Of what was it I was thinking?
So the meaning escapes.

The first white wall of the village . . .
The fruit trees. . . .

He often probes the interstices within the many and their essential unity but, like the old song, will not declare himself as the title, "Metaphors of a Magnifico" [19a], implies. The poems explore what their subjects contain both by themselves and in constructs, and their nature, consequently, forbids a patly discrete statement. The adjuncts of wholeness and multiplicity as both opposites and identities (but never negating powers) become a leitmotiv. Here, the cutting into arbitrary segments, the intrusion of futile echoes, the doubts at the end, and the deliberate flatness in links like "Of what was it I was thinking?" demonstrate the dangers which vers libre faces. Because a Magnifico need not deign to limit his metaphors, the permutations might roll onward: why not one man on one bridge into twenty villages, every journey being an identical quiescence for the travelers until its end when they resume their separate routes? The inconclusiveness of this one may derive from the Imagists' refusal to philosophize, but Stevens always fears imposing form and, likewise, peering into causality beyond what a moment presents. His special traits flourish outside formal structures; his designs take shape from within.

Often he aspires to capture and control that will-o'-the-wisp, organic form, which lured twentieth-century writers into devious ways. While a teasing concept, it may terminate in the license for palming off weaknesses as a strong independence. When embodied with authority, it stands magisterial and grand; in comparison most works of an expected design look like gelatinous concoctions dumped from tin molds. Stevens' derivative poems in the *Harvard Advocate* between 1899 and 1901 and his silence until 1914 prove that he endured a long apprenticeship before devising his mature style. His undergraduate "Ballade of the Pink Parasol" transposes Austin Dobson's "The Pompadour's Fan," although indicatively Stevens departs from the strictest rhyme scheme required by a ballade. Dobson endowed the fan with a tawdry romance, the practical nineteenth century looking nostalgically back on the rococo eighteenth in the manner of Max Beerbohm's caricature "Mr. Austin Dobson and Mr. Edmund Gosse, Composing a Ballade." Before the nineteenth century had quite vanished Stevens summed up its sophistication centered on a pink parasol, a view of the "Ballade," one trusts, not unduly dependent upon the uses to which James about this time was putting the same object in the hands of Madame de Vionnet. Nothing came to Stevens ready-made: "When I was here at Harvard, a long time ago, it was a commonplace to say that all the poetry had been written and all the paintings painted." [218b] Even the juvenilia place single lines with assured deftness. "Red roses, I wonder, red with the Spring. | Red with a reddish light?" [18] heralds forty years later, "Like rubies reddened by rubies reddening." [346a] The locale, "Outside the Hospital," also predicts later disturbing landscapes; here the blind girl receives flowers from a man without legs. A line in "Adagia" succinctly illustrates why Stevens could not limit himself to pantoums and sestinas: "Thought tends to collect in pools." [170b] Many poems must have introduced themselves to him without a credential. If they sometimes lack final statements, the counterpoise does not mean that he prized fragments but, rather, shows his honesty in never feigning an emotion or blocking off the limits of a genuine one. He could, however, always contrive a suitable garb for his prescience, if not in the strictest measures. A fair number of the compositions, in fact, exemplify an organic form, irregular as they strike the eye at first glance.

Facility in rhyming puts almost as heavy a curse on the English poet as no talent for it. The old debate between Daniel and Campion about its value could profitably be resumed. Futile though the regret is, one cannot help lamenting both the contemporary taste which forced Pope to waste ingenuity in a field where he least excelled and the changing pronunciation which shackles some of his more telling syllepses. English rhymes will, generally, sound either expected or overly ingenious. W. H. Auden's fluency in forms begot stunning insights originally; over the years these have tarnished with deplorable rapidity. Poets have often regarded their task wryly, e.g., Jonson:

> *Rime, the rack of finest wits,*
> *That expresseth but by fits,*
> > *True Conceipt,*
> *Spolying Senses of their Treasure,*
> *Cosening Judgment with a measure,*
> > *But false weight.*
> *Wresting words, from their their true calling;*
> *Propping Verse, for feare of falling*
> > *To the ground.*
> *Joynting Syllabes, drowning Letters,*
> *Fastning Vowells, as with fetters*
> > *They were bound!*

"Phases," Stevens' very early appearance in a national magazine—*Poetry*, of course—rhymes strictly most alternate lines, some of which hint at less traditional effects [4b]:

> *Vines with yellow fruit,*
> *That fell*
> *Along the walls*
> *That bordered Hell.*

The typography and rhymes do not coincide; *yell*(ow) links with the second and fourth lines and joins the third in consonance, while the rhythm is iambic dimeter. He avoids, in the main successfully, overly mechanical rhym-

ing, although strains to bring off a pattern may reach
extremes. Oddities, like the following, occur infrequently
[133a]:

> The grackles sing avant the spring
> Most spiss—oh! Yes, most spissantly.
> They sing right puissantly.

The comparative freedom from fretting about stanzaic
units allows him to exploit individual lines at which he
excels and which set the tone for all the poems. The
external structure may creak or the final impact bog down,
but no poem lacks the redeeming cadences which he alone
can invent. Of course, ahead of the poems themselves
stand the frequently praised titles with their startling
promises. Merely glancing down the table of contents in
any of his books heralds the pleasures within. That he
could hit upon this number, all in the same manner, and
yet vary it when restricted to short phrases proves his
control over attitudes and vocabulary. If only the titles
existed, they would represent a unique accomplishment,
although no one would dare guess to what sort of work
they belong. Nowhere else in literature, probably nowhere
else in any art except the names by which Klee designated
his paintings, does such brilliant compactness index the
whole. As with Klee, especially his drawings, so with Stevens, the precise relationship between several slight lines
and a pretentious concept may put an unbearable strain
on the object in living up to the prologue even satirically.
After the resounding "Two Illustrations That the World
Is What You Make It," "The Constant Disquisition of
the Wind" and "The World Is Larger in Summer" follow
soberly. By themselves the two poems present adequately
their topics, but the response they deserve does not come
up to what one might have anticipated. The titles, whether
playful or intense, belong indispensably to their subject as
an integral part. If they rarely describe obviously and if the
poems seldom exhaustively define them, at some point a
suitability illuminates both, as with "Metaphors of a Magnifico."

Prestidigitation by its nature cannot endure though it may enchant. If one accepts the extrinsic difference that romantic poets deal in words and phrases to the detriment of structure, while classicism demands an impersonal totality, Stevens stands near the border line, perhaps on the romantic side. The two terms have, obviously, endured overuse until they count for little. With its mannered grace, nevertheless, his work comes closer to classical virtues than does that by his contemporaries. Probably his lasting fame will rest on the longer poems where groups of lines slowly accumulate meaning by examples, not statements. Among the very few instances in this century of a single diction which sustains true originality are: "The Comedian as the Letter C," a journey both picaresque and philosophic; "Notes toward a Supreme Fiction," a discourse on poetry where every dictum presents itself through an instance; "Esthétique du Mal," a reverie both on and beyond time; and "An Ordinary Evening in New Haven," a trenchant reprise of developed themes. With all the freshness of discovery the corpus evolves in a persuasive culmination [325-26a]:

> *The greatest poverty is not to live*
> *In a physical world, to feel that one's desire*
> *Is too difficult to tell from despair. Perhaps,*
> *After death, the non-physical people, in paradise,*
> *Itself non-physical, may, by chance, observe*
> *The green corn gleaming and experience*
> *The minor of what we feel. The adventurer*
> *In humanity has not conceived of a race*
> *Completely physical in a physical world.*
> *The green corn gleams and the metaphysicals*
> *Lie sprawling in majors of the August heat,*
> *The rotund emotions, paradise unknown.*
> *This is the thesis scrivened in delight,*
> *The reverberating psalm, the right chorale.*

"Scrivened in delight," it connotes the same interplay between book and scribe, words and calligraphy, text and marginalia, the physical and the transcendent which marks an illuminated manuscript. At a time when incompleteness

of subjects and treatment predominates, when the poignant confession hides in a deliberate lacuna, when poets
compose their own fragments, when the sole positive is
denial, a tribute to wholeness, however romantic its trappings, satisfies continually. It arises from the sounds that
create their consistent world in terms of each poem, which
has no end except realizing itself, and that become entities
while always celebrating the actual. "Eventually an imaginary world is entirely without interest." [175b]

v

Although Stevens' special vocabulary and structure comprise his basic traits, others contribute persistently
to his distinctive craftmanship. Indifference to academic
references further removes him from the more celebrated
Imagists. The subjects which his exemplary technique
takes for its discourse come from any categories of experience. The passages quoted have evinced his wide, if eclectic, knowledge. In spite of his familiarity with culture, he
asks less extraneous information than any worthwhile poet
since Wordsworth. The frankly charming "The Prejudice
against the Past" [368–69a] starts:

> Day is the children's friend.
> It is Marianna's Swedish cart.
> It is that and a very big hat.

One need not spot the Swedish cart as the object on which
Marianne Moore centers her own "Carriage from Sweden." The hat belongs to a philosopher, as one learns later;
beyond that object its owner claims no being. Shall one
recall a portrait of a philosopher with a hat or Stevens'
frequently crowning intellectual heads with a cover: "Ra-
tionalists, wearing square hats, | Think, in square rooms?"
[75a] The point is that no buried clue lurks in an anagram
or behind the lines. Both cart and hat warn precisely
against the folly of those who embalm artifacts from the
past among untouchable treasures. Similarly, Stevens may
mention Franz Hals, Nietzsche, Picasso, or that "a
hand, | In a black glove, holds a novel by Camus" [457a],

but the general context sufficiently places such allusions
without pedantic footnotes. Lines borrowed directly from
other poets, William Carlos Williams or W. B. Yeats,
recognize their origins by italics. Some assimilated adornments, if extracted, might surprise one, such as when
Stevens recalled, "the words Catching at Good-bye refer to
a popular song entitled Good-bye, Good-bye Harvest
Moon. I suppose I had in mind the way that particular
song kept coming back to mind." [178d] Without the
direct authority it would have taken a bold guess to venture
that a popular song inspired the phrase, especially because
Stevens probably remembered incorrectly "Shine on, Shine
on, Harvest Moon." Anyone amused by subconscious va-
garies could find the transference indicative of Stevens'
temperament; anyone convinced that Stevens enjoyed private jokes with prying enquiries may judge the reference
far-fetched. Neither conjecture adds to the poem.

On spying the Swedish cart one might assume that
Stevens merely repeats Miss Moore's observations; their
nearness in lists of contemporary poets has stressed their
affinities. They do share many traits, but the way of handl-
ing references confirms their independence. Miss Moore
studies a single thing, a steam roller, Ireland, an ostrich, or
Yul Brynner. Afterwards, she groups about her topic facts
and theories culled from the unlikely sources credited in
her notes, about one of which, on a cat called Peter,
Stevens comments slyly, "But this amusing stroke is, after
all, a bit of probity, whatever else it may be." [254b] Her
finished mosaic displays in collage the being and importance which the disparate items contained less beguilingly
from the outset. She elects to deal with matters which,
through all juxtapositions, retain their identity and does
not often modify them by objects introduced through
metaphors. For Stevens subjects alter through comparisons
with diverse things or moods, and his discourse may shift
entirely. Also, Miss Moore sets her poems more decidedly
in time than does Stevens; the Swedish carriage summons
to contemporary Brooklyn the histories of the country
where it originated and the one which exhibits it:

and yet, in this city of freckled
integrity it is a vein

of resined straightness from north-wind
  hardened Sweden's once-opposed-to-
  compromise archipelago
of rocks. Washington and Gustavus
Adolphus, forgive our decay.[19]

He rejects even a tangential contrast. Pledged to his striking vocabulary, he honestly plays only the role of poet
without decking himself in faded romances and others'
discarded adornments.

Poets in this century have posed themselves before borrowed backdrops and donned a bewildering repertoire of
personae: Ezra Pound stuck that title on one collection of
his poems, and exposing Hugh Selwyn Mauberley's "identity" promises to elicit enough literary detectives to staff a
modest Pinkerton Agency; W. H. Auden, capable of ven-
triloquism expert enough for the music hall, has attributed
three personalities, boy, prelate, and old peasant woman,
to T. S. Eliot; E. E. Cummings swings between a plebeian
carping and a lover's gallantry; Edith Sitwell, with her
Sengerphone, hid behind a curtain for a façade; W. B.
Yeats contrived permutations through true and false
masks—the list could run on. Because these poets, almost
as avidly as novelists who acknowledge James their master,
shun making statements with their own voices, to mount
an attitude they drag forth objects venerated by the past
and emphasize how tawdry in contrast the present has
grown. Sometimes deliberately, sometimes unintentionally, their manner likewise dims the accumulated luster of
ancient epochs. In the twentieth century the device has
engaged almost every art; Giorgio de Chirico, during his
most celebrated phase, for example, relied upon classical
ruins and lost splendors amid steep perspectives of waste
space. The penchant may smack of wit or vulgarity. For a
publicized instance: the unnamed woman in "A Game of
Chess" of *The Waste Land* lures back some snows of
yesteryear. According to the superfluous notes the passage

derives from *Women Beware Women,* but because *The Tempest* dominates the poem the game between Miranda and Ferdinand recalls an innocence unknown in modern London. Through parodied lines the woman in her chair before the table also invokes Cleopatra's throne. Should one play by Middleton and two heroines from Shakespeare prove insufficient, the scene, along with meter, vocabulary, and actors, shifts to a pub; through the farewells at closing time Ophelia's "good-night, sweet ladies" also resounds. Other legendary women likewise flit about in the game of verbal cache-cache. Without undervaluing either the profundity or the notable skill which composed the poem, one may still glimpse too large a crowd in this ghostly carnival for the implied discomfort. One's impatience does not rest upon ignorance of the sources; the more echoes one catches, the more muddled the jangle which overtones cause.

For tastes educated by twentieth-century art, Stevens' lack of erudite notes consequently renders more enigmatic his attitudes. His reticent spurning of autobiography rules out an easy reliance on what he has read, where he has traveled, or his creeds in politics and art. Assuming that he reiterates the clichés of his period will not help, either. When Randall Jarrell says about "Loneliness in Jersey City" that it depicts "that particular countryside which, I think, God once sent angels to destroy, but which the angels thought worse than anything they could do to it,"[20] one gets the commentator's picture of Jersey City rather than the poet's. Jarrell's gambit, a common one for him, resurrects a stereotyped line on which vaudeville once traded, Jersey City, New Jersey, vying with Reading, Pennsylvania, as the nightmare of the hinterlands. Several of Stevens' poems depict places around Reading without relying on routine jokes. Jersey City occurs as a convenient locale; perhaps Stevens wrote his report there in room twenty-nine three; probably he did not. To apprehend the loneliness one need know no more about Jersey City than what one learns from the stanzas; summoning too many associations will distort it. In the next chapters compari-

sons with other poets, novelists, artists, or philosophers do
not generally insist on a direct borrowing but merely name
a familiar point from which to gauge more concisely his
meaning. His preface to Valéry's *Dialogues* repeats the old
complaint of interpreters' crediting poets with an excess
erudition.

> In 1930, Louis Séchan published a work on *La Danse
> grecque antique*, which contained a chapter on Valéry's
> *Dance and the Soul*. M. Séchan was Professor of Greek
> Language and Literature at the University of Montpellier.
> He sent a copy of this book to Valéry, who acknowledged
> it in a letter, which it seems worth while to copy at length,
> as follows:

> I thank you greatly for your attention in sending me your
> fine work on Greek dancing. I learn from it many things
> I ignored—and even ignored about myself. Your kind
> chapter on my little dialogue generously attributes to me
> much more erudition than I ever possessed. Neither
> Callimachus nor Lucian, Xenophon nor the Parthenia was
> known to me; and would not in any case have been of
> much use to me. Documents in general impede rather
> than help me. They result in difficulties for me, and
> consequently in peculiar solutions, in all those composi-
> tions in which history must play some part. [280b]

From whatever books and paintings he drew his nourishment—and a meager Quellenforschung can stretch attenu-
ated passages out of Baudelaire, Mallarmé, Bergson, and
Valéry which parallel his—the poem itself emerges as
objects subtly fused by his own cadences. The past, as in
"The Prejudice against the Past," never lies quite depleted
save as an illustration of how it is misunderstood. The lost
pink parasol of the undergraduate verse must come to rest
in a living hand and, reciprocally, present must permeate
the past. Far from being at war, the two complement each
other in the limits of the line.

vi

In the description of how he dispenses with allusions, his general attitude toward other epochs has emerged
as well. "Each age is a pigeon-hole" [157b], and remains,

therefore, largely sealed off. Obviously Stevens does not lack some sense of history any more than did Elizabethan dramatists. The view in "The Prejudice against the Past" creates it as a direct force, not a faded souvenir. Summoning up other eras, he may betray naïveté, such as when he expatiates on the seventeenth century.

> Pretty much all of the seventeenth century, in France, at least, can be summed up in that one word: classicism. The paintings of Poussin, Claude's contemporary, are the inevitable paintings of the generation of Racine. If it had been a time when dramatists used the detailed scene directions that we expect today, the directions of Racine would have left one wondering whether one was reading the description of a scene or the description of one of Poussin's works. The practice confined them to the briefest generalization. Thus, after the list of persons in *King Lear*, Shakespeare added only two words: "Scene: Britain." Yet even so, the directions of Racine, for all their brevity, suggest Poussin. [172c]

Any self-respecting graduate student in English could point out that Shakespeare's hand had, alas, little to do with the list of persons and that directly naming the place represents a printers' convention. (And ascertaining where that practice originated would give him a term paper in bibliography.) This quibble does not matter because Stevens' very point concerns harmony in the past, wherever its customs started. In his gaze time includes surviving entities, which exist as the living apprehend them; the past is the sum total of the present. "Confined by what they see, | Aquiline pedants treat" [368a] Shakespeare's texts as relics of typography. Stevens does not deny pedants their activities, but he knows that their methods stop short of relevant completeness. "All history is modern history" [166b], a verdict whose fuller scope the final chapter will show. One might, finally, recall T. S. Eliot's similar motif in *Four Quartets*: "History is now and England." [21]

vii

If time past belongs to any present moment, not medieval, Byzantine, legendary, or Arcadian, space exists almost as a continuum on a single plane. Presumably Stevens has mastered Bergson and believes "A journey in space equals a journey in time" [162b], one's position keeping up, willy-nilly, with the present. The poems, as has been shown, bear the markings from their day and land but not to the degree that they must flash the forged visas which regional novels need to prove themselves indigenous. Geographical names casually flash by: Pennsylvania, New England, the seven seas, the heavens, and many others. Such places betoken attitudes which conveniently center in generalized spots and do not hold up snapshots taken on one grand tour. This skill ultimately refines awareness of a quintessential nature, whether luxurious as the greenest continent or homely as Haddam, and must, consequently, reject the bagatelles on which mere local color draws. A passage from the version of "Owl's Clover" published by the Alcestis Press does not form part of that work in *The Man with the Blue Guitar*. It lists cities and countries before a final decay. Aware of the melancholy grandeur it conjures, one may count it, nevertheless, the kind of catalogue best left to Frederic Prokosch [53b]:

> *The heaven of Europe is empty, like a Schloss*
> *Abandoned because of taxes . . . It was enough:*
> *It made up for everything, it was all selves*
> *Become rude robes among white candle lights,*
> *Motions of air, robes moving in torrents of air,*
> *And through the torrents a jutting, jagged tower,*
> *A broken wall—and it ceased to exist, became*
> *A Schloss, and empty Schlossbibliothek, the books*
> *For sale in Vienna and Zurich to people in Maine,*
> *Ontario, Canton. It was the way*
> *Things jutted up, the way the jagged stacks,*
> *The foul immovables, came through the clouds,*
> *Colossal blacks that leaped across the points*
> *Of Boucher pink, the sheens of Venetian gray.*
> *That's what did it. Everything did it at last.*
> *The binders did it with armorial books.*
> *And the cooks, the cooks, the bar-men and the maids,*
> *The churches and their long parades, Seville*
> *At Easter on a London screen, the seeds*
> *Of Vilmorin, Verhaeren in his grave,*

The flute on the gramophone, the Daimlers that
Dissolved the woods, war and the fatal farce
Of war, the rust on the steeples, these jutted up,
These streaked the mother-of-pearl, the lunar cress.
Everything did.

That he deleted this part, a brilliant résumé of the European 'thirties, reaffirms how little it suits his characteristic modes.

Three poems printed sequentially all mention places in their titles: "A Dish of Peaches in Russia," "Arcades of Philadelphia the Past," and "Of Hartford in a Purple Light." The first examines a Russian quality which peaches exude beyond that country; Philadelphia has vanished into a past which none quite recalls; the light, having traveled from Le Havre and Norway, transforms Hartford by its masculine and feminine aspects. Indicatively, a peach may preserve a village, a metropolis vanish when no one sees it, and the sun rearrange a city: space reveals more than just immobile façades. Certain areas often harbor expected traits: Geneva conjures common sense, the South profuseness, Africa the primitive, New England austerity. Even the fixed landscapes frequently alter with surprising changes, a mingling connoted by the title "Forces, the Will & the Weather" [228–29a] when

> *There was not an idea*
> *This side of Moscow. There were anti-ideas*
> *And counter-ideas.*

resolves into

> *It was a shift*
> *Of realities, that, in which it could be wrong.*
> *The weather was like a waiter with a tray.*
> *One had come early to a crisp café.*

To turn back once again and cite the lines heading this chapter: however affected by a place, the poet cannot render it realistically; its transitory attributes must start it toward an imagined permanence. Although much of this poetic continuum is dramatized, it deliberately avoids specific characters and personal conflicts: "Life is an affair of people not of places. But for me life is an affair of places and that is the trouble." [158b]

viii

His two one-act plays, with a third, "Bowl, Cat and Broomstick," unpublished, belong to that period when English poets first became aware (by reports, one judges) of Noh and European experiments like *Igitur*, or, perhaps, merely Maeterlinck. They failed to transpose oriental stage conventions and did not heed Mallarmé's note "Ce Conte s'adresse à l'Intelligence du lecteur qui met les choses en scène, elle-même." [22] W. B. Yeats' early plays, with their characters never quite humanly conscious and speaking a language elusive to a point of inanity, set the pattern. The Provincetown Playhouse and other protesting groups on both sides of the Atlantic flaunted effects which, even to a critic well disposed toward one such company (the Irish Players), looked daft "with their blank faces and their stiff movements, taking up their cues so abruptly, and seeming not to hear anything said by their interlocutors." [23] "Three Travelers Watch a Sunrise" and "Carlos among the Candles" hint at many topics and present almost nothing, not even a noncommittal situation. Their dramatis personae glide through a vacuum—"Carlos among the Candles" being a monologue—although both have had productions. One may find them charmingly quaint, too delicate to qualify as closet drama, more like a peculiar display, perhaps a wreath composed of feathers worked into bunches so that they resemble flowers. To comprehend them asks tolerance of nearly all Stevens' idiosyncrasies, fine as a few passages may sound by themselves. For him "The eye sees less than the tongue says. The tongue says less than the mind thinks" [170b], and thus action entails too much hubbub, allegory risks oversimplifying. The excitements of dramatic clashes issue from fallibly human heads. Reading Stevens' plays, one feels that Valéry's genius-monster Monsieur Teste might have devised them, although, clearly, they exemplify that degree of ambiguity which made Teste spurn literature.

When the poems take the guise of meditations, the thinkers suit the topics contemplated. In a few, such as "Le Monocle de Mon Oncle," the sentiments converge upon a distinctive temperament; others, such as "The Comedian as the Letter C" or "The Man with the Blue Guitar" may lose sight of the protagonist or speaker for considerable stretches. To some commentators the method appears valid: "Although critics have complained about the weakness of the dramatic impulse in Stevens' work, very few have noticed that a large number of the poems are written from the point of view of a character, usually a character making an aside or meditating, interpreting, as if to himself. The 'I' of such poems, like the 'one' or 'he' or 'she' of others, is undoubtedly often very close to Stevens himself, but there can be no exact equation of person and poet." [24] The practice annoys others: "I am convinced that his favorite word is 'it.' He is, anyway, the great poet of the third person. However much he may conceive of the imagination as an instrument of profound insight, he uses it to arrive at the type of coherence that a philosopher is more usually intent on." [25] If the poems do not sketch actual places, neither do they hide in subconscious phantasies; almost as though he believed the theory that the eye emits its own beams, the ideal ground for many works falls almost halfway between a character and his milieu. This mode, nearly a still figure with life, cannot accommodate the disgruntled wishes of a Browningesque malcontent to brood interior monologues, an approach with which Ezra Pound, T. S. Eliot, and other Imagists frequently toyed. One of the few which depicts an individual, "To an Old Philosopher in Rome" [508–11a], does not name its subject, Santayana, whose life, to Stevens, exemplifies one "in which the function of the imagination has had a function similar to its function in any deliberate work of art or letters. We have only to think of this present phase of it, in which, in his old age, he dwells in the head of the world, in the company of familiar saints, whose presence does so much to make any convent an appropriate refuge for a generous and human philosopher." [147–48c] "Rome. . . .

newsboys. . . . The bed, the books, the chair, the moving nuns, | The candle" compose the décor. Santayana's remoteness from the world rules out some objects, but how many poets could resist the portentous details on which modern verse thrives? One senses "the majestic movement | Of men growing small in the distances of space," not the streets around the Colosseum nor the thoroughfare, which Santayana could watch from his room, on which the Germans left Rome and which Allied Armies then occupied in the Second World War. No separate pieces of furniture, no architectural backdrop reinforces the setting; Santo Stefano Rotondo and its baroque decorations, close-by, get no more notice than the Victorian parlor in the convent and its framed letter from Edward VII to the nuns. Presumably Stevens enjoyed Santayana's encouragement at Harvard, but no nostalgic sentimentality mars the poem. Elsewhere in another essay he keeps an aloof view, as well. "In the case of Santayana, who was an exquisite and memorable poet in the days when he was, also, a young philosopher, the exquisite and memorable way in which he has always said things has given so much delight that we accept what he says as we accept our own civilization. His pages are part of the *douceur de vivre* and do not offer themselves for sensational summary." [187b] The negatives indicating what "To an Old Philosopher in Rome" does not contain apply likewise to Stevens' characters; they too do not offer themselves for sensational summary.

In place of defined personalities, a troupe of generalized figures performs throughout the volumes [300a]:

> The captain squalid on his pillow, the great
> Cardinal, saying the prayers of earliest day;
> The stone, the categorical effigy;
> And the mother, the music, the name; the scholar,
> Whose green mind bulges with complicated hues.

With others, such as students, actors, the bourgeois, and, in a stellar role, the poet, these compose a cast, but the attitudes one adopts toward them must never disintegrate into a stock response. Like the locales, the stable characters

change mien constantly. Rarely do they occupy more than
two or three lines, and often they serve only for comparisons. Stevens employs them as he pleases: "Frankly, the
figure of the rabbi has always been an exceedingly attractive one to me because it is the figure of a man devoted in
the extreme to scholarship and at the same time to making
some use of it for human purposes." [185d] During the
Second World War the hero joins the company, and he
fits least readily with it, necessary as he is. He cannot have
an ostrich plume waving from his beaver hat and a cloak
flying behind him, but the poems assign him an idealized
stance which no member of the United States Army, not
even the model for a recruiting poster, could maintain in
this century. Perhaps the closest analogy appeared in an
advertisement for Brooks Brothers' uniforms, a drawing
which suggested that an officer had just purchased some
sleek battle gear, boarded an airplane, and near the front
was handing over, miles from any developing station, a
pouch of V-Mail film. Whatever Stevens means by "realism" and "reality," neither reproduces patronizingly person, place, thing, or event. His cast of characters more
closely corresponds with what one assumes—and whether
rightly or incorrectly hardly matters for this example—the
commedia dell'arte represented. Within arbitrary limits of
stock figures, the actors improvised traits. Nimbleness, the
moment, accidents, and spontaneity determined the enter-
tainment more than an inelastic script, and no two per-
formances quite duplicated each other. Stevens' figures
behave with sternness or frivolity in a sketched scene
unrestricted by cumbersome props. Milieux may, nevertheless, influence them. A formula such as this one makes the
device seem mechanical, and sometimes the commedia
dell'arte could not surmount its limits. At best, the cast
exceeded being a rack of puppets, which it always partially
transcended, and from its very restrictions conjured a
complex vitality.

ix

An executive turned experimental poet who in-
vents a special language, seeks organic form, scoffs at

faddish knowledge, lives inside the moment, transcends geography, and dispenses with individual characters does superficially resemble one of Pater's more affected disciples. Stevens, as a connoisseur, diverges from them because he does not divorce his artistic interests and mundane ones. From this vantage his role in business nearly explains why he wrote more effectively because of it; freed from any professional aesthetic pose, the self he contained could dispense with the usual badges which modern artists almost must flaunt. The philistine who shuns cultural labels and the exhibitionist who proclaims his right to them with every gesture, both put the museum apart from other experiences rather than among them: "Literature is the better part of life. To this it seems inevitably necessary to add, provided life is the better part of literature." [158b] Unassertively he declines to separate life and art along inflexible lines, while keenly distinguishing between them. Almost prescient of Malraux' establishing an imaginary museum without walls where all artifacts, removed from their autochthonous housings, compose a single cosmos, he independently improvised his own collection. A rectitude in regarding himself and his immediate world saves the poems from programmatic allegiances. In light of the attributes so far listed, one might consider "Anecdote of the Jar" [76a] to illustrate how such elements fuse, even to explain incompleteness.

> I placed a jar in Tennessee,
> And round it was, upon a hill.
> It made the slovenly wilderness
> Surround that hill.
>
> The wilderness rose up to it,
> And sprawled around, no longer wild.
> The jar was round upon the ground
> And tall and of a port in air.
>
> It took dominion everywhere.
> The jar was gray and bare.
> It did not give of bird or bush,
> Like nothing else in Tennessee.

No more than gags about mountain feuds will the tired Wildean paradox of nature's copying art exhaust it.

Diametric values have been attributed the jar, Tennessee, the poem as a whole, and Stevens as author. The moderately regular rhythm and casual rhymes suit a ballad, a tone which the unemphatic diction furthers. Self-evidently the *I* does not describe the author, and the scene does not tell merely about a single jar, hill, wilderness, and state. The stressing of *and*—a popular device at the time—contradicts the obvious antitheses, which unobtrusively reinforce each other: "round-slovenly," "wilderness-no longer wild," "round upon the ground-tall and of a port in air," "gray and bare-bird or bush." The single uncommon phrase, the vague "a port in air," heightens the significance of the jar without ludicrously increasing it beyond proportion. The period of history presumably does not matter; a pioneer mother or anyone since could perform this gesture, and no boundary divides *this* Tennessee from Kentucky, granted that another state would not serve so well. In a general way the outward signs all point toward Stevens' abiding practice; the meaning takes more devious turns. As the poem progresses, an antagonism between hill and jar mounts; the artifact triumphs, and, finally, Tennessee draws existence by being different from it. In one reading the created object of a culture, obviously foreign, holds sway over a landscape without an indigenous art. The wilderness welcomes a force which straightens it, and so a paraphrased "statement" implies the axiom that art ameliorates. On second thought, making it more like an anecdote and less like a fable, does "sprawl" improve upon "slovenly," does the gray, bare pylon in sterile domination charge the countryside with any glory? The shape looming on the horizon now depends upon a state whose specific traits it lacks. Does the austere jar grow poorer *in* the poem (in Tennessee) or merely to the mind of the *I* who disappears after the first line? If so, does he acquire knowledge or disillusion, truth or sentimentality? Another passage, in prose, may limit the conjectures without, however, yielding direct answers.

A number of years after "Anecdote of the Jar," Stevens' tribute, "John Crowe Ransom: Tennessean" [259–62b], speaks with precise economy. With its interlocking comments this piece nearly defies abridgment; although comparatively short, it extends a bit longer than a conscionable quotation tolerates. Because its dicta do aid an understanding of a place and attitude, to paraphrase it may illuminate the poem. It opens, "What John Crowe Ransom does is to make a legend of reality," and goes on to observe that he utilizes native materials. "They say that there are even more Ransoms in Tennessee than Tates in Kentucky," as the poet becomes nearly the shaper of his country. The meaning becomes sharper: "I don't in the least mean anything romantic. On the contrary, I mean a real land and a real people and I mean Mr. Ransom as the instinct and expression of them." One grasps a locale only by inhabiting it and, as one grows older, bestowing a life on it. Stevens here, as elsewhere, praises sentiment without sentimentality: "This is why trivial things often touch us intensely. It is why the sight of an old berry patch, a new growth in the woods in the spring, the particular things on display at a farmers' market, as, for example, the trays of poor apples, the few boxes of black-eyed peas, the bags of dried corn, have an emotional power over us that for a moment is more than we can control." Although Tennessee alters its citizens, including the Ransoms, poets must seek to define their own experience of their states, whereupon ironically, "Once they understand them it may be said that they cease to be natives. They become outsiders." If "outside," they remain where they started, still within. The poetic process itself, which nearly metamorphoses reality, transcends a corrupting realism and becomes true. "The greater the value he [Ransom] set on it, the dearer it became, the more closely he sought out its precise line and look, the more it became a legend, the peculiar legend of things as they are when they are as we want them to be, without any of the pastiche of which the presence vulgarizes so many legends and possibly everything legendary in things, not as they are, but as we should like them to

be." However accurately this critique describes Ransom—
and it seems quite apt—it likewise tells about Stevens
himself.

Tennessee, not, of course, his native state, embodies an
aspect of the United States, one remote from the climates
Stevens often sought. The jar represents an extrinsic element which does not match precisely "Imagination," "Culture," "Poetry," or a "European Temperament." When he
composed "Anecdote of the Jar," he let his enigmatic
observations center on the failure of feeling, a man with a
divided mind which apprehends art but which refuses to
deny his native heritage for its sake. Both landscape and
artifact have admirable qualities, which, unhappily for the
observer, refuse to coalesce. Later, the poems will develop
more fully the interplay between man and his surroundings
so that ultimately Stevens could salute Ransom's regional-
ism. The growth entails no drastic conversion but, instead,
a fusing of elements always present if sometimes in conflict. Appropriately enough, one of his last prose pieces
describes the state where he lived nearly forty years. It
concludes, with a note similar to that for Tennessee, on
returning to Connecticut: "Going back to Connecticut is
a return to an origin. And, as it happens, it is an origin
which many men all over the world, both those who have
been part of us and those who have not, share in common:
an origin of hardihood, good faith and good will." [296b]
Stevens, as a connoisseur, ever increases his grasp not just
over materials but in discerning essential resemblances and
harmonies. Were there a complete break in his style and
outlook this chapter would be wholly a fabrication; were
there no contrasts, the ensuing ones would require no
elaboration. On the other hand, he never codified a philosophic paradigm and rhymed by it. He wishes to extend his
appreciation as widely as possible but only within the
limits of fullest honesty, whatever divided loyalties he
must reconcile in himself. "The greatest conquest is the
conquest of reality. It is not enough to present life, for a
moment, as it might have been." [168b] Even if, dismiss-
ing Stevens' activities in insurance, one must search in-

tently for "realities," they do not lie in wholly remote regions. "Whatever I have comes from Pennsylvania and Connecticut and from nowhere else." [26] Before one surveys his total output toward the fictions and realities, a last specific, if elusive, trait requires preliminary notice.

x

If Stevens denies distant realms, whether past or future, in which present musings blur immediate objects and construct chimeras, at the same time he never concentrates on a single subject so intently that it juts forth isolated from all contexts. A prose description of a statue embodies the style:

> I have selected him [Verrocchio] because there, on the edge of the world in which we live today, he established a form of such nobility that it has never ceased to magnify us in our own eyes. It is like the form of an invincible man, who has come, slowly and boldly, through every war-like opposition of the past and who moves in our midst without dropping the bridle of the powerful horse from his hand, without taking off his helmet and without relaxing the attitude of a warrior of noble origin. What man on whose side the horseman fought could ever be anything but fearless, anything but indomitable? One feels the passion of rhetoric begin to stir and even to grow furious; and one thinks that, after all, the noble style, in whatever it creates, merely perpetuates the noble style. . . . It seems, nowadays, what it may very well not have seemed a few years ago, a little overpowering, a little magnificent. [8–9c]

Another sketch, by Henry James, surveys the same statue:

> I only know that in the afternoon, when the air was aglow with the sunset, I was standing before the church of Saints John and Paul and looking up at the small square-jawed face of Bartolommeo Colleoni, the terrible *condottiere* who sits so sturdily astride of his huge bronze horse on the high pedestal on which Venetian gratitude maintains him. The statue is incomparable, the finest of all mounted figures, unless that of Marcus Aurelius, who rides benignant before the Roman Capitol, be finer; but I was not thinking of that; I only found myself staring at

the triumphant captain as if he had an oracle on his lips. The western light shines into all his grimness at that hour and makes it wonderfully personal. But he continued to look far over my head, at the red immersion of another day—he had seen so many go down into the lagoon through the centuries—and if he were thinking of battles and stratagems they were of a different quality from any I had to tell him of.[27]

Granted the conventions of the genres and the dissimilar demands made by the essay and a novella, Stevens' and James' styles, their ways to see, react, describe, and express, touch closely. For both, the armed equestrian, as a vital but unknowable force, strides from a dim past into the present. Neither feels compelled to elaborate upon details, such as the design of the armor, the decorated saddle, the angle of the horse's head, and the church to one side. Just as James' prose to imperceptive readers sounds colorless because of its surface smoothness, so Stevens' bolder strokes mislead those who fail to connect them inside a pattern. James' sentences set sentiments against one another in strengthening qualifications; Stevens' lines place objects side by side to obtain, ultimately, an identical aloofness.

To further catalogue the typical images which Stevens' poems offer, one might divide the usual methods of emphasis into, roughly, four planes. The first, almost as though a magnifying glass were applied to it, offers striking details, whether concrete or general, straightforward or epigrammatic. The second, while congenial to highlighting, represents a whole through sketches. To take instances from another genre: the former method culminates in a trompe-l'oeil, where circus poster, grained oak, frayed twine, and dried herbs break from their frame, or, poetically, "staring forms | Leaned out, leaning," [28] with a power to haunt but not to enchant. The second blurs into the late impressionists' shadings but stays within the limits of its canvas. Behind the second level at a remote distance objects lose their corporeality and turn eventually into symbols—in one sense of the term—which assemble elusive and contra-

dictory concepts. For both James and Stevens the statue of
the condottiere exists within the second plane and refers
to the third. Ultimately, backing them all, however, may
lie or be posited a fourth, which resurrects the human
symbols into a transcendental eternity, obedient to
a sternly preordained cosmography set, one must, perforce,
assume, by a hand wholly beyond the horizon. The planes,
naturally, fade into one another, but most writers work
assuredly in one or two areas only; part of Shakespeare's
enduring mystery depends on his ease at ranging through
all four. The majority of twentieth-century poets have
utilized the first—hence their admiration for Donne's seeing "A bracelet of bright haire about the bone" [29]—and
then swung back to a mythic waste land or other legendary
kingdom. Stevens, even at his most Imagistic, rendering
Chinese effects of night, remains less frenetic: "A pool
shines, | Like a bracelet | Shaken in a dance." [74a] Be-
tween the lines glitter the elusive aspects of light. One
does not learn whether the pool, seen by night, glistens
because of moon, stars, or Chinese lanterns strung above
it. Is the bracelet made of jewels and, if so, what sort, or of
metal, and what kind? How fast does the arm move? The
questions are, of course, beside the point, but his images
lack the concrete quality on the first plane: "Arms that are
braceleted and white and bare | [But in the lamplight,
downed with light brown hair!]." [30]

Without recourse to a formula like the foregoing, those
who have judged the early poems pretty sounds and designs
fail to sense the symbolic areas behind them; those who
complain about later ones' waxing overly philosophic emphasize the metaphysical grounds from which the contents
evolve. A regularity of purpose, if not of presentation,
distinguishes all of them. The world and its arts, whose
boundaries shift freely, derive immanence through resemblance and analogy, the two concepts, as Stevens himself
tells in essay upon essay, which represent the matrix of
meaning and form. By working within flexible limits he
rings brilliant changes without violating either the sense or
the spirit. He manages an interplay between the two

planes which refer ultimately to a common source where each maintains its dignity. Rarely resorting to the pejorative, he starts on and returns to earth, which through its very atmosphere—one might notice the rich range of adjectives coupled with "air"—creates all values. The mythical kingdoms of dreams and eternity exist by negation.

> What a ghastly situation it would be if the world of the dead was actually different from the world of the living and, if as life ends, instead of passing to a former Victorian sphere, we passed into a land in which none of our problems had been solved, after all, and nothing resembled anything we have ever known and nothing resembled anything else in shape, in color, in sound, in look or otherwise. To say farewell to our generation and to look forward to a continuation in a Jerusalem of pure surrealism would account for the taste for oblivion. [76–77c]

The traits so far examined influence, then, at least in part, all the volumes not as rules of a game but as the idioms and idiosyncrasies which grace a modulated style. In this climate, again, Stevens differs from his contemporaries, at least from what much recent criticism has made them out to be. One suspects that modern literary historians share the prejudice of that ubiquitous, apocryphal youth who said he loved literature but hated to read, thereby reversing the nineteenth century which read ravenously but feared literature. Impatience with surfaces, a seeking to get behind the façade for a posited actuality, characterizes the present temper. Commentators compulsively seek out counters and then deduce absolute rules until enough pieces are traded with the poet in an imaginary game of chess to achieve a checkmate. Oddly enough, the very motives which briefly lured the new critics closer to the page have now led them away again in pursuit of mythical or ritualistic skeleton keys. At best, the image of the explicators at their chores resembles Piranesi's drawings where little scholars measure the worldly wreckage of an eternal city. Having abstracted a principle, they can spin phantasies from it, rather than trust any taste, and not bother about what any author, finally, says.

As a connoisseur, who condescends to mere pedants, Stevens enjoys nature and art without fretting over their precise boundaries. In his own generous terms he ponders the problems of how to convey spontaneous praise on the page at a time when no values will stand by themselves. The solution begins in Imagistic techniques. While his own idiom gains elegance, he places the subjects clearly and fully in the longer passages of his verse. The need for immediacy forces a refusal to rely on popular tricks: fragments from dead authors, setting up the past as a conventional backdrop to sketch a vanished nobility, geographical borders to denote political or religious allegiances, and a rivalry with the naturalistic stage in consistent characterization. This technique may suggest that he merely wandered through a fin-de-siècle twilight where poetry whispered nuances which mocked all commitments. Rather, he asserts his independence to see and say what the moment is without invoking absolutes. The insights which arise from this rationale save the surfaces and cohere into new patterns themselves far exceeding the accomplishments of other recent poetry. These first images of Stevens should become more understandable with the reading of the volumes which exhibit his method if not inflexibility. In an introduction to a book by a younger poet, twenty years after his own debut, he asked the pertinent questions.

What is there about a book of first poems that immediately interests us? For one thing, it is possible that we are going to have a fresh opportunity to become aware that the people in the world, and the objects in it, and the world as a whole, are not absolute things, but, on the contrary, are the phenomena of perception. In short, it is possible that a new poet is that special person at our elbow with his special, possibly even extraordinary, perception. . . . Since the perception of life is life itself, a book containing the first poems of a poet new to us has a natural and intense attraction. [266–67b]

As a man becomes familiar with his own poetry, it becomes
as obsolete for himself as for anyone else.

WALLACE STEVENS [220b]

As to the quality of the verse, I should like to say this: that
if it seems inferior to that of the original play, I must ask
the critic to observe that I had to imitate a style which I
had abandoned as unsuitable for other purposes than that of
this one play; and that to compose a pastiche of one's own
work some years later is almost as difficult as to imitate the
work of another writer.

T. S. ELIOT [1]

A HISTORY tracing English poets' progress, even as individuals to say nothing of them collectively, during the first
half of the twentieth century awaits its chronicler; the
chore still raises formidable barriers: sources, familiarity,
perspectives, and goals. The supposed obscurities of the
Imagists and other cults lent their work a specious affinity.
After many explications by critics and changes in the
authors, a partial picture starts emerging. T. S. Eliot's
metamorphosis offers the straightest approach: *The Cock-
tail Party* explains "Little Gidding," which clarifies "Ash
Wednesday," which leads back to *The Waste Land,* which
describes "The Love Song of J. Alfred Prufrock," whose
negations complement the moralizing in *The Elder States-
man.* The titles, of course, exist independently, but anyone
helped by diagrams will learn from chronological differences. With Stevens, congenitally incapable of playing old

possum, the collected works fit under one set of rubrics gracefully enough so that few uneasy backward or forward glances need round out his development, if that term does not assert too much. The late poems do expatiate upon the first ones but more as refinements than discovery. "A form of fire approaches the cretonnes of Penelope" [520a] could occur anywhere in his books, although the matters which it describes may have slightly altered. His notable consistency derives perhaps from the fact that only in 1923, at the age of forty-three, did he publish a first volume, *Harmonium,* a collection of pieces printed in periodicals during the preceding decade. Many poets have written themselves out before thirty; few have begun their work when older. That a limited, alert audience of contemporaries at once greeted him favorably, that magazines awarded him prizes attest recognition. One wonders whether the majority then responded to the whole book or only to the segments which realize impeccably the Imagists' credo. Viewed in totality, *Harmonium* expresses a finished aesthetic which asks minor refinements later. His other subjects may cause him to range farther afield, but the style can always accommodate them. Although renouncing the rather complacent limits of Imagism, he toyed with calling his final volume "The Whole Harmonium."

i

As reissued in 1931 *Harmonium* adds fourteen poems, although some antedate 1923, and rejects three from the first edition. *Ideas of Order,* published by the Alcestis Press in 1935 and by Knopf, who handled all trade editions, the next year, yields to some nervous assertions. In 1936, also, *Owl's Clover* came from the Alcestis Press; Knopf brought out a revised, one must assume definitive, version a year later in a volume called, for the other long poem in it, *The Man with the Blue Guitar.* Once Stevens had a poem published he seldom made major changes, but "Owl's Clover" proved nearly intractable. It is one of the few approved for a book excluded from the *Collected Poems. Parts of a World,* 1942, while unable to pull all its fragments into a unit, shows more integration. The two long poems, *Notes toward a Supreme Fiction* and *Esthétique du Mal,* issued in limited editions by the Cummington Press in 1942 and 1945 respectively, exhibit a new mastery, which the volume, including these and shorter pieces, *Transport to Summer,* confirmed in 1947. *The Auroras of Autumn* three years later reprinted "A Primitive like an Orb," which had appeared in a pamphlet by the Banyan Press. All these, with three exceptions, along with a group of new poems called "The Rock" comprise the *Collected Poems,* dated October 2, 1954, in celebration of Stevens' seventy-fifth birthday. A group of essays, *The Necessary Angel,* 1951, contains *Three Academic Pieces,* which the Cummington Press had printed in 1947; the other titles of this book all had first appearances elsewhere but as pamphlets or in a series of papers. The *Checklist* by Samuel French Morse gives thorough listings to 1954, and the volume *Opus Posthumous* contains heretofore uncollected or unprinted pieces.

To worry about a more precise chronology now would create unnecessary complications, even were it possible to arrive at one. Except for *Transport to Summer* none of the volumes indicates that the sequence as printed obeys the order of composition. To trace back to the periodicals which first published the poems would solve nothing because almost all appeared in little magazines, which might rush them into print, as *Poetry* sometimes did, or let them languish over several sporadic issues. A commentary may adopt the same informality, grouping them generally around their volumes without insisting upon an inflexible list. Moreover, the dating of many poems, even with manuscripts and documents available, must stay conjectural. Finally, because Stevens took some pains to give his separate volumes a unity, anchoring discussion around them will not contravene his own practices. A few departures from this plan will permit abiding concerns to enter this study more smoothly. Usually the titles which Stevens rejected for his books and which *Opus Posthumous* reprints may be picked up at random in roughly chronological order throughout appropriate chapters. The methods of citation should sufficiently stamp them, although often their special traits will indicate reasons for their having been omitted. The modulations of themes blend so well at most points that changes elude notice. As should become obvious, Stevens' mind, like James', never allowed a merely novel idea to violate it. His steady growth does not rely on sudden intellectual discoveries, the kind of conversion which literary historians relish documenting.

Harmonium stands by itself in modern letters. The title, as customarily with Stevens, quizzically identifies the contents. A harmonium, of course, is that small organ which held an honored place in Victorian parlors. Both object and room sound quaint by the time of the *Collected Poems*, but the discrepancy between the homeliness of the title and the recherché contents underlined the contrast from the beginning. A harmonium invokes the self-conscious modesty that amused poets in a period when advancing grandiose claims about their own importance, unacknowledged legislators of the world and such, had begun to cloy. While denying desire for the solemnity of a pipe organ, *Harmonium* softly says that no middle-class home ever sanctioned music quite so unfamiliar. For the popular drawing of Brahms at his piano above the room's antimacassars and macramé, it substitutes Peter Quince, casually out of A *Midsummer Night's Dream*, in rococo attitudes before an anachronistic clavier. One might recall, however, that concurrently Webern scored music to include a harmonium, part of the widespread impulse which coaxed new aesthetic possibilities from unlikely sources. The same wit prevails throughout; the poems present unexpected sounds and slyly parody the banal, doing for verse—to cite a different musical example—what Satie had done for music. "Trois Morceaux en forme de poire" would become *Harmonium* both for what it accomplishes in itself and as a repudiation of a mythic, Wagnerian earnestness. Sometimes it vexes with a deliberate perversity, as though a hymn played every Sunday evening has been transposed and left unresolved, and at others astonishes with intricacies worthy of the most theoretical ricercare. Reading into the title, as some have, an outright apology by a minor poet for his ineptitudes (equivalent to the advertisement of the period: "they all laughed when I sat down at the piano . . .") misses the point. An amateur by choice, Stevens does not shirk professional responsibilities, while refusing to forego the bizarre counterpoint which sober practices do not sanction.

One can scarcely avoid distorting or falsifying in an effort to devise comprehensive rubrics for the poems. Because his mastery frees him from extrinsic limits here, contrived categories must look arbitrary. Nevertheless, in order to detect the varieties, one has to impose groupings in despair of precise labels. To forestall the rigidity which a priori postualtes entail and to allow for the resemblances which cross boundaries, the following rules of thumb will not pretend to exceed a convenient device. Distinctions based largely on length and subjects may look wilfully naïve, above all for Stevens, who both compresses sweeping landscapes into a small compass and watches horizons dissolve or gather with the imperceptibility of light itself. The qualities of the air alter a whole country, or the entire scene contributes the prevailing atmosphere. Similarly, a single word, such as *fat*, ranges through unlikely contexts for praise and disapproval. From the poems themselves, as discrete units, an appreciation must begin. The philosophic realm in which they terminate does not swell out of a simple fiat or a borrowed spiritual absolute. Aware, then, of the deftness with which he coaxes nuances from a harmonium, one may take these types as approximately graded exercises which, like Bach's "Die Kunst der Fuge," give examples instead of rules and surpass their origins. At the same time, because Stevens advocated no program, certain classes will inevitably overlap, but the precepts of Imagism provide a persistent, if elusive, control.

Some do not exceed standard exercises in Imagistic techniques. The reader should, according to the formula, grasp in the round the flatly described object by blending the juxtaposed details, the taut lines, novel focus, and the unemphatic end. The primary appeal depends on a visual shock through a Gestalt response. Such poems challenge exegesis and win over it: either their effects leap forth spontaneously and disdain comment or they pose such enigmas that no critical hocus-pocus will resuscitate them. Some of these nearly achieve in their brevity a sense of spaciousness. Particularly, "The Load of Sugar-Cane" [12a] presents a tropical indolence where "the red turban | Of the boatman," which crowns it, rises to center the climate. "Ploughing on Sunday" by drawing upon essentially the same elements—water, birds, the light, and a worker— projects through exhilaration a bleak, expansive wilderness in the prairie before the coming of cults. In this poem the simpler, nearly regular, versification suits the uncomplicated vigor of the northern country. Contrasting with the land, the wind of "The Wind Shifts" barely surpasses that table of similes—the thus-and-so (preferably inanimate) does something like this . . . and that . . . (preferably human)—which often Imagists prized as the picturesque instead of shunning for the overworked pathetic fallacy it is. "Tea" anticipates the stock in trade of vocabulary and clipped lines which *Façade* features conspicuously, but it remains the kind of sketch which Edith Sitwell handles more adeptly. The Imagistic pieces may have struck Stevens as too slight in themselves; frequently for magazines he submitted several loosely related ones under a collective title. Of course, as already noted, the manner encourages patching up segments and forcing the reader to detect, or bestow, the order by himself.

One sequence called "Primordia," not reprinted as a group by him in a book, expresses a revealing side of his outlook infrequently recognized. (Three of its sections, however, do turn up as independent poems.) "The Load of Sugar-Cane" and "Ploughing on Sunday," as well as certain other ones also outside the suite, such as "The Silver Plough-Boy" and "In the Clear Season of Grapes" share with "Primordia" the motif drawn from a primitive United States. That he dropped the former from the 1931 edition of *Harmonium* and added the latter indicates, perhaps, his hesitancy regarding the subject, which links with a major trade-mark of the Chicago Renaissance by celebrating frontiers in a nearly New World. More effectively than Vachel Lindsay's homespun gossamers and Carl Sandburg's folksy raptures, Stevens' unconventional idioms can confront an essentially young country. "Primordia" falls into two sub-headings, "In the Northwest" and "In the South." Both revel in spaciousness, although the north keeps a remote aspect, and the south conjures older lands: "Frail princes of distant Monaco." [9b] Coming to grips with a generally inimical American soil indirectly determines many of his poems. Seriously as his native land may have stirred him, his attitudes toward it crystallized gradually. Years later, writing to Professor Poggioli about "The Comedian as the Letter C," he first said that Crispin lives "in the poetic American atmosphere as we all do," [2] then substituted *a* for *the* and deleted *American*. The interest always continues, but it enters poems evasively as a strand; it does not preempt an entire work outside the Imagistic pieces. Stevens' talents did not lend themselves to bathos as grandiose as Mount Rushmore, but neither, contrary to a philistine verdict, did he carve designs out of peach pits. He noted, "A public resemblance, by contrast, like the resemblance of the profile of a mountain to the profile of General Washington, exists for that great class of people who co-exist with the great ferns in public gardens, amplified music and minor education." [76c] Eventually a man can dwarf a mountain but not because of his public eminence. "Primordia" and the rest, more closely resembling the miniatures which Audubon put behind some of his drawings of birds, sketch private scenes. Stevens, like him, prefers scrutinizing, for example, the blackbird in its thirteen Imagistic poses. With this group the final attitude may praise, mock, question, or suspend judgment; if, generally, popular middle-class mores repel him, barbarity, per se, offers no refuge.

When, instead of praising, the verse regards accepted poetic clichés irreverently and frowns with a mature impudence, another tone emerges from Imagism. He enjoys satirizing trite ways of saying poetically "things that cannot be said" to demonstrate that, indeed, they cannot. Death, reduced to its lowest physical terms, remains a blank without a vocabulary. "The Worms at Heaven's Gate" [49–50a] introduces a certain Badroulbadour in an unwonted guise, bit by bit, through an efficient inventory.

The complete text goes:

> Out of the tomb, we bring Badroulbadour,
> Within our bellies, we her chariot.
> Here is an eye. And here are, one by one,
> The lashes of that eye and its white lid.
> Here is the cheek on which that lid declined,
> And, finger after finger, here, the hand,
> The genius of that cheek. Here are the lips,
> The bundle of the body and the feet.
>
> . . . .
> Out of the tomb we bring Badroulbadour.

A critic decided, "The sense of 'The Worms at Heaven's Gate' is almost destroyed by its isolation in anthologies, where it seems to mean that the sardonic worms are handing up bits of a corpse with ironic comments on their deterioration. For Stevens the beauty does continue, it survives corruption, and the worms, not sardonic at all, can only talk of beauty, not of death." [3] Apart from propounding a conundrum in epistemology, the reading removes the poem as far from Stevens' meaning as does its seclusion in anthologies. An outside measure gauges its standards more neatly than do human guesses about what chanting worms consider beautiful. For May, 1916, Poetry had promised to announce the outcome of a contest in which Stevens entered his play "Three Travelers Watch a Sunrise." It won, but the decision was deferred until June; the May issue carried Allen Upward's long lament over a boyhood friendship, "Baldur," philosophizing in the styles of three centuries. Badroulbadour rumbles in a long anagram on Baldur. The title may also allude to Aladdin's wife, daughter of the sultan of China, Badroulbadour being a variant spelling for Bedr-el-Budur (moon of moons), all associations of a sort appealing to Stevens. Badroulbadour can contain, of course, the Nordic as well as the Arabian names; either has a fleeting significance.

Whether coincidental or not, passages in Stevens' and Upward's poems reverse images: the denial of death, a persistent beauty, the grubs, and transfiguration. Parts of "Baldur" go:

> *but who will bear with me*
> *To breathe a more heartrending lamentation,*
> *To mourn the memory of a love divided*
> *By life, not death, a friend not dead but changed?*
>   *Not dead—but what is death? Because I hoard*
> *Immortal love, that withers not, but keeps*
> *Full virtue like some rare medicament*
> *Hoarded for ages in a crystal jar*
> *By wonder-working gnomes; that only waits*
> *The sound of that lost voice, familiar still,*
> *Or sight of face or touch of hand, to bring*
> *Life, like the dawn whose gentle theft unties*
> *The girdle of the petal-folded flowers,*
> *And ravishes their scent before they wake: . . .*
>
>   . . . . .
>   *Or is it worth*
> *The caterpillar's knowing, as it shrinks*
> *Within the coffin it has built, and dies*
> *Between the straightening walls, that they shall crack*
> *In ruins days or weeks or ages hence,*
> *And issuing from the dust a thing of light—*
> *Not it—shall drink the morning air and wave*
> *Its crimson banners in the sun?*

"The Worms at Heaven's Gate" appeared in *Others* for July 1916, perhaps a bit too soon to have permitted Stevens to have seen this poem. In his autobiography, however, Alfred Kreymborg reports that under his editorship *Others* published Stevens enthusiastically, and William Carlos Williams, guest editor for that issue, likewise encouraged him. The informality of its editorial practices would make a comparatively early printing not impossible; for example, the notice in the July issue of an erratum: "Attention is called to a serious error in the May-June issue. . . . God spare all authors, editors, publishers, printers and public!" Even if not a deliberate parody, the contrast between these two demonstrates Stevens' method. Neither poetry nor the fancy can penetrate too rarefied spheres; if they try, they, like the worms, have only empirical facts for metaphors, and actualities will mock the inflated musings. Poetry itself cannot prevail against a final decay; death is irredeemable physically and theologically. When Stevens boasts of a surviving beauty, it endures in the present because the poet recreates through his art the actual traceries left by an object which has itself vanished. The more solemn the tone which invokes poetic absolutes, the more haggard it must sound. As he repeats constantly: "The imagination is not a free agent. It is not a faculty that functions spontaneously without references. In IX [of "The Man with the Blue Guitar"] the reference is to environment: the overcast blue; the weather, that's it [sic] the stage on which, in this instance, the imagination plays. The color of the weather is the robe of the actor, which, after all, is a large part of him. The imagination depends on reality." [176d]

Another statement, "Disillusionment of Ten O'Clock," striking by itself but not representative enough to merit a place in the anthologies which feature it, contrasts the bourgeois town in a deathly sleep and a drunken sailor. The bizarre list of what the citizens might have dreamed criticizes their complacency when awake, but it does not recommend the old man's phantasies as the greatest good. The techniques of Imagism continue to dominate here as the single subject offers itself not in positive terms but by denial. Finally, the notable "Cortège for Rosenbloom" [79–81] succeeds by repeated *dead* and *tread* in conveying a funeral which modulates its procession until the pomps loom as preordained and final.

> And they bury him there,
> Body and soul,
> In a place in the sky.
> The lamentable tread!
> Rosenbloom is dead.

One saw dead Badroulbadour in bits, the slumbering town through what it cannot dream, but one does not glimpse Rosenbloom, who, despite his flowery name, certainly suggests a person of marked sobriety and age. The ceremony for one so briefly identified imparts a sense of awe, a little like that of a French précieux, who, experiencing a possibly genuine sorrow over a lost acquaintance and enlarging it to include all bereavement, does not command a vocabulary equal to a lament. Here, again, the poem playfully makes the point that it must obey its inherent limits and forego an excessive curiosity about locked spaces.

Attitudes toward death and the unknowable reach a facetiously grotesque plane, but the outré fascinated Stevens from the early prose sketch "In the Dead of Night," where he contrived high jinks in the manner of Victorian whimsey. There the outlandish behavior depended on a servant's plot to poison his employer's family; instead of proving fatal the substance released inhibitions. One hesitates to label other items grotesque indiscriminately because the taste for it fluctuates from age to age—hence the unstable reputation of Mannerism—and from reader to reader. A hasty verdict based on conditioned responses can mislead seriously. Often, although by no means predictably, a convoluted segment terminates in an ultimate statement; where rhetorical extremes imply just mockery will cause disagreements. On the other hand, simplicity may fall apart, and a straightforward sentence through its flatness may ridicule a failure of the imagination. Were the tone always quite uniform, its degrees would provoke less controversy and in the process, likewise, lose a prime attribute. An uncomplicated affair, "Life Is Motion" [83a], unlike "Primordia" satirizes the ungainly frontier and its animal spirits as Bonnie and Josie celebrate the marriage (of flesh and air) in Oklahoma with an operatic "Ohoyaho." Mostly, the grotesque pieces represent yielding to momentary high spirits, a delight in pyrotechnics, because a sterner judgment weeded most of them from the collections. Some touch on love, a topic which Stevens generally presents in a respectful burlesque, as when he envisages a "Romance for a Demoiselle Lying in the Grass" [23b] and concludes, "Clasp me, | Delicatest machine." The sheafs of poems which he offered journals under a single title, such as the wink toward Dickensian whimsey, "Pecksniffiana," and his askew glance at his lute with a single string, "Sur Ma Guzzla Gracile," do not sustain the same intensity of caricature throughout. No signs automatically mark the degree of extravagance sought.

The same noncommittal device shields the few short pieces in *Harmonium* which focus on living figures. Generally his avoiding force, at this time, keeps the satire sedate, and unintentional parody may contribute further an unresolved note. Such poems resemble most the speaker in "Carlos among the Candles" and share affinities with other works of the period which depend on revealing details. When the type succeeds, as it fitfully does for Edwin Arlington Robinson, it produces the wonders of an "Eros Turannos"; when it goes awry, as it almost inevitably does in Edgar Lee Masters, it becomes moralizing delivered from tombstones. Often Stevens names his personages in titles: "Another Weeping Woman," "From the Misery of Don Joost," "The Apostrophe to Vincentine" (the form apologizing for not having grown into a villanelle), "Jasmine's Beautiful Thoughts Underneath the Willow," "Two Figures in Dense Violet Night," and "Two at Norfolk." Their scattered, striking phrases do not directly converge on the persons, and the whole collapses in a vacuum because the characters themselves belong to no discernible life. To read a vast symbolism of opposing attitudes into them—a more nearly valid practice with late works—requires bringing a mass of suppositions from scattered hints. "Last Looks at the Lilacs" [48–49a], to consider one, mocks a "caliper," a term which indicates power and abstract thought, boring a "divine ingénue" until Don John, who has sympathies with summer, will embrace her. The taunting of the pedant and the rhapsodizing over the young girl convey expected views. Here, possibly an allegory should shadow seasonal traits from these figures, but to elaborate soon becomes either banal or pointlessly forced. For the reader himself to set the lilacs in context asks the very sentimentality which Imagism sought to exclude. "Last Looks at the Lilacs," ultimately, only sketches the unlikelihood of a romance between age and youth. In any event, enough poems pair their polarities directly.

ii

Clearly delineated opposites belong to a way of noting which Stevens terms an "anecdote" in titles: "Earthy Anecdote," "Anecdotal Revery," "Anecdote of Men by the Thousand," "Anecdote of Canna," "Anecdote of the Prince of Peacocks," "Anecdote of the Abnormal," and "Anecdote of the Jar." The last, discussed in the preceding chapter, may represent the model for their scope. A set stanzaic form does not determine them; externally these seven poems share little, some more strictly measured than the majority in *Harmonium*, others in vers libre. Nor does the anecdote take a special subject or development; at first glance these pick different topics. All do pretend to a superficial slightness, brief jottings which underline deeper implications. In the Imagistic poems a single item fixes everything else, and from it an awareness of the context or its inscrutability arises. The anecdotes oppose two objects side by side without necessarily concluding the antagonism between them. The two perspectives from a double vantage send forth lines leading to more questions than answers. The topics favor general conjectures and usually turn upon diametric poles like reality-illusion, art-nature, waking-sleep, tangible-transcendent. Keeping the possibilities manageable may ask a greater care from the reader than the poet himself exercised. Just as *Harmonium* has voices beyond that adaptable instrument's, so these anecdotes tell no tales but allow the speaker his say without moralizing. True to the anecdotal frame, a concluding surprise, not fully prepared for in the telling, frequently rounds them off either through dropping the irreconcilables or with a sudden resemblance between opposites. At its worst it disintegrates into poetizing according to O. Henry; at its best it permits Stevens to balance doubt and praise without condescending testimonials.

Not all anecdotes carry the designation in their titles. "Homunculus et la Belle Étoile" [25–27a] extracts as much as the manner will yield in *Harmonium* and achieves a precise enigma, exquisitely cool in its suspensions. Man and star brashly invoke a traditional microcosm and macrocosm; the opening lines present a remote geography through an equally distant vocabulary. "In the sea, Biscayne, there prinks | The young emerald, evening star." Florida provides waters, which deck the evening star, and, becoming emerald, connote the simple fecundity of the sea and the people on whom the reflected glitter shines. Even the driest philosophers may stumble across it and not scan it indifferently, although they cannot quite encompass its riches.

> *It is better that, as scholars,*
> *They should think hard in the dark cuffs*
> *Of voluminous cloaks,*
> *And shave their heads and bodies.*

The hortatory tone persists as long as the thinkers contemplate the sky, where they perhaps find their studies less literal than supposed. While a sympathy of spontaneity joins uncritical people and the evening star, the scholars, set off from them, discern other depths within it, which it may or may not contain.

> *It is a good light, then, for those*
> *That know the ultimate Plato,*
> *Tranquillizing with this jewel*
> *The torments of confusion.*

The suspended ending derives from the archness which marked the poetry of the early twentieth century and intrudes into Stevens' work sporadically. Does *good* mean beneficial for philosophers (and others) as they are or does the star ambiguously point them from their torments to a new serenity? The *ultimate Plato* rings with a misty preci-

sion and also pulls in the music of the spheres. Does this
star, therefore, deny the philosophers' Plato or raise to
quintessence all thought? Such teasing lends the anecdotes
an innocent distrust of platitudes, a common enough pose
at the time. Stevens hides behind his own reticent aplomb
without any reassuring winks.

To critics who seriously want a single or limited number
of meanings for every line, his polite withdrawals may
prove distracting. If one abandons the unwarranted belief
that this volume repeats the same dogma in every poem,
then one starts seeing the elaborate innuendoes. Discoveries about the world, always offering fresh surprises, defy
one creed. Many poems delineate abstract forces which,
although the concept may irk humanists, such as the
philosophical homunculi, arise, swell, alter, and cease without reference to people. An early reviewer favored the
humanly centered "Last Looks at the Lilacs" and complained "But when we have gone all through Mr. Stevens,
we find ourselves putting to him the same question that he
himself, in the last poem of his book, puts *To a* [*sic*]
Roaring Wind [113a]:

> *What syllable are you seeking,*
> *Vocallissimus,* [*sic*]
> *In the distances of sleep?*
> *Speak it."* [4]

Were a reply to drift from the distances of sleep, who, save
the poet, would interpret it? If inhabiting the distances of
sleep, how does the wind roar? A vocalissimus hardly lacks
syllables, however confused their ordering. Does the command result from the poet's own anxiety about the message
or a care for all speech? As printed originally "To the
Roaring Wind" formed a tailpiece for "Primordia." To
beg an answer from the wind after nine short images about
the northern and southern United States perhaps heightens the irony of seeking in a landscape what it cannot
yield. The independent existence of the poem, nevertheless, warns against both looking for a complete credo in
any one title and ignoring the limits which Stevens sets on

single items. The jar and Tennessee do not resolve their animosity; la belle étoile influences those below it contradictorily; a wind, dreamed by the poet, searches for words: the anecdotes reach precisely the faith which sustains skepticism.

At the outset Stevens worked contentedly in playing one absolute off against another; he perfected this technique until a defter finesse modulates tensions between less blatant polarities. For example, "Les Plus Belles Pages" [244–45a] offers a variety of diametric quantities, which commence, "The milkman came in the moonlight and the moonlight | Was less than moonlight," then moves on to consider related items, since nothing exists by itself, until it reaches a solitary Aquinas and concludes, "Theology after breakfast sticks to the eye." Although Stevens disliked offering prose paraphrases, he wrote out a short sketch for this one, in part [293–94b]:

> Apparently the poem means that the conjunction of milkman and moonlight is the equivalent of the conjunction of logician and saint. What it really means is that the interrelation between things is what makes them fecund. Interaction is the source of poetry. . . . The principle finds its best illustration in the interaction of our faculties or of our thoughts and emotions. Aquinas is a classic example: a figure of great modern interest, whose special force seems to come from the interaction of his prodigious love of God. The idea that his theology, as such, is involved is dismissed in the last line. That the example is not of scholarly choice is indicated by the title. But the title also means that les plus belles pages are those in which things do not stand alone, but are operative as the result of interaction, inter-relation. This is an idea of some consequence, not a casual improvisation. The inter-relation between reality and the imagination is the basis of character in literature. The inter-relation between reality and the emotions is the basis of the vitality of literature, between reality and thought, the basis of its power.

The "explanation" brilliantly expands without in the least impoverishing the work. To expect readers to reach such a synopsis unaided makes, perhaps, an exorbitant demand upon them and certainly on the anecdotal form. Fortunately, the longer pieces expatiate upon the shorter.

iii

The Imagistic traits so far isolated frequently help throw light on the ambitious works. Because *Harmonium* incorporates an ambiguous totality which twentieth-century authors sometimes seek, one must read nearly each page of the book with the données from the whole in mind. The further hazard of their being no consistently offered philosophic frame means that much remains tentative. Of the three kinds so far labeled—one reason for distinguishing among them—each projects its own development in the unity of Stevens' outlook for this book and the later ones. The Imagistic pieces can swell to offer their catalogues still almost freed from other commitments; they exemplify nearly the sole successful instances of this sort of writing. Among the most vexing, others, not grotesque throughout, sardonically record an imbalance between objects which should reinforce each other. Although no poems trace conflicting characters, some sketches—the woman of "Sunday Morning," the Uncle with his monocle, a high-toned old Christian woman, and Crispin—exist less shadowy when placed beside their progenitors. Finally, the anecdotes expand their duality until their structure becomes contrapuntal, although, as the note on "Les Plus Belles Pages" says, a few lines may compress major themes. The chief works embody the concept which Stevens gave his introduction to Valéry's *Dialogues:* Gloire du long Désir, Idées. One dare not, however, extract the ideas from their necessary constructs; otherwise they want glory and extension. As devoutly as Mallarmé and Valéry, Stevens believed that one makes poems with words, not ideas. The coupling of ideas and desire locates the climate, one where the rules of logic blend with the landscape and where, at the same time, emotions arise from serenity, not excitement.

The long Imagistic poem which does not disintegrate into a lumber-room represents an arduous feat of poetic legerdemain. This sort of composition never recognizes what it is about; the objects never coalesce with the usually abstract subject. The kaleidoscopic patterns steadily metamorphose the topic without commentary. Marianne Moore, who, Stevens said, "makes the most lavish snake-charmer look like a visitor" [250b], uses it as her principal style, but, as already noted, she relies upon quasi-academic references and documents. Stevens' most famous example, probably his best known poem, "Thirteen Ways of Looking at a Blackbird," with an exhilarating freedom of technique presents the views not in excelsis but through what they derive from and change within their habitat. The ranges through such varieties of meaning and sound impart to the blackbird by its very ubiquity a transcendence; here as in the anecdotes the rhetoric may contradict the subject. It partakes of the quality of a Ravel waltz: the medium cannot encompass the most ambitious levels of artistic intensity, but brilliant improvisation on hackneyed models imparts a nobility or sentiment. "Thirteen Ways of Looking at a Blackbird" [92–95a] makes nearly ideal use of the material: from the short, expected "The river is moving. | The blackbird must be flying" to the decorative "bawds of euphony | Would cry out sharply." By excluding any outright statement, the images here create a rich fusing of reality with response to it. "Metaphors of a Magnifico" aims at an identical effect, except a statement of purpose there becomes mixed up among the men, bridge, and village and so blurs surfaces.

If "Thirteen Ways of Looking at a Blackbird" by modesty achieves grandeur, "Six Significant Landscapes," almost as pretentious as their title, could comfortably contain several more or be reduced by a couple. In each a fluttering motion—of wind and water, a pool, ants, stars (twice), and a half-moon—contrasts with man, woman, or manufactured item. Some belong more properly to the anecdotes. Just what significance, apart from the point that under given circumstances any aspect of the world need not lack mystery, they possess appears neither in the poems nor through what connects them. A similar weak-

ness, intensified, mars the only nearly tiresome group Stevens ever wrote. Called "New England Verses" [104–6a],
they ostensibly parody New England primers with their
primitive couplets, although, unlike the ancestor, not on
Biblical themes. With predictability each of the antithetical titles, "The Whole World Including the Speaker,"
"The Whole World Excluding the Speaker," "Soupe aux
Perles," "Soupe sans Perles," dangles its two lines, and the
joke becomes pallid before the final sixteenth. In stretching
the discrepancies between title and couplet a shrewdness
of sorts arises, but the contrasts or similarities within the
paired stanzas strike one as either so obvious that they
seem not worth making or so tangential that anything can
be made of them. The rhymes contribute little except
"Iliad-penny pad," which gives the whole thing away. As a
modern parody on rustic belief, they may amuse, but as
poems which wrench a slick sophistication from an archaic
piety, they sound decidedly kittenish. Stevens parades a
series of effective images only with an emotion, which
may, however, be ephemeral as clouds, stretching across
them.

iv

The same Imagistic manner, then, can accommodate a work as poised, ebbing, clear, and faultless as "Sea
Surface Full of Clouds." [98–102a] In arrangement his
most inflexible poem, it triumphantly traces mornings in
the Pacific through five lambent aspects. Each section has
eighteen lines in six groups of three, irregularly rhymed,
the first two of which announce, within three variants, "In
that November off Tehuantepec, | The slopping of the sea
grew still one night." Dawn's arriving upon the deck
makes the poet think of chocolates and umbrellas. The
green ocean resembles in its tossing different machines;
frequently with Stevens waves stand for almost mechanical
repetitions. The clouds reflected in the water impart a cue
for sentiment through metaphoric flowers and allow the
poet to identify what aspect of himself responds to the
scene, a line in French, always the twelfth. The concluding

six lines trace the patterns through the heavens and ultimately resolve sea, sky, and, by implications, poet. In a
later poem a similar line, "The waves | Were mechanical,
muscular" [81b], implies that their surgings do not, with
their variety, descend into a mere ticking but offer a
reliable flux, a counterpart for the imagination. "Sea Surface Full of Clouds" in its impeccable bounds exemplifies
the elegant precision of organic form which almost every
poet strives for. The wonder is that all the self-imposed
patterning contributes freshness and excitement in every
line either by the novelties, the echoes, or both. It nearly
proves that the greatest freedom lies in severe obedience,
at least sometimes, for poetry.

The first stanza with "rosy chocolate | And gilt umbrel-
las" becomes innocent spontaneity so that the smooth sea
mirrors the clouds as flowers and "Poured brilliant iris on
the glistening blue." In the next, "chop-house chocolate
| And sham umbrellas," a sinister quiet impedes the
clouds with a heavy worldliness until the sky clears and
clarity returns. The fashionable "porcelain chocolate | And
pied umbrellas" contradictorily bring ambiguities with "silver petals of white blooms," as the poet, through them,
identifies love. The time here seems pre-dawn, and white
on shadows moves sensuously. The flowers remain hidden
until the sky, "A blue beyond the rainy hyacinth," colors
them in the first light. "Musky chocolate | And frail um-
brellas": intellect and wit possess the ocean and reveal
human indifference; the tortured images of water at last
yield to the simple air so that the green murkiness in the
ocean becomes, "Mile-mallows that a mallow sun cajoled."
"One thought of Chinese chocolate | And large umbrel-
las"; clowns and circuses predominate from a sense of
chagrin until the whole vanishes in the unity of sea and sky
"and from the two | Came fresh transfigurings of freshest
blue." Whatever uncertainties one harbors about the value
of synaesthesia as a poetic device, it here justifies itself:
day provides light, which the poet defines by a subjective
response, whereupon he turns back to the ocean for deeper
discoveries. Arbitrarily as the associations alter between

the stanzas, the continuing form emphasizes the unpredict-
ability of the weather and the emotions, both disciplined
by poetic awareness alone. No immediate cause for the
traveler's experience, no ulterior significance of chocolate,
umbrellas, clouds, and flowers disturbs the poem, which
stays uncommitted throughout. Its statements and methods incorporate Stevens' abiding theme, the interchange
between milieu and insight. "Take, for example, a beach
extending as far as the eye can reach, bordered, on the one
hand, by trees and, on the other, by the sea. The sky is
cloudless and the sun is red. In what sense do the objects
in this scene resemble each other? There is enough green
in the sea to relate it to the palms. There is enough of the
sky reflected in the water to create a resemblance, in some
sense, between them. The sand is yellow between the
green and the blue. In short, the light alone creates a
unity." [71c]

Obeying the authority of his own feelings, Stevens found
the données of Imagism congenial. This discipline must
often be content with fragments, just as: the Magnifico's
metaphors do not, cannot, exhaust the chosen place; the
ways of looking at a blackbird, even with awareness of
absences, keep lighting on accidental qualities; the New
England verses might as well expand to twenty-six couplets; the six landscapes do not hint what bestows their
numerical significance. He, of course, did not versify the
diary of a Cook's tour, but had the voyage lasted longer
and the sea during that time have borne more clouds and
moods, would a different poem have emerged? The rigorous composition of "Sea Surface Full of Clouds" mitigates
a seeming discipline, but do all its limits, in the last
analysis, look arbitrary? The question resolves into: can a
formal poem retain the sweep of the weather? In another
connection Stevens said, "An imitation may be described
as an identity manqué. It is artificial. It is not fortuitous as
a true metaphor is. If it is an imitation of something in
nature, it may even surpass identity and assume a praeter-
nature. It may very well escape the derogatory." [73c] "Sea
Surface Full of Clouds" rightly belongs on this uncommon

eminence; a history about vague reveries could sustain itself
in no other manner. Resourcefulness can contrive an infi-
nite number of ways to write a poem, and the search for
the unique form, while generally doomed, if it succeeds
gains commensurately. In spite of critics' efforts to weigh
down the poem with a specious dignity by bestowing a
philosophic message upon it, it mocks all inflexibility
through its very structure. The essentially fugitive nature
of the moods, when frozen within the formal rigidity, flocks
into their casual sequences. Irresolution itself functions
dramatically by the contrasting line in French to indicate
how dependent upon the shifting clouds and waves man's
self-knowledge is. Although Stevens, happily, seldom sticks
epigraphs on his poems, for this one he might have borrowed from Baudelaire the final response of the stranger
who declares: "J'aime les nuages . . . les nuages qui
passent . . . là-bas . . . les merveilleux nuages!" [5]

If he loved clouds, no spurning of the world drove him
to it; the ocean itself offered tokens which became the
land. Consider, as well:

>Gloomy grammarians in golden gowns,
>Meekly you keep the mortal rendezvous,
>Eliciting the still sustaining pomps
>Of speech which are like music so profound
>They seem an exaltation without sound.
>Funest philosophers and ponderers,
>Their evocations are the speech of clouds.
>
>So speech of your processionals returns
>In the casual evocations of your tread
>Across the stale, mysterious seasons. These
>Are the music of meet resignation; these
>The responsive, still sustaining pomps for you
>To magnify, if in that drifting waste
>You are to be accompanied by more
>Than mute bare splendors of the sun and Moon.

There lingers about this the trappings of a divine academic
festival, although without the title it looks strangely jagged
and broken; "On the Manner of Addressing Clouds"
[55–56a] fuses its qualities. Envisaging clouds as robed
grammarians introduces a modest conceit; exploring its

connotations matches the quality of "Sea Surface Full of Clouds"; having the cloud-scholars borrow from man's speech becomes anecdotal. Taken in these three ways, whatever extraneous problems the poem contains soon disappear. What remains, including the much-explicated phrase "funest philosophers," makes a precise statement whose nature, rather than idiom, invokes paradox. To inscribe philosophic order on clouds stretches an uncommon metaphor, but their grandeur, superficial until the world responds, qualifies it sufficiently. One feels that basically Stevens shares postulates with Bishop Berkeley now and then, that whatever exists is in the eye of the beholder but maintained in the ensuing poetry. The second passage, repeating many of the same phrases, with puns on *mortal* and *still*, draws the inferences. The glory of clouds lingers on earth beyond their brief drifting across the sky and will rebound again for their magnificence. The last line picks up the opening contrast of splendor amid gloom. Clouds make man conscious of pomps, even with overtones of the French phrase, pompe funèbre, and he in turn celebrates them; the language stresses a playful ceremony; the poet creates the clouds as regents, then serves them, and ultimately, when they have vanished, preserves them.

Once again, other passages help illuminate the purport of a poem. An undergraduate quatrain, "Go not, young cloud, too boldly through the sky . . . | For eastward lies the night," [6] may imply a related thought, but it too patly delivers the arch warning. A quite late prose passage explains more fully the metaphysical groundwork. "To see the gods dispelled in mid-air and dissolve like clouds is one of the great human experiences. It is not as if they had gone over the horizon to disappear for a time; nor as if they had been overcome by other gods of greater power and profounder knowledge. It is simply that they came to nothing." [206b] In their decline these gods sink without the clamor of a Götterdämmerung; like clouds, they merely dissolve. Because of the human faith which once paradoxically bestowed almost enduring life on the fancied immortals, their loss has reality, and Stevens concedes that man's knowledge likewise shares the poverty. "It left us feeling dispossessed and alone in a solitude, like children without parents, in a home that seemed deserted, in which the amical rooms and halls had taken on a look of hardness and emptiness." [207b] Once they had vanished, man obviously could not summon them back and, instead, had to compose his own world. Stevens pursues the subject further to ally the old gods more closely with abiding clouds; perhaps from the outset the divine beings connoted gratuitous aesthetic delight. "To a people of high intelligence, whose gods have benefited by having been accepted and addressed by the superior minds of a superior world, the symbolic paraphernalia of the very great becomes unnecessary and the very great become the very natural." [208b] The clouds, too, always shine with a real grandeur but rooted in a human contriving, whether for deities or aesthetics.

v

The primacy which certain poems attribute to the external clouds (and gods) does not have as a corollary that Stevens subscribes to a deterministic attitude and subdues man under blind cosmic powers, Ananke in "Owl's Clover" notwithstanding. Frequently, man creates gods and, through grammar and rhetoric, makes logical the sky. Knowledge starts from the world and its atmosphere, and the disembodied mind comprises a ruling, but not wholly sovereign, part of life. A "Theory" [86–87a] in its totality runs:

> I am what is around me.
>
> Women understand this.
> One is not duchess
> A hundred yards from a carriage.
>
> These, then are portraits:
> A black vestibule;
> A high bed sheltered by curtains.
>
> These are merely instances.

The same human impulse which conceived duchesses created carriages to accompany them; the poem turns on its
belief in the fitness of things. To posit a suitability does
not assert that whatever exists must be harmonious or in a
causal relationship, although resemblances may often beget true insights. In contrast with the reassuring knowledge
which arises from external wholeness, a terror can adhere
about inflexibility or tatters. "The Snow Man" [9–10a]
subtly evinces the remoteness at which Stevens excels; by
qualifying the actual it circumscribes a metaphysical blank.
What symptoms accompany the failure of response? In a
winter climate one must experience a cold sharper than
snow and ice produce to grasp what it is *not* to imagine
"any misery in the sound of the wind," whose melancholy
a "snow man" cannot understand: "And, nothing himself,
beholds | Nothing that is not there and the nothing that
is." Sharing some of the same figures and treatment of
them, this poem parallels the concluding part of Keats'
"Stanzas" ("In Drear-nighted December") :

> *The feel of not to feel it,*
> *When there is none to heal it,*
> *Nor numbed sense to steel it,*
> *Was never said in rhyme.*

Although an alternate reading only recently favored, the
first line of the quoted part appeared in versions published
during the nineteenth century. Beyond Keats' view, perhaps only implicit in Stevens', who can assert what phantasies might *not* spin around the snow man's icy brain? He
partakes of that inhuman winter which made him and can
compose no poems. Whether, like a duchess, the snow
man depends on his season, the end does not affirm,
although to enquire about his melting in spring becomes
irrelevant. Similar symptoms for summer ennui motivate
"Banal Sojourn" [62–63a], where the brilliant colors,
which in examples so far quoted have accompanied suave
comforts, flash falsely while "The grackles crack their
throats of bone in the smooth air," one of those amazing
descriptions with enduring authority. No mystery from

winter has survived, and "One has a malady, here, a malady. One feels a malady," a less ingenious phrase for absence than in "The Snow Man." Stevens' special accents emerge clearly here if one lets Keats' "Stanzas" exemplify mystery and John Crowe Ransom's "Winter Remembered" analysis:

Better to walk forth in the murderous air
And wash my wounds in the snows; that would be healing;
Because my heart would throb less painful there,
Being caked with cold, and past the smart of feeling.

If, for Stevens, an inadequacy of emotion upon confronting externals verges on terror, a finicky solicitude about them becomes ridiculous. "Floral Decorations for Bananas" [53–54a] has a speaker who complains, "Well, nuncle, this plainly won't do," and not at all plainly continues a euphuistic mockery, which exaggerates, without invalidating, the contention that before the heavy bananas "The women will be all shanks | And bangles and slatted eyes." The finale in a riot of overstatement appropriate for the bananas and yet more revealing about the fastidious speaker's taste assigns misshapen tropical leaves resembling toucans as a suitable accompaniment. On the other hand, "Anecdote of Men by the Thousand" [51–52a], like others so titled, contrasts two theories: characteristics of a place largely depend upon its inhabitants, who, in turn, draw their distinguishing features from the land where they live. "The soul, he said, is composed | Of the external world." Which ultimately determines which the poem does not indicate. Like Proust, Stevens constantly responds to "the *Duft* of towns." [83b] The postulate can reach Cusanus' intensity when man's very presence draws up the world through himself to consciousness, a figure comparable with the jar and Tennessee, although unhampered by the muted antagonism between those two forces. If "Anecdote of Men by the Thousand" said the last word on whether one defines a place as Lhassa because of the dresses its women wear or whether the women adopt their fashions because they live in Lhassa, the later poems would not have had to be written, or they would reinterpret pat formulae. Throughout *Harmonium* affinities bind man and his habitat, a network most strongly and hauntingly projected through the uncanny "Tattoo" [81a]:

> The light is like a spider.
> It crawls over the water.
> It crawls over the edges of the snow.
> It crawls under your eyelids
> And spreads its web there—
> Its two webs.

From here the webs fasten both to the brain and external objects so that the beholder's eyes expand throughout his body and his world. In summer, a snow field, the tropics, or Lhassa, much as man expresses his soil, the earth informs the soul harboring his knowledge. The next group, which anyone who believes that Stevens assigns chief authority to the imagination should consider carefully, indicates a distrust of those who start only with the ego and qualifies such generalizations as: "For Wallace Stevens, imagination is 'the only clue to reality,' and he is primarily a *realist*. This is, perhaps, his chief divagation from such a school as 'symbolisme,' and it is, after all, an important one. And yet, for him, as for the 'symbolistes,' imagination is 'the only genius.' For him, also, to think of the imagination 'as a part of life, is to realize the extent of artifice.' It is through such artifice as poetry, then, that Stevens seeks to investigate and enjoy reality." [7]

vi

"Gubbinal" [85a], a designation presumably derived from the Gubbins, who represented to the British what the Boeotians did to the Athenians, concedes that "The world is ugly, | And the people are sad" because someone insists—by denying the brilliant sun, flowers, animals, and fire which the verse shows—that all is lackluster. The lines repeat themselves not to extract new pleasures as elsewhere, but for a flat acceptance. "The Man Whose Pharynx Was Bad" [96a] complements "Floral Decorations for Bananas"; both use a sated man who recoils in distaste from an external excess. In the latter the speaker deliberately exaggerates the lurid bananas to establish his own discernment. In the former, depressed by "The malady of the quotidian," the man lets bleakness crush him, just as the one of "Banal Sojourn" could not respond adequately to profuseness. Whereas both "Floral Decorations for Bananas" and "Banal Sojourn" force the individual to wince before the lushness he sees, here the barrenness does not itself induce melancholia. Like "The Snow Man," the one with the bad pharynx experiences accidia, but "I am too dumbly in my being pent," proves him unable to appreciate any weather: "Perhaps, if winter once could penetrate | Through all its purples to the final slate." He wishes not for another time but for another self, the same longing which motivates "Anatomy of Monotony," when the spirit makes the body restless with the earth, the body having first stirred the spirit to discontent. The poems which show beginning from outside and within both enlarge upon the grotesque pieces. One might take the derivation of the term *grotesque* as indicative: Renaissance painters applied it to the Roman decorations surviving on the walls in buried ruins. For Stevens the grotesque may depict an inner phantasy quite shut off from the exterior world or the fixing on merely part of one's environment, a minor segment, at that. Just as the grotesque went beyond its origins, so some of his poems in this vein look substantial.

When asked to select his favorite poem for the anthology *This Is My Best*, he named "Domination of Black" and explained his choice with a mild manifesto.

The themes of life are the themes of poetry. It seems to be, so clearly, that what is the end of life for the politician or the philosopher, say, ought to be the end of life for the poet, and that his important poems ought to be the poems of the achievement of that end. But poetry is neither politics nor philosophy. Poetry is poetry, and one's objective as a poet is to achieve poetry, precisely as one's objective in music is to achieve music. There are poets who would regard that as a scandal and who would say that a poem that had no importance except its importance as poetry had no importance at all, and that a poet who had no objective except to achieve poetry was a fribble and something less than a man of reason.[8]

This is the complete document. To argue that a plea for pure poetry came forth to refute a squabble about politics may sound obtuse. Nevertheless, this time (the reply dated August 24, 1942) saw the height of a controversy over whether the French avant-garde had caused their country to collapse and whether expatriates had undermined the United States. Allen Tate put it in heuristic satire:

> *In this bad time no part*
> *The poet took, nor chance:*
> > *He studied Swift and Donne,*
> > *Ignored the Hun,*
> *While with faint heart*
> *Proust caused the fall of France.*
>
> *Sad day at Oahu*
> *When the Jap beetle hit!*
> > *Our Proustian retort*
> > *Was Kimmel and Short,*
> *Old women in blue,*
> *And then the beetle bit.*
>
> *It was defeat, or near it!*
> *Yet all that feeble time*
> > *Brave Brooks and lithe MacLeish*
> > *Had sworn to thresh*
> *Our flagging spirit*
> *With literature made Prime!* [9]

By his choice Stevens presumably wanted to ally himself, as usual, with those who insist upon the primacy of poetry. He could, had he wished, have picked one, especially from among those composed during the preceding decade, which points toward more practical matters. "Domination of Black," as a flowing pattern of sound and images, traces an autumnal design: leaves mirrored in fire by night blend into a peacock's tail until the bird's traditional dark cry

matches the hemlocks outside the window. The repetitions
echo and expand the quiet scene, which by itself contains
nothing awesome, to dramatize a fear lying beyond mere
headlines. The inner musings, which incite restlessness,
occur without an immediate prompting. Undoubtedly
sheer darkness and all it represents, more powerfully than
any other vacancy, entail themes and adjuncts which Stevens does not care to explore in *Harmonium*. He once
assigns to one of three New England women a belief about
"that ever-dark central, wherever it is, | In the central of
earth or sky or air or thought" [108b], but himself chooses
to realize "That the sense of being changes as we
talk, | That talk shifts the cycle of the scenes of kings."
[109b] Even the chant "Swatara, Swatara, black river"
[428a] settles on a man walking beside it. Only toward the
very end do some poems consider blank darkness. Here
"Palace of the Babies" [77a] employs a similar theme less
elusively. It begins, "The disbeliever walked the moonlit
place, | Outside the gates of hammered serafin." The
moonlight, as part of night, rocks and spins; these maternal
actions summon phantasmagorial babies, a more vital force
than the molded effigies. Stevens' ability to portray a
moderate anxiety and then to define by austerity a still
more buried terror combines a sternness in vision and style
too infrequently credited him. The night nurse and charges
do not comfort the disbeliever, while in his mind, suspiciously veiled by a hat, "The clambering wings of birds of
black revolved, | Making harsh torment of the solitude,"
lines complementing the end of "Homunculus et la Belle
Étoile." In both "Domination of Black" and "Palace of the
Babies" an awareness of personal inadequacy causes fear.
Again, contrary to opinions usually advanced, no refuge
from this inner ennui beckons in an empyrean of pure
escape. Rhetoric mocks the quotidian and the transcendent.

vii

"To the One of Fictive Music" [87–88a] reverses
the direction of the more ambitious "Sea Surface Full of

Clouds" and "On the Manner of Addressing Clouds,"
where movement begins against the sky and descends to
an observer who interprets its blue shadings in human
attitudes. Here the poet considers an impossibly remote
ideal, "Sister and mother and diviner love"; all the trade-
marks of a pseudo-Biblical incantation follow, the repeated
words (*and* eleven times in nine lines) and rhymes which
stumble over each other. Should this rhapsodizing strike
one as a bit too exquisite, more wondrous than explicable,
like the wrath of Die Königin der Nacht in *Die
Zauberflöte*, the effect of tessitura probably is intentional.
Man, in contrast with the fictive creature, tortures earth
until it resembles him, "Gross effigy and simulacrum."
The muse of fictive music has no name, like a true deity,
and no being, more elusive than the cloudy grammarians.
The third stanza less ornately but with greater awe sets the
ineffable figure close to the head of all creation, immortal
or human, while it concedes that man cannot avoid finding
his speech in the world. The final section, then, as though
recognizing that this embodiment, if that term is not too
crude, crushes by its perfect clarity, suddenly begs for a
figure whom Klimt alone could have depicted with full
justice, "On your pale head wear | A band entwining, set
with fatal stones." The uncanny power of the next, the
final, two lines almost reconciles one to the rest, "Unreal,
give back to us what once you gave: | The imagination
that we spurned and crave." Whereas sun and moon
rounded off the passage of the clouds, here the abrupt shift
from the invocation fails to complete or dismiss the subject. Presumably the new aspect belongs to the one of
fictive music and not another power; she should be protean
enough to assume the guise. For the continuity of the
piece the rapid transfiguring makes autocratic demands
upon a reader's generosity. Does the *unreal* refer to the
first or the second embodiment or to all aspects of the one
of fictive music? Does the request beseech the old aspect
or the new? Was the imagination spurned because of
euphoria or ignorance? If the imagination has been refused, does this poem lack it was well; if so, where can one

find it? Perhaps the same paradox caused Stevens to print two parts of "The Man with the Blue Guitar" as "The Place of Poetry—Inaccessible Utopia."

A tentative outline of what "fictive music" means will limit guesses.

Early music presents many insoluble problems to those who set out to reconstruct and interpret it. In few of the problems, however, is it so hazardous to attempt any definite codex of law and practice as in that of *musica ficta*—i.e. the insertion of accidentals into a text. That composers, from the earliest times, intended such occasional modifications to be made by the performers is beyond any possible doubt: indeed the ancient name for an accidental (*signum asininum* or "ass's mark") is clear evidence that its insertion by a composer was a reflection on the competence of the singer. But there is little or no agreement among the old theorists as to the laws of interpretation; which seems to imply either that there was no unanimity in practice or that the theorists themselves suffered from the malady endemic to their tribe. For it is characteristic of all theorists to epitomize and codify the very usages which the creative minds of their contemporaries have decisively abandoned. Nor is there, at the present day, any solid agreement among the most thoughtful students of ancient music—no two of whom would, in all probability, produce an identical "fair-copy" of any given manuscript from the earliest times down to Orlando Gibbons. The most reasonable course, therefore, is to attempt to state impartially the conditions of the problem and the difficulties inherent in its solution.

"Music is called *ficta* when we make a tone to be a semitone, or, conversely, a semitone to be a tone." And the problem for the student consists in this: since the composer did not (or seldom did) tell the performer, by means of accidentals, when these changes were to be made, how could the performer know? [10]

Analogously, Stevens' fictive music has nothing to do with a dying fall, an unheard melody, what vibrates in the memory, or something in the deep heart's core. It represents the taste and knowledge which can interpret properly an imperfect world and its incomplete arts. (When Yeats' line, incidentally, does get into a much later poem, it creates another sound: in Holland one Hans by a frozen sea listens to a roaring wind [a vocalissimus?] and remembers to "*hear it* as it falls *in the deep heart's core.* | A steamer lay near him, foundered in the ice." [421a]) Like the snow man's feeling the nothing that is, the imagination here invokes everything, part of which is not. The very bravado implies that the worship of anything too remote and disembodied ends in futility, that a muse must exceed unadulterated ectoplasm. Fictive music requires a score before the imagination can insert the accidentals, and fictive, after all, carries overtones of mere sham.

"Poetry is the supreme fiction, madame," begins Stevens' monologue to "A High-Toned Old Christian Woman" [59a], and the frequently quoted comment is cited for reaffirming the view that he prefers the impressionistic to the documented, the fictive to the factual, the frivolous to the devout, the pagan to the Christian. In this poem he does choose but not without irony, and the anecdotal manner reappears. "To the One of Fictive Music" defines the almost unknowable through insubstantial terms; here two contrasting pleasure domes of eternity, built up by opposing forces, show palms "Like windy citherns hankering for hymns" and palms "Squiggling like saxophones." The two heavens, in resembling the courts of fashionable hotels, stand now as a touching tribute to the jazz age and H. L. Mencken's Bible Belt. Even the saints, "disaffected flagellants," "whip from themselves | A jovial hullabaloo among the spheres." The tone mocks not only genteel standards but also the flashy language of the speaker whose "fictive things | Wink as they will." The woman and speaker presumably agree that both the nave and the peristyle of their respective religions can exist, whether they suggest a "haunted heaven" or a "masque | Beyond the planets." The banter implies, furthermore, that the high-toned old christian woman has lived a number of years, and her tolerating the man's impertinences measures her sophistication. Baudelaire's concepts run through Stevens', and the dandy's desire to shock the bourgeois takes a variety of forms; here, the poetry accommodates it but need not restrict itself to it. If Stevens delights in haughty sounds and concepts, with the same equipment he can also recognize their limits; whereas Baudelaire, for all his relish of irony, must at some point take himself seriously, Stevens cannot always regard even poetry without noting that it inspires peculiarities, which he may defend or dismiss.

Also combining fervor and detachment, "Peter Quince at the Clavier" [89–92a] interprets anew the relationship between music and the world. Not so clownish as in Shakespeare, the player equates the sounds with the desire he feels: "Thinking of your blue-shadowed silk, | Is music." The next section, an andante passage, depicts Susanna wandering beside her pool. Upon her discovery of the elders, "A cymbal crashed, | And roaring horns." An interlude of stinging noises ensues. In the fourth the tempo of the first returns reflectively:

> Beauty is momentary in the mind—
> The fitful tracing of a portal;
> But in the flesh it is immortal.
> The body dies; the body's beauty lives.

Fictive things descend from diverse lives and origins, as poets have known ever since they discovered that verse bestows its own eternity, not, however, quite beyond change. The merely imagined cannot endure; what once lived may, in memory, enjoy a life through its former being and the poetry it inspires. The high-toned old woman's dreary heaven, if altered to an actuality, might shock her; Susanna, however shaming her episode by the pool, vibrates constantly, therefore partaking of the immortal, in the mind; "[music] plays | On the clear viol of her memory." Similarly, Badroulbadour to the cataloguing worms resembles any other corpse; human speech alone could keep her alive. This poem, if a bit soft in its syllables and tending toward a sentimentality, because Susanna's figure depends on associations from outside the poem, does present a nearly ideal construct for *Harmonium*. The poet-musician muses on a figure who lives for the present

through his artistry. He, nevertheless, stays a clown and his
instrument, a clavier, renders the lush melody crisply;
irony frees him from commitments.

viii

No evasion will avoid a central conflict of *Harmonium:* a sporadic annoyance with the daily scene and
the persistent refusal to counterfeit another. Terming it
conflict exaggerates the tension because the poems do not
resolve into a squawking debate where one side demolishes
the other. Instead, at their best they present this world as
so washed and glistening that thought of and hope for any
better one must sound pallid and deluded. Although frequently scorn and parody provide a comic mask for the
poet, at least he flees to no traditional theology as a solace
upon losing this life. The famous, often explicated, "Sunday Morning" [66–70a] dramatizes his qualified kind of
epicureanism but always in reasonable figures. Sitting in
the Sunday sun, a woman decidedly not old, nor self-
consciously high-toned, nor christian lives through her
musings, just as Peter Quince did through his clavier. The
opening sketches a well-appointed room, probably a sun
porch, with tropical comforts: peignoir, coffee, oranges,
and the light. "The green freedom of a cockatoo | Upon a
rug," introducing a design in the material, a shadow, or,
most likely, a bird out of its cage, provides a counterpart of
the Christian dove. From these agreeable objects her
thoughts turn to the harsh symbols in a church she will
not attend: death, Palestine, blood, and the sepulcher.
The knowledge that "Divinity must live within herself" in-
augurates a list of the emotions for the living. Jove, whose
sky no longer separates earth from paradise, joins the two
elements and denies "this dividing and indifferent blue."
Memory alone, under this dispensation, must order the
passing seasons, which imply the changes and entail consciousness of death, the literal end of everything for her.
Nevertheless, boredom with things celestial would attend
a heaven of perpetual June: "Death is the mother of
beauty." Acknowledging that the acceptance of change

must in itself become her true faith, "Sunday Morning" closes with a declaration, "We live in an old chaos of the sun, | Or old dependency of day and night." This human bravery sustains the wilderness itself as the spirit becomes the undulations of pigeons sinking downward at evening. Their softer plumage recalls the iridescent cockatoo with which the poem opened. The credo, made with utter calm, substitutes belief in earth for any less transitory havens where souls dwell. In its willingness to glorify the fleeting, it recognizes its own dangers and, within limits, tests its evidence. The last stanza, while by no means contradictory, brings the subject round to a familiar landscape and leaves a certain hesitancy.

The theme of "Sunday Morning" has bemused writers with degrees of urgency for centuries, and in this one, especially, poets and novelists have probed it. Valéry in "Le Cimetière marin" trenchantly arrives, like Stevens, at an acceptance of life and flux. "Sunday Morning," when published by *Poetry* in 1915, lacked three of the eight stanzas in *Harmonium*, and the final version rearranged the initial five. It seems, however, that Stevens had submitted the poem originally with its eight stanzas, and Harriet Monroe, wielding her editorial scissors, cut and pasted. *La Nouvelle Revue Française* printed "Le Cimetière marin" early in 1920, so there can be no likelihood of any direct influence. Nevertheless, the French text touches on many similar figures and thoughts.

> Maigre immortalité noire et dorée,
> Consolatrice affreusement laurée,
> Qui de la mort fais un sein maternal,
> Le beau mensonge et la pieuse ruse! [11]

The American has:

> Death is the mother of beauty, mystical,
> Within whose burning bosom we devise
> Our earthly mothers waiting, sleeplessly.

Another parallel cluster occurs when, earlier in the same stanza, Stevens writes:

Is there no change of death in paradise?
Does ripe fruit never fall? Or do boughs
Hang always heavy in that perfect sky,
Unchanging, yet so like our perishing earth,
With rivers like our own that seek for seas
They never find, the same receding shores
That never touch with inarticulate pang?

Valéry describes his human status in these terms:

Comme le fruit se fond en jouissance,
Comme en délice il change son absence
Dans une bouche où sa forme se meurt,
Je hume ici ma future fumée,
Et le ciel chante à l'âme consumée
Le changement des rives en rumeur.

Different as their methods are, Valéry capitalizing on the
actual place, Sète, at every point and Stevens departing
from the sun porch immediately, the subjects naturally
offer the same patterns to a twentieth-century intelligence.
Thus, Valéry starts with the sails like doves on the water:
"Ce toit tranquille, où marchent des colombes, | Entre les
pins palpite, entre les tombes," and concludes, "Rompez,
vagues! Rompez d'eaux réjouies | Ce toit tranquille où
picoraient des focs!" Stevens, after the cockatoo at the
outset, ends his on the same note:

And, in the isolation of the sky,
At evening, casual flocks of pigeons make
Ambiguous undulations as they sink,
Downward to darkness, on extended wings.

Yeats, on the other hand, rejected terrestrial flux and took
Valéry to task.

Then after certain poignant stanzas and just when I am
deeply moved he [Valéry] chills me. This metropolitan,
who has met so many reformers, who has learnt as a part
of good manners to deny what has no remedy, cries out
"Cruel Zénon! Zénon d'Elée", condemning that problem
of a tortoise and Achilles because it suggested that all
things only seemed to pass; and in a passage of great
eloquence rejoices that human life must pass. I was about

to put his poem among my sacred books, but I cannot now, for I do not believe him. My imagination goes some years backward, and I remember a beautiful young girl singing at the edge of the sea in Normandy words and music of her own composition. She thought herself alone, stood barefooted betwen sea and sand; sang with lifted head of the civilisations that there had come and gone, ending every verse with the cry: "O Lord, let something remain." [12]

Later for Stevens, when "She sang beyond the genius of the sea" [128a], a great deal remains, more than Valéry concedes, if less than Yeats requires.

An allied poem, one of Stevens' most directly bitter, "The Bird with the Coppery, Keen Claws" [82a], while fixing steadily on the subject and not hinting that these birds pass through images toward an allegory on religion, obviously draws more than a tropical forest above which "A parakeet of parakeets prevails." Blind and almost paralyzed, similar to the parrot Loulou which replaces the Holy Ghost in "Un Coeur simple," he exacts the will from lesser birds by his intellect, whose mysterious ways underscore the irony of his supernatural power. As the title implies, not only does intelligence beyond the point of knowing distinguish this "pip of life amid a mort of tails," but the coppery, keen claws grasp implacably both for descriptive detail and cruelty. To equate this parakeet with a single interpretation of the paraclete disrupts the poem; such obviously is the primary meaning, which extends to any rigid orthodoxy: the principle which prohibits seeing and tasting anything except an ascetic's dry shell. Stevens' sensibilities contrive a pity for poverty without descending to the meager. Here at the apex of his exotic forest a dread dreariness rules but does not negate the rest. The activities which the divine bird fails to notice set off his meanness. In Stevens' abiding view, man must be held responsible for his gods, and the bird depicts a thoroughly human contrivance. Not all faith need embody such sterility, and the foliage persists no matter what its head represents. Transcendence made incarnate tells more about the worshippers than about the unseen substance itself. Belief can, likewise, inspire joy: "This happy creature—It is he that invented the Gods. It is he that put into their mouths the only words they have ever spoken!" [167b]

ix

Almost at an opposite pole philosophically, inside the restricted range of *Harmonium*, "Le Monocle de Mon Oncle" [13–18a] places its shifting thoughts within a defined individual; informed, proper, a bit too diffident, and alert for every irony. "The Love Song of J. Alfred Prufrock" comes to mind, but Stevens shuns T. S. Eliot's tidy despair. Granted that nothing in the poem precisely licenses the guess, if a youthful rapture inspires an idealist to lose himself apostrophizing "To the One of Fictive Music," then his uncle broods superciliously through his single eye upon a lady whom he both spurns and craves. Unlike religion—or, better, belief—a topic to trouble Stevens increasingly, love seldom enters the later poems except indirectly. The opening invocation sounds too courtly even for a troubadour's Platonic lament, "Mother of heaven, regina of the clouds," but soon it destroys this pose. "And so I mocked her in magnificent measure. | Or was it that I mocked myself alone?" The second stanza, its concise insights into resigned weariness suiting a generation which made premature old age a specialty, expresses annoyance because of annoyance notably: "Shall I uncrumple this much-crumpled thing? | I am a man of fortune greeting heirs," and his propriety condones indifference to the spring. A couplet compactly draws upon terms, and themes, which Stevens has already annexed as his own, "Yet you persist with anecdotal bliss | To make believe a starry *connaissance*." Four ensuing sections define the woman when young and how, although changed, she survives not as Badroulbadour does to the worms but, rather, Susanna for Peter Quince. Rhetorically stressing the ironies and assured of how staid his passion must be, he envisages it not as a star fit for "fiery boys" but the flickering of a firefly. Throughout, surfaces and textures engender spiritual contrasts. Beau Brummell's Bath, his Arcadian refuge, conjures "mountainous coiffures," but the artificial fashion collapses before an erotic memory, "Why, without pity on these studious ghosts, | Do you come dripping in your hair from sleep?" "There is a substance in us that prevails," frequently quoted as an affirmation, in context ineffectually negates alarm about impotence by continuing:

> When amorists grow bald, then amours shrink
> Into the compass and curriculum
> Of introspective exiles, lecturing.
> It is a theme for Hyacinth alone.

After the deliberate procrastination, the theme advances again in the seventh section; so far the speaker has regarded chiefly himself and the inconveniences of love a bit narcissistically. The nature of this passion now engages him: "The mules that angels ride come slowly down | The blazing passes, from beyond the sun." The fantastic touch borrows attitudes from poems on more nearly outright religious matters. Between an effete heaven and a vigorous earth, the speaker becomes a meditating scholar rather than impetuous poet and searches inadequately again among motives for his indecision: it may come down to the epigram, at twenty the poet is always right, at sixty the doctor never wrong. Love remains quasi-physical, not vanishing in an aura of disembodied metaphors. Sex, strikingly depicted for *Harmonium* in the tenth section, is immediately qualified by the eleventh because for this man animal force alone cannot explain away refinements of the senses: "Clippered with lilies scudding the bright chromes, | Keen to the point of starlight." Caught between alternate selves, a dark rabbi trained in his youth and a rose rabbi still annotating beauty for his own reflections, he concludes the irony of extreme detachment, "until now I never knew | That fluttering things have so distinct a shade." Echoing "Sunday Morning," the monocle concentrates on nuances equated with settling pigeons. As a stylized portrait through thin strokes each part contributes its correct sub-

tlety, although so minutely do the hesitations rebound
that the whole becomes petulant, almost, in a term applied
rashly to Stevens, rococo. Moreover, a vagueness about the
basic situation detracts from the poem: is the man married;
does he have his wife or another woman in mind; does
much of it fade into an allegory; does the title imply that
the uncle speaks in his own voice or that a younger poet
has borrowed a single myopic aspect for his own exquisite
soliloquy? Often the hermetic epigrams, while amusing by
themselves, rage against man's having experienced this
much and, alas, no more; the modified interior monologue
plays at Watteau's pastoral sensuality. Through the stirrings of age, it shows that a futile regret may be worn
comfortably; as such, it need not apologize for itself.
Stevens probably, however, never quite trusted himself on
the subject love.

Another poem treating it, "Red Loves Kit" [30–32b],
appeared in 1924 and, although available for later books,
was not reprinted by him. The title itself, presumably a
phrase chalked on a wall, makes a disclaimer of romantic
transports. In its general pattern, if shorter, it resembles
"Le Monocle de Mon Oncle." The discourse, presented by
an unidentified speaker, dissects a less contemplative pas-
sion than the uncle's. "That you are innocent | And love
her still, still leaves you in the wrong." The abruptness
harks back to Browning and Meredith without their
crudely simplified analysis of motives. The second stanza,
which shifts its focus from the man to the woman, once
again praises a bit too lavishly but this time foregoes
deliberate mockery. Quite suddenly, the third stanza turns:
"Rest, crows, upon the edges of the moon, | Cover the
golden altar deepest black." The concluding part, the best
in the poem, then shows night disturbed by the flying
birds, as, once again, the phenomenon of natural darkness
produces a terror based on human inadequacy. The subject
of love quite vanishes, and "Red Loves Kit" ends oddly,
"fecund in rapt curios." "The Woman Who Blamed Life
on a Spaniard" conjures similar images of birds to flutter
away the force of love. That Stevens handles so gingerly

the matter which traditionally occupies poets has contributed to his reputation. The aesthetic climate in which he
elected to dwell, as has been seen, does not favor it. The
traditional romantic lover either projects his feelings outward onto the world or withdraws for a subjective life.
Stevens chose less passionate intensities. Failure to identify
his preference for the grotesque can lead to awkward
misreading: "The central concern of Stevens' poetry, the
concern that underlay Crispin's voyage and the poet's
meditative argument with the woman in "Sunday Morning," as well as most of the more or less curious divergen-
cies of his career, is a concern to be at peace with his
surroundings, with this world, and with himself. He requires for this an experience of the togetherness of himself
and Nature, and interpenetration of himself and his environment . . . something to satisfy the deeply ingrained
longings of his religious feeling." [13] The assumption that
all matters in the major poems of *Harmonium* must end
fervently—as has been shown—causes unnecessary apolo-
gies and leads to misunderstanding its principal adornment
disastrously.

x

"Alas! Have all the barbers lived in vain | That
not one curl in nature has survived?" [14a] complains the
uncle, who would probably sneer at a natural curl as
excessive. How profoundly the longest poem of *Harmonium* differs stands forth when one remembers that
Crispin in "The Comedian as the Letter C" [27–46a]
starts life as a barber, a counterpart of Beaumarchais'
Figaro: he possesses "a barber's eye," has been "lutanist of
fleas," and shares Figaro's second métier, "The valet in the
tempest was annulled," and, at times, "the knave, the
thane." Crispin merely borrows a French term for valet, a
type common in French drama, and bears Count
Almaviva's servant's Franco-Hispanic origin, "cap of
Spain," going from "Bordeaux to Yucatan, Havana next."
He does not step directly out of Beaumarchais, Mozart,
Rossini, or another theatrical predecessor, but a line from

Le Barbier de Seville (Act I, scene ii), "Je me presse de rire de tout, de peur d'être obligé d'en pleurer," might serve as the epigraph for this poem, just as with "Le Monocle de Mon Oncle" behind the crispest sigh there lurks mockery. Self-awareness in both rules out sentimentality. The title has caused some critics to throw up their hands as though confronting meaningless whimsey. The *Dictionnaire Larousse*, in one of its surrealistic landscapes inhabited by things whose name begins with the letter in the ensuing section, shows for *C* a comédien (perhaps clown) prancing on the lower serif of the letter *C* beside a carafe and ringing a cloche, thus nearly filling it out to an *O* or zero. Demonstrably in the picture the individual must, willy-nilly, partake of the objects around him. Perhaps the letter *C* also hints, analogous with Rimbaud's assigning vowels their colors from a child's alphabet book, that an acrobat conforms to his nature by contorting himself: arms along the ground, body arched, and feet dangling over the head —thus a *C*.

The décor depicts sketchily the eighteenth century, and the action traces a man of wit, common sense, taste, and imagination from the old world to a literally new one. In a sense it is a picaresque poem. A favorite interpretation of it makes it Stevens' autobiography manqué. This questionable reading violates many données consistently applied in *Harmonium*. Although stretching the letter *C* into Confession can explain parts, they overlook Crispin who, cypher though he may be, deserves as much respect in his own guise as does Figaro. Stevens went out of his way to mention, "There is another point about the poem to which I should like to call attention and that is that it is what may be called an anti-mythological poem. The central figure is an every-day man who lives a life without the slightest adventure except that he lives it in a poetic atmosphere as we all do. This point makes it necessary for a translator to try to reproduce the every-day plainness of the central figure and the plush, so to speak, of the stage." [169d] The poem has six parts, designated by Roman numerals, which, through an aphoristic sentence, Stevens divides into two groups of three. The movements fall, rather, into three distinct segments. Thus, both I and II present an alternative which Crispin cannot rise to. The third explains his weaknesses and the fourth his extravagances when he takes another path. The concluding V and VI trace a continuous development but need the opening two as an ironic counterbalance.

The initial statement could well lead off a number of poems in *Harmonium:* "Nota: man is the intelligence of his soil, | The sovereign ghost." The vocabulary partially disqualifies the definition; as a disembodied intelligence man fades into a specter, less than a plain central figure. Acceptance of his own power, nevertheless, guides Crispin until a bit too late he discovers his errors. The urbane Figaro, advising an amorous Count Almaviva, could succeed as the intelligence of his soil in eighteenth-century France but as a potential colonist must call upon other resources. Crispin himself enters the poem aboard ship. Unlike a poet's in a preceding century, his is not "The Mind, that Ocean where each kind | Does streight its own resemblance find"; [14] "the eye of Crispin, hung | On porpoises, instead of apricots." If the "wig | Of things" at home, the nostrums of his native land cannot encompass the porpoises' snouts among foreign waves, "Inscrutable hair in an inscrutable world." No longer plying his barber's trade, his intelligence cannot comprehend the watery element as the thing-in-itself. The god assigned this part, Triton, a deity wholly dissolved in his element, occupies Crispin's thoughts until, reversing the imagery of "Sea Surface Full of Clouds,"

> *nothing of himself*
> *Remained, except some starker, barer self*
> *In a starker, barer world, in which the sun*
> *Was not the sun because it never shone*
> *With bland complaisance on pale parasols,*
> *Beetled, in chapels, on the chaste bouquets.*

The man who in Europe manipulated his surroundings with insouciance must, at sea, fall back upon himself. This self rejects, perforce, the imagination and searches for a new ordering among objects remote from those it has known. The ocean offers, the title of this section, "The World without Imagination."

The second part, "Concerning the Thunderstorms of Yucatan," shows so rich and teeming a land that it proves as fruitless as the blank, mechanical ocean. Crispin visits this country in a detour, having named Carolina his goal from the outset. The pallid intelligences of this soil, "Maya sonneteers | Of the Caribbean amphitheatre," still observe conventional diction in their thoughts and poetry by hymning the "night-bird," a deliberately vague term to set off against one of those shockingly garish images which delight Stevens, "As if raspberry tanagers in palms, | High up in orange air, were barbarous." Such lines simultaneously imply four contradictory meanings: flatly improbable; a denial of vocabulary by rhetoric because, surely, they *are* barbarous; establishing a land which just might contain such phenomena; and a reproof to those who fail to see or, on viewing, deny because of their conditioned dullness. Severance from the expected during the voyage out has disabused Crispin, who never could incorporate this teeming climate: cleverer than its poets and more effete than its foliage. On such earth he can no longer bask in the tried proverbs, and the equatorial sun stirs wishes beyond his powers of attainment. "The fabulous and its intrinsic verse | Came like two spirits parleying." Opulence overwhelms him, and he captures only trivialities. A storm then arises with primitive mysteries beyond Yucatan, proclaimed by the violent god, Vulcan, who, unlike Triton, lives divorced from the element he commands. Crispin, in the refuge of a cathedral, although not to worship, has left his native Europe, the sterile ocean, and, now, this overpowering fecundity behind. His education must take a different tack: "Approaching Carolina."

Up to this time Crispin has attempted to incorporate the external world with himself. He wanders onward to a climate less austere than the sea and less lush than Yucatan, "America was always north to him, | A northern west or western north, but north." The third section, under the

guardianship of the moon, projects an unwritten book to
which Crispin might have contributed. (The sun has so
far dominated the poem.) He now sees himself "between
two elements, | A fluctuating between sun and moon,"
with the sun illuminating the external, the moonlight
mediating between the external and himself. No more
than Yucatan does Carolina deliver to him the ideal climate. After being invested with a provincial grandeur, the
north turns out raw in commerce; yet, "It made him see
how much | Of what he saw he never saw at all." In the
long apology for Crispin as poet, one might recall that
Stevens stresses him as an "every-day" man. The term poet
does not mean, primarily, the craft of composing but how
Crispin sees and reacts; as an ironic comedian he would
produce, at best, prose poems. Poet and realist, applied to
Crispin, resemble metaphors, the former the failure in
practical matters but the appreciator of innuendoes, the
latter a success with affairs and a dolt before subtleties,
both, in their way, clowns. So, too, Carolina stands not
just for the United States itself but a new twentieth
century, and Crispin almost personifies the man of sensibility from another day lost in its crassness. The last three
sections, then, reverse the opening with "The Idea of a
Colony," which starts, "Nota: his soil is man's intelli-
gence. | That's better. That's worth crossing seas to find."
Neither taking such truisms at face value nor equating
them with Stevens' whole outlook, one notices that this
manner more nearly resembles the method which *Harmonium* regards favorably. Crispin throws aside the old shib-
boleths: "Here was prose | More exquisite than any tum-
bling verse." His pleasures, of an undetermined sort,
become inner strivings against easy clichés. A disorder
equal to Rimbaud's beguiles Crispin. The practice comes
down to simplicity just as earlier it had swollen with
extravagances. Both, ultimately, defy order by imposing a
severe rigidity on man and place. The prose colony allots
each individual almost a parody of what surrounds him,
from the Carolinas down to Brazil and the pampas. A
slight motive for Crispin's wanderings at last appears.

He could not be content with counterfeit,
With masquerade of thought, with hapless words
That must belie the racking masquerade,
With fictive flourishes that preordained
His passion's permit, hang of coat, degree
Of buttons, measure of his salt. Such trash
Might help the blind, not him, serenely sly.
It irked beyond his patience. Hence it was,
Preferring text to gloss, he humbly served
Grotesque apprenticeship to chance event,
A clown, perhaps, but an aspiring clown.

Crispin now strives to enhance whatever his adopted country provides, and this part, indicatively, concludes on the
word "exact." The last two sections exercise Crispin's
talents as a literalist. A decline from his first hopes settles
him in "A Nice Shady Home," the fifth section, treating
bourgeois values; the remainder offers a more nearly unified
man who draws his forces together. The question remains
whether he could have achieved more, granted his potentialities and experiences.

The descent does not ridicule what he aspires to but
fails to live by. He resumes his European habits and busies
himself once again in the daily quilts and salad beds.
Entailed by domesticity, he marries and plays the part of
paterfamilias: "For realist, what is is what should be."
Some critics, seizing a casual simile, invoke Candide (via
Pope and the Age of Reason) as a key to Stevens' own
preference for this mode. Both protagonists, as children of
the eighteenth century, undertake romantic quests and
end up—happily?—in gardens. Otherwise, they differ notably, and Crispin keeps his affinities with Figaro, in the first
part scheming, in the second married. The final section,
"And Daughters with Curls" recovers, not just ironically,
Crispin's former desire for artifacts but born in nature. In
one sense man brings the intelligence from his soil, as an
earthy phrase depicts the daughters "Leaving no room
upon his cloudy knee, | Prophetic joint, for its di-
viner young." Their curls survive without barbers
whether "Anabasis or slump, ascent or chute," all part of

Crispin, "Four questioners and four sure answerers." The French turnip reproduces in the new world a turnip; an instructive exercise, a bit too long to present here, can trace the color purple as it kaleidoscopically recurs in, among other items, plums, balustrades, light, and the turnip. Ultimately, the poem shows acceptance of the possible and rejects miracles: "So Crispin hasped on the surviving form, | For him, of shall or ought to be in is." Stevens revels in resemblances, which imply continuity and may border on metamorphoses; he shuns the fancies which explain away the actual. Far from echoing *Candide*, "The Comedian as the Letter C" implies that this one may be the best of all *possible* worlds, whatever man makes of it, and it of man. So, too, the men offering their orgiastic chant in "Sunday Morning" sang [70a]

> *Their boisterous devotion to the sun,*
> *Not as a god, but as a god might be,*
> *Naked among them, like a savage source.*

Crispin's adventures trace many themes, but to assign him a narrowly mythic or autobiographical role violates all the other words Stevens wrote. "So may the relation of each man be clipped," the allusion to a barber sustaining the irony, after "The relation comes, benignly, to its end." Crispin represents every man of taste with instincts a bit more ambitious than his talents will accommodate, but the common romantic failing does not verge on tragedy here. He turns up in another poem with the indicative title, "Anecdote of the Abnormal." [23–24b] It employs a Harlequin-like personage who composes his own world, sometimes conforming with the senses, sometimes in defiance of them, and suddenly concludes:

> *Crispin-valet, Crispin-saint!*
> *The exhausted realist beholds*
> *His tattered manikin arise,*
> *Tuck in the straw,*
> *And stalk the skies.*

Realism still corrupts reality. "The Comedian as the Letter C" offers a catalogue of the ranges in *Harmonium*. The

descriptions give the direct, primary qualities which Imagism advocated, but, if only through absences they become
a bit grotesque. The anecdotes present their by now expected polarities, here between soil and intelligence, without a victory for either. Its length permits it to make a
somewhat philosophic point without preaching and to
shrug off the vanity of grasping the quite transubstantial.
The two parts contrast the folly of beginning from within
and the difficulty of accepting the world in all its rawness,
necessary as such a process may be. Crispin cannot escape
Carolina and embrace the moonlight in which he delights.
Religion provides only shams, but love does not exceed
material comforts, a kind of reality which thrives on
worldly symbols.

Beyond offering a summary, "The Comedian as the
Letter C" signals a turning point, with Stevens never a
violent shift, in his poetic outlook away from the clown
whether as a doomed aspirant or the sardonic compro-
miser. In this sense, then, the poem does become anti-
mythological because it fully depicts a disinherited
twentieth-century comedian only to deny that this congenial imago exerts abiding power. The comically assumed
modesty behind many pieces in *Harmonium* tends to
abate. Later volumes trade on neither the clown's pathos
nor resilience nor juxtaposings of the two but place the
poet solidly on earth where he can live as, simultaneously,
the intelligence of his soil and the recipient of its wisdom.
Stevens, obviously, still relishes ironies, but his faith in a
freshly defined imagination allows him to see roundly.
Although other problems remained, and new ones con-
fronted him, having established himself beyond the clown,
he could work them out poetically and yet not break with
this early style. His very awareness of saying a tender
good-bye to Crispin explains why he could explore modern
man as a comedian and then eventually shake off anxiety
and claim the noted serenity which relatively few contemporary artists command. With this trait, especially, Stevens
differs from many modern poets, who have appropriated
the clown for romantic personae—the scarecrow in excel-

sis: one moves from W. B. Yeats among myths and school children, to T. S. Eliot's hollow men's dream kingdom, to Petrouchka's ghost stalking above the deserted carnival, through a tribe of nineteenth-century Pierrots, to reach, finally, a mythic Hamlet amid flights of angels. Stevens' detachment, his remoteness from autobiography and rituals, saves his poem from being one more prolonged romantic sigh, but the word comedian here, however much it hurts, is not pejorative.

The image of *Harmonium* should have emerged by now. In it all the contributing themes have a dual aspect. One can list them in separate sentences. It speaks for a man who believes in things he cannot wholly champion and who rejects superstitions firmly but reluctantly. He starts from "reality"—daily experience, a bit repellent and unpoetic—which, nevertheless, his candor cannot deny. To seek sanctuary in a disembodied imagination, a tempting alternative, would exile him among delusive shadows. One must live by poetry, conscious at each moment that it has no efficacy in miraculously altering physical qualities. If traditional religions preach a meaningless faith, a crusade against them enlists uncongenial allies. Reason, presumably, advises abandoning attempts to reconcile such opposites, but, then, it also would cheerfully surrender poetry to escape ambiguities. Passionate love, sometimes considered a solace, responds to an ego and, thus, terminates in a fantastic subjectivity. Putting on a clown's mask may protect the defenseless sensibility which speaks truth through anecdotes, although the gesture, at last, becomes an evasive refusal. This list summarizes the romantic ironists' common complaints, but one discovery saves Stevens from their ineffectuality. His belief in words and his mastery over them permit him to avoid worrying about the dilemmas publicly. Instead of begging pathos, he concentrates on a vivid abstraction. Like a central fulcrum, a poem, through words, can balance all worlds without belonging to or renouncing any. The poem, being chiefly about itself, gives the power to sustain all in unison, comparable with Beethoven's work, which, as Nietzsche observed, is music about music. The rich varieties of *Harmonium* prove how satisfying this stratagem can be inside a limited range. Nevertheless, between 1923 and 1935 the United States and its literature endured many changes. *Ideas of Order* could no more just continue *Harmonium,* which, as re-printed in 1931 showed no important changes apart from adding fourteen poems and dropping three, than wholly break with it. William Carlos Williams quotes a letter from Stevens: "Given a fixed point of view, realistic, imagistic, or what you will, everything adjusts itself to that point of view; and the process of adjustment is a world in flux, as it should be for a poet. But to fidget with points of view leads always to new beginnings and incessant new beginnings lead to sterility. . . . Well a book of poems is a damned serious affair." [15] *Harmonium,* then, keeps a point of view cognate with later volumes.

> The ancient symbols will be nothing then.
> We shall have gone behind the symbols
> To that which they symbolized.
>
> WALLACE STEVENS [102b]

> The social man, then, lives in a world of symbols, and
> though he presses other things into his service, such, for in-
> stance, as kings, footmen, dogs, women, he finds in art his
> richest reservoir of symbolic currency. But in a world of
> symbolists the creative artist and the creative man of science
> appear in strange isolation as the only people who are not
> symbolists. They alone are up against certain relations
> which do not stand for something else, but appear to have
> ultimate value, to be real.
>
> ROGER FRY [1]

A TRULY METAPHYSICAL HISTORY of aesthetics staggers the
mind. Taine's temporal triumvirate, race, moment, and
milieu, reign over chronologies of the arts and enforce
their Procrustean whims. To propose a survey treating
masterpieces as finite entities which in a transcendent
body manifest and obey their own laws, bearing the same
repeated configurations and relationships to man's actions
as, for an astrologer, the patterns of stars and planets do
sounds eccentric. Such a process might, nevertheless, formulate concepts basic for appreciating certain artists, such
as Stevens. In composing *Harmonium* he self-consciously
liberated himself from the social symbols which Roger Fry
describes, and, consequently, scorned mere realism as a
corruption of any true reality. Granted that his poems use

counters and fitfully draw upon the French symbolistes' techniques, they cannot reflect just the contemporary scene with all its counterfeits. One might recall the coinage "status symbol" to name the opposite of what he seeks. His images show objects important by themselves and aspiring to become poetry, not advertisements for products anyone may purchase as signs of worldly prestige. The concomitant aloofness permits lodging the charge of social snobbishness, false as it is, against him. His tastes derive from pursuits generally thought highbrow, but he avoids the fussy insecurity of the middlebrow and—in the incisive epithet devised by a reviewer for a scholar whose life exists as a footnote to literary morality—the flatbrow. One commentator has observed accurately, "Any poetry relies, if not on the authority, at least on the companionship of some other articulation of chaos than its own, and Wallace Stevens has written his poetry in the congenial company of at least five other fictions which are in their kinds supreme. These are namely: Law, Money, Music (of the 'fictive' sort), Metaphysics, and Civilization—this last in the sense of refined connoisseurship and full consciousness. . . . One minor beauty of this company is that it relegates to secondary or even fainter importance the less supreme, more preliminary, and less consciously fictitious fictions which have most guided contemporary poetry."[2] Stevens himself said, with a directness which must pain self-styled liberals, flatbrows, bohemians, and sociologists, "Money is a kind of poetry" [165b] and, by direct implication, not a symbol for something else. He built up this poet's courage through the years; obviously Crispin the comedian could not serve to declare it.

i

To a degree Stevens analyzes his brand of reality more sternly than his contemporaries do, but in presenting it he must snub as banal most fictions publicly agreed upon as comprising commercial and popular "reality." He does not pretend that poetry, or anything else, will easily make visible a higher, absolute truth about the actual, based on the social scene but washed and straightened. Things as objects for poetry occupied him all his career, and in this vein he seems happiest. Nevertheless, the next three volumes, *Ideas of Order, The Man with the Blue Guitar*, and *Parts of a World*, depart sometimes in search of other provisions from almost patented symbolism. The unity of *Harmonium* relies upon a central outlook capable of multiple variations. A statement by its author on the dust jacket of the trade edition claims a more nearly integrated concept for *Ideas of Order*. Important but not generally available, it merits full quotation.

> We think of changes occurring today as economic changes, involving political and social changes. Such changes raise questions of political and social order.
>
> While it is inevitable that a poet should be concerned with such questions, this book, although it reflects them, is primarily concerned with ideas of order of a different nature, as, for example, the dependence of the individual, confronting the elimination of established ideas, on the general sense of order; the idea of order created by individual concepts, as of the poet, in "The Idea of Order at Key West"; the idea of order arising from the practice of any art, as of poetry in "Sailing after Lunch."
>
> The book is essentially a book of pure poetry. I believe that, in any society, the poet should be the exponent of the imagination of that society. *Ideas of Order* attempts to illustrate the role of the imagination in life, and particularly in life at present. The more realistic life may be, the more it needs the stimulus of the imagination.

This caveat, on the basis of what the volume offers, sounds like whistling in the dark. The concept of a "more realistic life" defies exegesis as triumphantly as the most obscure poem. The gesture did not ward off attacks from reviewers either honestly committed to a Marxian bias in literature or joining a fashionable swing toward the left.

The next volume contains only four main sections: "The Man with the Blue Guitar," "Owl's Clover," which for its initial appearance in a magazine and the Alcestis Press edition singled out a *New Masses* writer, Stanley

Burnshaw, as a fleeting target, the shorter, "A Thought Revolved," and the brief, "The Men That Are Falling." The purposes of this volume, also according to Stevens' own comment on the ephemeral dust jacket, are:

> In one group, *Owl's Clover*, while the poems reflect what was then going on in the world, that reflection is merely for the purposes of seizing and stating what makes life intelligible and desirable in the midst of great change and great confusion. The effect of *Owl's Clover* is to emphasize the opposition between things as they are and things imagined; in short, to isolate poetry.
>
> Since this is of significance, if we are entering a period in which poetry may be of first importance to the spirit, I have been making notes on the subject in the form of short poems during the past winter. These short poems, some thirty of them, form the other group, *The Man with the Blue Guitar*, from which the book takes its title. This group deals with the incessant conjunctions between things as they are and things imagined. Although the blue guitar is a symbol of the imagination, it is used most often simply as a reference to the individuality of the poet, meaning by the poet any man of imagination.

The ambition outstrips the implicit assumptions in *Harmonium*. Crispin as an "every-day man" met failure; the player can boast, "You as you are? You are yourself." [183a] *Parts of a World*, as the title implies, searches again for a solid center from which poetry emanates. An author's claims about his work do not necessarily coincide with others' opinions, and *Parts of a World* may fall short in fulfilling the unity to which its title aspires. "Owl's Clover," one of the few dropped from the *Collected Poems*, probably never sounded right to Stevens, although considerable merit distinguishes passages. To whatever external stress these books bend, they continue still the style, vocabulary, manner, and types of *Harmonium*.

Primarily Imagistic exercises, if by now slightly more complex, appear throughout *Ideas of Order*. A relative austerity distinguishes some both in what they select and how they present it. The thought behind "How to Live.

What to Do" [125–26a] could derive from Robinson
Jeffers when a tolerant mood freed him. A sternly black
landscape, guarded by a monolithic outcropping, which
places two people who have quit "the muck of the land,"
provides "heroic sound | Joyous and jubilant and sure."
"Some Friends from Pascagoula," another instance of Stevens' teasing use of American place names, isolated primitive nobility, here in the descent of an eagle, which exists
only as a vivid memory. A similarly uncomplicated sun
drives away old doubts, although in the process it banishes
all thinking, as it walks in "The Brave Man." "A Fish-
Scale Sunrise" [160–61a] proclaims an end to night's revels
when "The sun rises green and blue in the fields and in the
heavens. | The clouds foretell a swampy rain." To insist
that none of these images could have appeared in *Harmonium* lets a thesis dominate over judgment. They offer the
world in a less benign aspect, and even the South menaces
with poverty. At the same time, they do not support the
commonplace that Stevens gave up his rhetorical explora-
tions in these volumes. The way of seeing remains the
same; it takes other subjects and turns toward diverse
objects, since, as he concedes, a bit reluctantly, "Everyone
takes sides in social change if it is profound enough."
[173b]

The external world looks harsh and grotesque. *Harmonium* has the chiding "Frogs Eat Butterflies. Snakes Eat
Frogs. Hogs Eat Snakes. Men Eat Hogs" [78a], where the
swinish rivers puzzle the man who "Knew not the quirks
of imagery" and take their part in destroying him. "Mud
Master," more extremely, equates a muddy river and a
muddled mind. Obedient to light, green leaves and peach
buds may eventually spring forth from the banks, but
whether this mud master of summer will touch the intelligence no one asserts. Other contrasts set off the two
volumes. The earth-mother "In the Carolinas" from *Harmonium* wears an unaccustomed loveliness, but "Meditation Celestial & Terrestrial" [123–24a] by an almost painful riot, after a winter of reason and rations, accepts
"summer, the drunken mother." Likewise, in "The Sun

This March" [133–34a] an inner darkness shrinks from spring, and expecting salvation may ask for the wrong favor. A sinister throb lurks in the call, "Oh! Rabbi, rabbi, fend my soul for me | And true savant of this dark nature be." The dark rabbi of winter and the drunken mother of summer both overpower by their assurances, almost in defiance of the usual svelte comforts. "Re-statement of Romance" [146a] through its contrasts pretends to arrive at a resolution in human terms. Beginning with the belief that night cannot know itself any more than the speaker in the poem can understand himself, it continues to the romantic commonplace of the isolated individual's needing a reflection to establish an identity. The person whom the speaker addresses, one neither of clouds nor fictive music, may help the two of them, in their loneliness, to achieve a human insight, while darkness and its implied stars become a mere backdrop against which both now "see" each other. This union remains incomplete; they stand "Supremely true each to its separate self." The stress upon personal dependence with none of the joy accompanying physical elation repeats the timidity which both winter and summer could engender.

Anecdotes, their polarities as unresolved as winter and summer, continue but in more pallid shades with the decidedly melancholy, slightly bitter, "Gray Stones and Gray Pigeons." The former Florida colorings enter "Winter Bells" chiefly through a liturgical religion which a Jansenist atmosphere cannot tolerate. Similarly "The Reader" [146–47a] finds himself perusing a somber sky, and "A voice was mumbling, 'Everything | Falls back to coldness,'" the heavens indifferent to the autumnal gardens. "The Pleasures of Merely Circulating" [149–50a] exemplifies the mixed feelings behind many poems. Here, happily, the effects fill almost adequately the brief scope. It opens with a kind of circular dance, mingling gardens, angels, and clouds. The final four lines likewise indulge in that mixture of opposites which intrigued Stevens at this time: "Mrs. Anderson's Swedish baby | Might well have been German or Spanish." Yet, in the middle part, thus qualifying it as anecdotal, other images circulate to another point, hardly pleasurable:

> *Is there any secret in skulls,*
> *The cattle skulls in the woods?*
> *Do the drummers in black hoods*
> *Rumble anything out of their drums?*

The decidedly "dark" intrusions yoke opposites more violently than before and, one suspects, not just because of a bearish stock market or lengthening bread lines. The volume closes with "Delightful Evening" [162a] on the extreme "The twilight overfull | Of wormy metaphors." Whatever wryly ironic weariness the anecdotes of *Harmonium* have, the colors flash predominant brilliance, if only to dramatize its absence. Here somberness prevails, and indulgence of pejoratives lends these poems their special qualities. The poet's stance has altered from a buoyant comedian's to a sardonic annotator's.

ii

Satiric verse sharpens its edge to a witty musical staccato, and its diction jumps with a less controlled detachment. "The American Sublime" [130–31a] throws up its hands before a vista.

> *When General Jackson*
> *Posed for his statue*
> *He knew how one feels.*
> *Shall a man go barefoot*
> *Blinking and blank?*

The equestrian pose summons the frontiersman surprised by an elevation to a height he cannot support. Stevens' prose again presents the general.

There is in Washington, in Lafayette Square, which is the square on which the White House faces, a statue of Andrew Jackson, riding a horse with one of the most beautiful tails in the world. General Jackson is raising his hat in a gay gesture, saluting the ladies of his generation. One looks at this work of Clark Mills and thinks of the remark of Bertrand Russell that to acquire immunity to eloquence is of the utmost importance to the citizens of a democracy. . . . Treating this work as typical, it is obvious that the American will as a principle of the mind's being is easily satisfied in its effort to realize itself in knowing itself. . . . The statue is neither of the imagination nor of reality. That it is a work of fancy precludes it from being a work of the imagination. A glance at it shows it to be unreal. The bearing of this is that there can be works, and this includes poems, in which neither the imagination nor reality is present. [10–11c]

"The American Sublime" ends on the not quite facetious questions, "What wine does one drink? | What bread does one eat?" with full awareness about the quality of food procurable in this climate. Behind them may lurk a Biblical answer, which no one at the time accepted: "Take no thought for your life, what ye shall eat, or what ye shall drink."

Stevens elsewhere puts his equestrian statues, for which he has a fondness, through paces worthy of a caracole. "Owl's Clover" erects marble horses for a central image, and one stands in the provocatively perverse "Dance of the Macabre Mice." [123a] It seems best to quote the whole poem because it expatiates upon General Jackson and public figures.

In the land of turkeys in turkey weather
At the base of the statue, we go round and round.
What a beautiful history, beautiful surprise!
Monsieur is on horseback. The horse is covered with mice.

This dance has no name. It is a hungry dance.
We dance it out to the tip of Monsieur's sword,
Reading the lordly language of the inscription,
Which is like zithers and tambourines combined:

The Founder of the State. Whoever founded
A state that was free, in the dead of winter, from mice?
What a beautiful tableau tinted and towering,
The arm of bronze outstretched against all evil!

The poem incorporates Stevens' tricks at a middling level: placing unexpected creatures in a heightened atmosphere, the foreign word (hardly a startling one by itself but beguiling in the line), repetitions, and the musical instruments. Less predictable novelties intrude; the incongruity of releasing mice upon a statue, although with parallels in surrealism at this time, risks a greater contrast than any in *Harmonium*. Turkey weather, presumably, belongs to the colorings of a mottled winter day, as, again, the creatures express their climate. The irony which this Monsieur's statue conveys requires less pointing than General Jackson's. The raised sword must replace the tipped hat, but the surprising extension stretches the bronze arm outward against all evil, exclamation point. This punctuation, elsewhere in the poems, reinforces, principally, a shout. The word evil does not matter in *Harmonium*, and its emphatic entrance here indicates a depth. Shall one take the founder of the state for a good man upon whose country a later blight has fallen or for a fool who hoped any state and statue could free itself from the pirouetting, macabre mice? As an adjunct to "Anecdote of the Jar," without its detachment and as a prediction of the similar, if better modulated, "The Blue Buildings in the Summer Air," it demonstrates the quality of this volume.

Grotesque pieces contribute a decided rhythm to *Harmonium*, and some available ones did not get into it; composing in this vein amused Stevens during this decade and part of the next. Outside *Ideas of Order*, among pieces appearing in *Opus Posthumous*, the scorn sounds less equivocal. "The Drum-Majors in the Labor Day Parade" [36–37b] lists nearly a flat conversational transcript of a suffering employer who finds, justifiably, "The parade's no good." "Lytton Strachey, Also, Enters into Heaven," worth preserving if it went no place beyond the title, through the biographer stares down several of Stevens' bêtes noires: those who glorify indigenous American vulgarities, as Vachel Lindsay did when he translated General Booth; theologians who make heaven a haven for their own spirits; celebrators of streamlined skylines; and those who insist Stevens should adopt popular idioms merely to keep up with the times. The grotesque tones frequently make *Ideas*

of Order itself lively. Throughout the two long poems of
The Man with the Blue Guitar, as well, bizarre under-
cuttings and counterparts introduce jagged edges. In that
volume, also, the four poems loosely comprising one group,
"A Thought Revolved," take up pure poetry and to it
oppose the impure, commercial actualities. The first, "The
Mechanical Optimist," one of his least indicative pieces,
fits with the leftist satire in the 'thirties, and presumably
on this misreading it has broken into anthologies. (One
does not want to carp unduly at the anthologists, whose
selections seldom have done Stevens justice; they face an
impossible chore. Those titles which the browsers can
grasp without knowing much of his work do not incorporate his most basic concerns. The more telling ones do not
unlock themselves in isolation.) Besides "The Mechanical
Optimist," the other three in the suite "A Thought Revolved" keep the same tartness toward the kitsch on public
display and nearly a romantic longing for a good which the
world cannot grant.

Most deliberately, "Five Grotesque Pieces," some a mere
panache of sounds, flaunt extravagances. Among them,
"What They Call Red Cherry Pie" [75–76b] takes phrases
which would flit about Stevens in a businessman's restaurant, and from such offhand scraps, e. g. "Meyer is a bum,"
he gestures, like Geoffrey of the undergraduate story, at
composing himself with the scene. It veers dangerously
close to Robert Frost's territories: "He says "That's what I
call red cherry pie.' | And that's his way. And that's my
way as well." Yet, one mode never restricts Stevens, and
from these satires emerge later achievements, some admittedly as idiosyncratic as these. One must write off "She
was all of her airs and, for all of her airs, | She was all of
her airs and ears and hairs" [74b], and the later "In
Hydaspia, by Howzen, | Lived a lady, Lady Lowzen,"
[272a] as lines which Lyly might have blotted out. Practicing repetitions, rather than echoes, he transcends mockery
but does not always spin the evocatively haunting lines he
sought in this vein. "Ghosts as Cocoons" comes close, if
taken by itself, to an incantation, a practice on which

Imagism, because of its mania for constructing single icons, always teeters. For example, works by Ezra Pound or Edith Sitwell, when either too many objects crowd round the subject or the verses stretch out in homophony, become almost Gregorian. This chanting, outside liturgical confines, soon yields private poetry, verse whose objective details vanish in parochial devotions. Intentionally or not, in "Ghosts as Cocoons" [119a] the dimensions of the subject elude the author. An awaited bride has not arrived. She represents autumn or the passing of summer or one on whom a consummation depends. The title, perhaps, implies the necessity for turning the incorporeal into the actual. If the one of fictive music inspires rather too intricate promises, here, after a furor of praise, she is a "ghost of fragrance falling | On dung," both "pearled and pasted," decked in the genuine and fake. Meanwhile, other types in *Ideas of Order* explore significant advances, if, once again, no style claims total authority everywhere.

Two poems with one title, "Botanist on Alp" [No. 1 and 2, 134–36a] measure the present and its weariness with a future which will merely extend its ills.

> *Panoramas are not what they used to be.*
> *Claude has been dead a long time*
> *And apostrophes are forbidden on the funicular.*
> *Marx has ruined Nature,*
> *For the moment.*

Despite the darkness of the botanist's and others' minds, the atmosphere, long after Claude's serene landscapes, retains freshness.

> *Yet the panorama of despair*
> *Cannot be the specialty*
> *Of this ecstatic air.*

"Lions in Sweden" [124–25a] garrulously words through similar possibilities about present and future. The older allegorical statues which once adorned banks and public buildings undergo demolition by sophisticated ridicule: Fides ("the sculptor's prize, | All eyes and size"), Justitia, Patientia, and Fortitudo. The modern lions in Sweden, the concept itself a fanciful one, serve no better. Nevertheless, desire for an older nobility of expression persists as the poem closes:

> And the whole of the soul, Swenson,
> As every man in Sweden will concede,
> Still hankers after lions, or, to shift,
> Still hankers after sovereign images.
> If the fault is with the lions, send them back
> To Monsieur Dufy's Hamburg whence they came.
> The vegetation still abounds with forms.

In these three poems out of the fuller awareness, which arises by projecting present dullness into a future made drearier by it, the present enjoys an ironically tarnished luster. Stevens cannot mourn a vanished past very long, and, consequently, somberness does not prevail.

Of the poems which pit the present against a generalized past and future, the carefree "Sailing after Lunch" [120–21a] comes closest to scoring its point. At first the poet complains that nothing in its disjointed state pleases him: the limping boat, the inadequate lunch, the ramshackle country, the weight of dead history. A welcome freshness of concept and vocabulary breaks the giddiness:

> To expunge all people and be a pupil
> Of the gorgeous wheel and so to give
> That slight transcendence to the dirty sail,
> By light, the way one feels, sharp white,
> And then rush brightly through the summer air.

Unlike "Botanist on Alp" [1 and 2] and "Lions in Sweden," this poem finally reconciles the discords in a precarious balance. Nothing in *Ideas of Order* long stays steady; moods can switch easily from gaiety to ennui. "Waving Adieu, Adieu, Adieu" [127–28a]—and one may expect the day soon when a study of Stevens' infrequent but outrageous puns will come forth—repeats farewell to earth. Being inured to others' rehearsals for death, about which no training can guarantee proficiency, establishes the irony. The plea asks an enjoyment of this world when confronting an absolute negation without a heaven afterwards. Bidding good-bye to the earth, "One likes to practice the thing. They practice | Enough, for heaven," sways between amusement at one's own pieties and contempt for others'. Reducing an experience generally counted overwhelming to banter does not fully prepare for the startlingly direct close, "what spirit | Have I except it comes from the sun?" "Sad Strains of a Gay Waltz" [121–22a] utters an unabashed cri de coeur, "Too many waltzes have ended." The Weltschmerz initiates a series of Stevens' usual images turned inside out until the teeming grotesques vanish with a promise uttered in the face of despair, "The epic of disbelief | Blares oftener and soon," lines which, unfortunately, tend toward the trite and sentimental.

"Mozart, 1935" [131–32a] fares little better. The modern poet-pianist suffers in the present with "its hoo-hoo-hoo, | Its shoo-shoo-shoo, its ric-a-nic"; here the nonsense culminates in nonsense, much like an uncle's dismissing his niece's addiction to jazz. The outburst does not go beyond the prattle of its own words and makes him ridiculous for venturing where he has no business in the first place. The syllables of adolescents' music, having come from the vacuum in a hack's head, will not grow more ludicrous when mimicked by intelligence. The man waving adieu, practicing a final death, turned toward a positive sun; here, the appeal to a young Mozart cannot muster an equal promise and moans because too many waltzes have ended and Claude's serenity has faded. A long distance lies between Mozart's besieged attic and Peter Quince musing at his secluded clavier. In "A Fading of the Sun," itself an ominous concept, chaos also prevails with the mass misery of the 'thirties. The goodness of affirmed simplicities—tea, wine, bread, and meat—rings as passionately as any proletarian work in this period; at least, it tries to. Just how, poetically, one arrives at this faith nothing in the poem quite indicates. One may now advance the generalization that, although troubled by his times, Stevens did not have his doubts draw their reduced nourishment from a panic before economic collapse as such. A skepticism about external social symbols always marks his work; when he tried to enlarge, somewhat, his grasp of their significance, he could encompass neither graver cynicism nor, at this moment, an affirmative credo. "The act of thinking of the life of the rich is a poetic act and this seems to be true whether one thinks of it with liking or with dislike. The same thing may be said of the act of thinking of the life of the poor. Most of us do not share the life of either the one or the other and for that reason both are unreal. It is possible, too, to think of the national economy as a poetico-economy." [240b] This statement, although made in 1948, harks back ten years for its origins. He thought as a poet in terms of actualities, not for what they meant symbolically but for what they could provide his art. Had the poetry offered a political tract, it would not waver in its allegiances; he trains his sensibilities on the scene and refuses to dramatize himself or others.

iii

The convincing "A Postcard from the Volcano" [158–59a] grimly redeems the despairing pieces, although they serve as essential overtures to it. The time depicts a future strewn with wreckage of present culture. The waltz which the world danced on the edge of a volcano finally ended, but a meager life continues. Children, innocently playing among the skeletons and shambles, will not consciously know who prevailed there. Before being overcome, nevertheless, "we" had shaped the world and "left what we felt | At what we saw." The line mirrors T. S. Eliot's "for the roses | Had the look of flowers that are looked at" in "Burnt Norton." Becoming specific, the landscape discloses a ruined mansion, "And what we said of it became | A part of what it is," a complementary aspect of Peter Quince's musings. The decaying walls keep ghosts in the almost lovely ruin:

> A dirty house in a gutted world,
> A tatter of shadows peaked to white,
> Smeared with the gold of the opulent sun.

The diametric appeals of a tender sentiment set in dissonants on the *t, d, k,* and *g* sounds reinforce rage at waste.

The belief garners as much as "Sunday Morning" allows, but it fails to salvage enough. Stevens does not, however, join T. S. Eliot's like preoccupation about man in time only to renounce both at the end of "Burnt Norton":

> *Sudden in a shaft of sunlight*
> *Even while the dust moves*
> *There rises the hidden laughter*
> *Of children in the foliage*
> *Quick now, here, now, always—*
> *Ridiculous the waste sad time*
> *Stretching before and after.*

Although slight in scope, "A Postcard from the Volcano," better than any poem he had published up to its time, strikes the conjunction of themes which lead him into the later, more fully expounded philosophic poems. It utilizes the abiding concerns of *Harmonium*, how man and his world interweave, but the backward perspective from a destroyed future illustrates more convincingly that an aesthetic can and shall persist. Deliberate frivolity or remote overstatement no longer must serve as defensive masks.

Three longer poems of *Ideas of Order* shake off the nagging uneasiness which blurs the short ones. In part this clarity bathes the scene because the Caribbean area, away from the disturbing north, induced the moods, but southern indolence does not everywhere prevail. Stevens scorns prefabricated counters, and "Farewell to Florida" sketches an unexpected aspect of the region. The one who bids good-bye to the personified state from the sea experiences neither the sporadic enthusiasm of Crispin nor the pleased wonder welling beneath "Sea Surface Full of Clouds." The matching of Florida against the north shows neither in an especially favorable light, the former overly exotic and rich, the latter coldly mean. The indecisiveness sighs relief at a deliverance from an intolerable lethargy, if the escape promises no better climate. Titles of the more affirmative indicate the impetus: "The Idea of Order at Key West," "Evening without Angels," and "Academic Discourse at Havana." One cannot suppress a wish that an

older semi-tropical culture, perhaps Egyptian, had im-
pressed Stevens; the loss of élan and surprise would have
found adequate compensation in a less frantic struggle to
assimilate a novel scene and its landmarks. The Caribbean
atmosphere infused with Spanish Catholic beliefs cannot
as usable dogma rouse sympathy in him. Also, however
brilliantly he extracts general qualities from the climate,
around Florida there linger impressions of week-ends in
bogus villas designed by Mizner, and ultimately it shrinks
into less than a charmed land: "Eldorado banal de tous les
vieux garçons. | Regardez, après tout, c'est une pauvre
terre." [3]

"The Idea of Order at Key West" [128–30a] modulates
its pitch between details and essences with a clarity which
clutching after such insubstantial qualities seldom attains.
The first line tells the situation—"She sang beyond the
genius of the sea"—and then expands infinitesimally to
capture the informing spirit which infuses the evening
beach. Singer and song symbolize nothing beyond themselves, "The sea was not a mask. No more was she." These
entities do not improvise a graphic value in which they
stay parts; they partake of an abiding order, and, thus,
become valid in themselves. In being realized, the voice
animates the land and water, which generate it. Finally,
"She was the single artificer of the world | In which she
sang." The sensation here complements "A Postcard from
the Volcano," persuading how, by image and statement,
the interplay of feelings and objects composes a subject
whose importance one can only feel. Metaphysical though
this substance may be, it dominates over casual actualities.
When this music pervades Key West, the two walkers,
poet and philosopher, can interpret not only the night but
also the town, expressed in the lights from the fishing
boats. It inevitably concludes on a famous passage:

> *Oh! Blessed rage for order, pale Ramon,*
> *The maker's rage to order words of the sea,*
> *Words of the fragrant portals, dimly-starred,*
> *And of ourselves and of our origins,*
> *In ghostlier demarcations, keener sounds.*

The passage says plainly that the order alludes to intui-
tively discerned harmonies, not daily events and their
cacophonies. Inevitably "The Solitary Reaper" has
occurred to some critics for a comparison, and, perhaps,
aspects of the two poems can illuminate each other.
Wordsworth's philosophizing, however, embraces a deliberately willed outlook and excludes some matters so he can
arrange the rest; Stevens' "rage for order" does not reject
and allows the possibility of changes. If "The Idea of
Order at Key West" presents a knowledge of evening,
"Evening without Angels" [136–38a], despite its title,
looks at the light. After instances of the difficulties which
merely living in the light and air entail, since they transcend man, the poem returns to night. The frequently
advanced claim that Stevens prefers night to day, imagination above reason, does not dictate the movement here.
Discovery of night depends on day, and at the end one
confronts human darkness "Where the voice that is great
within us rises up, | As we stand gazing at the rounded
moon." "Academic Discourse at Havana" [142–45a] least
effectively sketches the majority of themes for this volume:
the south, the general poverty in spirit, the happiness
which has dissolved with a hazy past, the vulgar intrusion
into everything by politics, and, finally, the poet as the sole
one who, through composing upon these matters, can
implant a new outlook. First published in 1923 but included in neither edition of *Harmonium*, its very roughness
affirms both his early concern with such topics and his
insecurity about presenting them. For example, the opening and some ensuing passages, such as, "Life is an old
casino in a park," express a facile regret in tinseled decoration. Frequently the wit knots a brow too quickly outraged
by lack of order.

iv

The arrangement of the pieces in *Ideas of Order*
imposes no absolute precedence, and subjects arise almost
casually. If so sure of himself that he could risk anticipa-
tions, as with "Academic Discourse at Havana," Stevens'

order, dependent upon reasonableness and imagination, should have the same quality of coherence after *Harmonium*. The risks of extending this method stand out fully in "The Man with the Blue Guitar." Here, an extreme relaxing of structure produces the rather terrifyingly free "Like Decorations in a Nigger Cemetery." [150–58a] The title proclaims how much this poem differs from *Harmonium*. Both imply a unity of desired effects, but in this one harshness, which jams together discontinuity, if not fully orchestrated, becomes nearly atonal. His genuine interest in, and affection for, neatness notwithstanding, the structure of individual poems caused him increasing trouble. As already observed, they tend toward looseness, as in "Metaphors of a Magnifico," or seek an absolute exactitude, as in "Sea Surface Full of Clouds," or tie images together under one title, as in "Primordia." While extending his range in subject and attitudes, he quite forsakes absolute control. In separate works a growing reliance on Roman numerals to distribute stanzas suggests how haphazard the structure sometimes becomes, and "Like Decorations in a Nigger Cemetery," as its gaudy title implies, revels in incongruity. Badly undervalued, it remains an ideal poem for the United States in many ways, another instance of how Stevens explores stealthily.

In the fifty short sections a few images and themes join as leitmotivs: the autumnal season, the poet wearily questioning himself, the creeping decay, and evasions about commitments to any standard. Books which scrutinize Stevens' work intently, nevertheless, ignore or slight this one perhaps because "The Idea of Order at Key West," as a poetic summary of his outlook between *Harmonium* and *The Man with the Blue Guitar*, fits more neatly into schemes. "Like Decorations in a Nigger Cemetery" does not appear to have any notable ideas of order buried beneath it. Stevens probes persistently chaos and dogma until they nearly touch, and so, for his full growth in terms of practice, this poem becomes almost crucial. It displays remnants from *Harmonium*—"the rules of rabbis, | Happy men, distinguishing frost and clouds"; "The hunter shouts as the pheasant falls. | Consider the odd morphology of regret"; "the ocean of the virtuosi." Mingling among these, others predict later concerns: Ananke, "the ruins of a new society"; "The comedy of hollow sounds derives | From truth and not from satire on our lives." Not trying to reconcile the forces—and yet including unfinished patterns—provides the segments an uncanny force without precedent in *Harmonium* and stages almost a rehearsal for the long poems later.

The opening passage summons up precisely the kind of misted, if vigorous, vistas by which Stevens identifies the native landscape:

In the far South the sun of autumn is passing
Like Walt Whitman walking along a ruddy shore.
He is singing and chanting the things that are part of him,
The worlds that were and will be, death and day.
Nothing is final, he chants. No man shall see the end.
His beard is of fire and his staff is a leaping flame.

Although other sections amplify these phrases, nowhere does one encounter how to select details for a ready understanding. Through the relaxed form the poet's exultation accompanies bravado with the effort, almost certainly doomed to failure, of fusing elements which cohere by none of the usual rhetorical standards. The Roman numerals dividing the sections provide, at most, very casual props. The whole range of his styles contributes to this nearly overwhelming display, which always builds upon a knowledge of its futility. Patterns may or may not relate parts; do the singing birds against leaden pigeons (in XIII and XIV) become oriole and crow against a surrealistic barnyard (in XXV and XXX)? Nothing long remains steady, although the poem never lapses into mere metamorphosis, so that the Walt Whitman sun (after a probably unintentional passage to India) reappears in XVII (here given complete):

> *The sun of Asia creeps above the horizon*
> *Into this haggard and tenuous air,*
> *A tiger lamed by nothingness and frost.*

Days pass thus—months, perhaps—in their novelty and
with less fanfare than before. Although man remains "the
abstraction, the comic sum," his weather and surroundings
less delectably beckon and lower with a deeper menace
than any horizon which Crispin saw. Nevertheless, flashing
like an aurora in November, former images occur with
sharpened emphasis. For example, when chrysanthemums
cannot disguise "the clanking mechanism | Of machine
within machine within machine," the ocean-machine of
"Sea Surface Full of Clouds" clicks again. Although a
work too special, too fully absorbed into Stevens' most
elusive language—and then limited to aspects of that—it
looms like a rugged apex of style.

> It needed the heavy nights of drenching weather
> To make him return to people, to find among them
> Whatever it was that he found in their absence,
> A pleasure, an indulgence, an infatuation.

Never easy, often obscure, the whole work predicts his
maturing practice. Whereas *Harmonium* isolated images
under the aegis of a single topic or constructed parallels
and contrasts, the later manner, for a time, simply offers
defiant phrases. It expands from a poetic sensibility of
detachment to one which can indulge emotional power
while staying still disengaged. After such an undertaking
most poets would face choosing a Messianic vocation or a
Trappist's vows. Stevens' solution, as usual, reasonably
capitalized on working through the unresolved, implied
elements.

All four poems of *The Man with the Blue Guitar* try to
have it both ways: to maintain the freedoms inherent in
Harmonium but, at the same time, to bear with more
coherence upon the problems which the world pressed
against *Ideas of Order*. Inevitably the quest requires a
more spacious world. His long poems later indulge digres-
sions which may dilate the movement and thought without
detracting from either. In "Owls' Clover" and "The Man
with the Blue Guitar" the incidental aperçus nearly con-
vince one of their rightness, but, contrariwise, the main

arguments flounder on confused premises. Both nearly wear out their contents before the end, if inventiveness seldom flags. As already mentioned, Stevens cut and trimmed the six main parts of "Owl's Clover" without satisfying himself about them. Deciding which text to use could lead to one of those fruitless editorial debates. *Opus Posthumous* prints the longer version, and citations will, whenever possible, refer to it for convenience. While one must be grateful for having any version widely available, an earlier state should not displace the one which its author at one point established between boards and then dropped without further public comment on which he preferred—or whether, as seems more likely, he wanted to consign all of it to oblivion. Whatever its shortcomings, it makes an essential link in his development. The structure of "The Man with the Blue Guitar" falls between "Like Decorations in a Nigger Cemetery" and "Owl's Clover," more integrated than the former, less given to a single topic than the latter. Neither of these, however, pretends to present a necessary totality. Whereas a philosophic analysis almost broke down before the longer poems of *Harmonium* and some in *Ideas of Order*, the thought behind "Owl's Clover" separates too readily from ornament. At times this disparity may contribute to the theme, but elsewhere it opens doors betraying a makeshift jumble behind the scenes.

v

The dominant figure about which "Owl's Clover" revolves shows some sculptured horses of heroic proportions. Stevens' methods offer no consistent picture of them, piece together all their attributes and observe their many angles and lighting as one will. Their marble wings make them akin to Pegasus and the function of poetry itself. The first section, "The Old Woman and the Statue" [43–46b], Stevens once elaborated on. "The old woman is a symbol of those who suffered during the depression and the statue is a symbol of art, although in several poems of which *Owl's Clover* . . . consists, the statue is a variable symbol. While there is nothing automatic about the poem, nevertheless it has an automatic aspect in the sense that it is what I wanted it to be without knowing before it was written what I wanted it to be, even though I knew before it was written what I wanted to do." [219-20b] The beginning picks up the usual themes from the horses pawing upward in their stone flight set against the park which they, likewise, share. The plaza remains theatrically empty, as though the curtain rises on a set which the audience applauds for its own graces.

A static vista by itself has never ushered Stevens to his greatest triumphs, and in this case the striving skirts disaster. Although the sculptor has allowed for moderately free exchange between his work and its surroundings, invading this public privacy shuffles a crone: "But her he had not foreseen: the bitter mind | In a flapping cloak." For a while the verse coming to grips with such a reality in a rarefied atmosphere may remind one of nothing so much as the old Ballet Russe de Monte Carlo (whichever branch reached its heyday during the middle 1930's) solving unemployment by Serge Lifar's choreography and Eugène Berman's décor. Whatever motivated it, the results of this encounter must look specious. Less than a victim of sudden poverty, she joins the familiar figures in other galleries, those whose perceptions will not let them see and react to the simple wonders of gardens and art. No fairy godmother, basket with apples for sale, government pension, or social service volunteer will alleviate her haggard hate: "nothing of herself except | A fear too naked for her shadow's shape." The locale of the park stays vague, but surely this extreme destitution conjures Petrograd and an old serf. Her blankness envelopes the statue in night. At this point all three Weird Sisters and Hecate could hardly work a denser havoc: "The harridan self and ever-maladive fate | Went crying their desolate syllables." Granted Stevens' occasional relish of overstatement, such excess loses all touch with satire. Not only does she blacken the afternoon but also night, which would otherwise blend with the statue. Obviously this lumpen figure has not stepped from a WPA mural, and she represents a poverty of response inherent in anyone. Nevertheless, by designating

physical and imaginative destitution, she barely sym-
bolizes—rather allegorizes—and so woefully lacks relevance. Here, instead of stinting himself before an object
which he admires, Stevens strives for sympathy with a
subject whom he cannot accept. She rouses neither terror
nor sorrow but looks almost quaint, probably no more so
decades after the appearance of the poem. Her malev-
olence enshrouds the park, but, being a mere cypher, she
projects no real force. Her portrait proves how gauche
Stevens becomes when he deliberately seeks an apparent
sociological counter.

Much of "Owl's Clover" falls uneasily among utterances
which center now upon public polemic, then obvious
symbols, or private ruminatings, or accouterments around
the statue. Various phrases, owl's clover, itself, for example,
vary with contexts. It suggests, according to Marianne
Moore, who specializes in this kind of insight: "Those
who dare to forget that 'As the man the state, not as the
state the man,' who divert 'the dream of heaven from
heaven to the future as a god,' are indeed the carnivorous
owl with African greenness for its repast." [4] Owl's clover is
a plant and medicinal in the treatment of scrofula. Camouflaging a similar tonic as poetry does not agree with Stevens' usual practices. Moreover, does the owl flying across
many of the other poems correspond with this one? Happily, things pick up somewhat after the lamentable beginning. The rightness of surface and emotion moves once
again in phase as the public and the semi-private join. The
second part, called eventually "The Statue at the World's
End" [46–52b], fatalistically consigns the world and statue
to a future scrap heap. Stevens had entitled this part "Mr.
Burnshaw and the Statue" originally in the pique he had
with a reviewer for the *New Masses*. The relationship of
Mr. Burnshaw to the thesis and surface of the poem is, at
best, tangential.

> *The thing is dead . . . Everything is dead*
> *Except the future. Always everything*
> *That is is dead except what ought to be.*
> *All things destroy themselves or are destroyed.*

With the last statement one can hardly quarrel. The horses suffer in an age dominated by the proletariat and look like mere confections, pipe dreams, antiques, or ruins. A cosmic ritual of forgetfulness occurs around the plaster, which has superseded the marble, as a monument to the Masses takes its place. Such a tribute cannot endure either; it will reach an early end: gratuitous destruction culminates in destruction only. Having advanced to this point, were there no further compromise, the poem would have to end, but since time does not, neither does the discourse with the topic, "It is only enough | To live incessantly in change." The problem of how to face impermanence reiterates the themes, essentially, of "Sunday Morning." The matter, which has plagued Stevens increasingly—and will continue to—becomes one of discovering the order within the transitory, as, for example, seasons. Casually, by one of those revealing images, he isolates a common emotion in a fresh way: "Men gathering for a mighty flight of men, | An abysmal migration into a possible blue?" Sections cut away, but reprinted in *Opus Posthumous*, suggest a further allegory. Just as a statue represents a true and a false aspect of masculine creativity—the individual artist and the simulacrum of a public hero like General Jackson respectively—so dancing women here counterbalance the hag's lack of grace in the first part. The pattern, however, contributes no discernible value.

The third section, "The Greenest Continent" [52–60b], echoes the theme from *Heart of Darkness*, as the European intelligence, the ideal of the eighteenth century, confronts spatial rather than temporal illogicality. (Were Stevens given to political prognostications, his insight would uncannily show the emerging nations of the 'sixties.) The progress within the sections tolerates dizzying leaps, but, in general, the first explores a confused present, the second speculates on an uncreative future, and Africa, in the third, involves conflicts fought largely in the past and inherited by the present. "The heaven of Europe is empty. . . . | There was a heaven once." The indicated omission in these lines originally encased the part quoted in section vii,

Chapter 1, above, for one example of what the final version excludes. The rational Europe, which never existed, save, perhaps, in an encyclopaedist's mind, catches up golden moderation so exquisitely that a devout antediluvian paradise for a naturally good man pales when set beside it. In Africa the jungle sprawls, and the aspiring horses of the north find no haven. Its natives perpetuate their primordial culture, one worthy of Piero de Cosimo's rout before the discovery of honey, "And Africa, basking in antiquest sun, | Contains for its children not a gill of sweet." The belief from other poems re-enters; a finality in death, not a true fertility, lends Africa its sprawling greenness, its hysterically lithe vitality which composes arabesques of the illiterate. Into this indigenous jungle descend angels of Europe in a parody of colonization and *Paradise Lost*. "Angels tiptoe upon the snowy cones | Of palmy peaks sighting machine-guns." Like the macabre mice, these celestial inhabitants enjoy an ambiguous triumph, and Africa retains its antagonisms. The horses, always in an aura of nobility, could not survive in this climate. Nothing proves quite indestructible, and just as a place lives in the objects to which it gives rise, so the objects must translate their milieux.

The section concludes on one of Stevens' strangest passages; trenchant in itself, it compares with little else he says by describing Ananke, Necessity, which has ordained both the statue and its locale. Obedient to the general, never the particular, indifferent to nuances as well as inflections, more obtuse than the old parakeet in "The Bird with Coppery, Keen Claws," as unfeeling as an insulated Snow Man in a jungle, a principality for a decidedly dividing and indifferent heaven, changeless amid flux: Ananke rules only barbarous fatalists. Recognizing necessity in this guise would never bestow any freedom. It may reincarnate the inhuman Jove from "Sunday Morning," although the awe in this litany grants no release by orgy of the men who there praise a deity. Ananke is "origin and resplendent end of law, | Sultan of African sultans, starless crown." From references to Nietzsche throughout the

prose and poems, one assumes that Stevens has read him
and may have based the alliance of Africa and fate on the
passage which compares Bizet (*Carmen*) and Wagner.

> Mit ihm nimmt man Abschied vom *feuchten* Norden, von
> allem Wasserdampf des Wagnerischen Ideals. Schon die
> Handlung erlöst davon. Sie hat von Mérimée noch die
> Logik in der Passion, die kürzeste Linie, die *harte* Noth-
> wendigkeit; sie hat vor Allem, was zur heissen Zone gehört,
> die Trockenheit der Luft, die *limpidezza* in der Luft. Hier
> ist in jedem Betracht das Klima verändert. . . . Ihre
> Heiterkeit ist afrikanisch; sie hat das Verhängniss über
> sich, ihr Glück ist kurz, plötzlich, ohne Pardon. . . . Wie
> in seiner lasciven Schwermuth selbst unsre Unersättlich-
> keit einmal Sattheit lernt!—Endlich die Liebe, die in die
> *Natur* zurückübersetzte Liebe! . . . Sondern die Liebe
> als Fatum, als *Fatalität*, cynisch, unschuldig, grausam—
> und eben darin *Natur!* [5]

As elsewhere, when one suspects a source, Stevens' redac-
tion employs only the basic concepts and enlarges upon it
independently. The African deity, too, for him, mirrors
the images of its human creators. Africa worships fate, and
this religion says more about Africa than Truth, although
aspects of Ananke may exceed geographical boundaries. As
another analogy, a comparison between "Gold Coast Cus-
toms" and "Owl's Clover" might identify mutually two
poets who in early attitudes and vocabularies share qualities. Edith Sitwell concentrates her intense imagery as she
superimposes Africa on England in a shifting montage.

> *And the rickety houses*
> *Rock and rot,*
> *Lady Bamburgher airs*
> *That foul plague-spot*
> *Her romantic heart.*
> *From the cannibal mart,*
> *That smart Plague-cart,*
> *Lady Bamburgher rolls where the foul news-sheet*
> *And the shambles for souls are set in the street.* [6]

Lady Bamburgher's opposite number in "Owl's Clover"
becomes a mordantly reflective man known as the Bulgar,

who introduces the mass of people under a socialized
Central-European government, quite as chaotic as colonies
under African mindlessness. In this next section a somewhat impoverished present takes over by a discourse on
economic matters. To entitle a sociological tract in poetry
"A Duck for Dinner" [60–66b] sounds peculiar, perhaps
less for some other writers than for Stevens. A bitterness,
underscored by failure to transpose concepts into the usual
idiom, brings this part close to pathos. The discrepancy
between emotion and style does not argue such passages
more deeply felt; if one dare make a conjecture on this
point, the poet probably sensed his mind had recoiled and
so sought a disguise in vehemence bordering the trite.

> O buckskin, O crosser of snowy divides,
> For whom men were to be ends in themselves,
> Are cities to breed as the mountains bred, the streets
> To trundle children like the sea?

(The final version modified this part slightly, but it seemed
unnecessary to switch to *The Man with the Blue Guitar*
for the citation; generally the changes entail excisions.)
Between the inscrutable jungle of Africa and a rapacious
society where for the masses "Their destiny is just as much
machine | As death itself" stands the statue of horses, now
meaningless. The park again claims the scene, a place of
distraction with a concert featuring " 'Concerto for Air-
plane and Pianoforte,' | The newest Soviet reclame," as
the populace amuses itself, but Stevens dispatches such
satire more neatly in prose vignettes. Neither Africa, un-
thinking, unchangeable, unconscious of its useless past
and unproductive future, nor the atrophied European genius can realize a millennium beyond a Soviet pettiness.
Conjectures fade and, despite all threats, the statue rides
again victorious in its own right through a passage of
mystic prophecy. It sounds resolute enough for an over-
stated finale. In structure "Owl's Clover" faces repeated
hazards. The sixth, concluding part in this section already
begins ironies which qualify the preceding vision. In a
quotidian park the statue now represents a glory quite as

false in terms of aesthetics as of economics; strangely enough, as in other passages, the theme sounds better in its later variations than upon its first appearance. Art triumphs in its own right, but the people remain uncomprehending; "We must have the throstle on the gramophone. | Where shall we find more than derisive words?" Crispin's voyage, of course, never took him this far into darkness.

"Sombre Figuration" [66–71b] rounds out the conjectures so far presented; it cannot resolve all matters, and Ananke and the statue reign supreme over their diametric polarities. A new concept appears, a subman, who stalks through ensuing poems with an unassigned prerogative, at times sinister, at others reassuring.

> We have grown weary of the man that thinks.
> He thinks and it is not true. The man below
> Imagines and it is true, as if he thought
> By imagining, anti-logician, quick
> With a logic of transforming certitudes.

The subman does not quite fuse matters; he resides within each individual, perhaps an inner darkness by which to order experience in a new way, very distantly related to Jung's collective unconscious. This second self brings "turgid tunes, | As of insects or cloud-stricken birds" with a barbaric sway. If the one of fictive music inspires an excessive awe, the subman frequently induces knowledge akin to terror; this feeling springs not from ignorance but after confronting truth. Some of Stevens' insinuating lines describe the mutations of this figure in his most explicit statements. Although too schematic a development, having achieved this much almost implies that through "Owl's Clover" Stevens had freed himself for "The Man with the Blue Guitar."

> He turns us into scholars, studying
> The masks of music. We perceive each mask
> To be the musician's own and, thence, become
> An audience to mimics glistening
> With meanings, doubled by the closest sound,
> Mimics that play on instruments discerned
> In the beat of the blood.

If the subman can imagine, he cannot create from nothing; the European with his culture and the American of Continental tastes vanish in a mist. Yet, no escape from past into future will ease the present. The rotating scene finally comes full circle to the initial one, which, having been subjected to many distortions, now becomes one blackbird's way of looking at statuary: "in a crow's perspective of trees | Stands brimming white" the group which came from the sculptor's mind and must exist there. "Owl's Clover" ends on a series of tentative guesses which, in terms of the poem itself, present neither irrefutable answers nor points for departure. The imagination by itself will solve nothing, but without it nothing can evolve. The final statement dismisses conjectures rather than providing a conclusion.

The vacillating tendency of *Ideas of Order*, particularly "Like Decorations in a Nigger Cemetery," continues. "Owl's Clover" deals with certain subjects which assume preternatural importance. The statue, prevailing only in the present, suffers a diminution from the weakening of temperaments which create its kind, the world as it is, the corrosion by time itself, and programs about the future. The artifact, nevertheless, still retains power, although almost freed from the impetus which first made it and whose vision it continues to transmit. The trouble throughout rests on Stevens' efforts to bring the external in line with his poetic beliefs; Ananke and the subman both should define such aspects, but they cannot and consequently appear irreconcilable in the poem as well as out of context. The topic of poetry alone weakly counterbalances disorder. If "Owl's Clover" stays fragmentary in spite of its author's efforts to pull it into line, "The Man with the Blue Guitar" [165–84a] attempts no final integration. Just as its central image, the blue guitar, borrowed quite freely from Picasso, stands for imagined qualities, which ring spectacular changes, so the poem demonstrates instances without worrying nicely about their exact relationships. In this freedom it shares greater affinities with "Like Decorations in a Nigger Cemetery" than "Owl's Clover," but the

guitarist's control over the images functions more persistently than the marble horses can. Stevens' publishing it as
a sequence in a magazine while omitting sections included
throughout the final form (with three left over for *Opus
Posthumous*) indicates the relaxed attitudes. His own
notes for this poem, the longest translation in *Mattino
Domenicale*, help clarify many passages but leave others
ambiguous. One letter says, "You will understand that in
converting a poem, written and thought out in the peculiar
figurations of poetry, into plain English, one's explanations
are bound to call for a certain amount of tolerance," to
which Professor Poggioli adds "Passo volentieri al lettore
questo consiglio di prudenza e di discrezione." [170d]

vi

It begins with an explicit statement of an interview between the poet and his audience, the latter wanting
"A tune upon the blue guitar | Of things exactly as they
are," although for Stevens no one can describe poetically
things or people with realistic exactitude. To mock such
an unrealizable goal, the owl (of "Owl's Clover?") metaphorically turns up, a talisman on a peasant's house for
warding off evil: "To nail his thought across the door, | Its
wings spread wide to rain and snow." Neither superstition
nor psychology will reveal man. Moreover, the plea for
things as they are amounts to a popular desire for sentimental reassurances from a medium which cannot tolerate
them. Stevens then arrives at the crux of what he does
with poetry and the trials it entails: depicting most objects
as meaner than they are betrays the imagination; things-
in-themselves scarcely exist for his universe, at least when
isolated; indiscriminate praise will not piece together a
world; reason, while one cannot totally depart from it,
guides deceptively. At best there remains an imaginative
force, which the blue guitar becomes; it represents the
quantity to mediate between externals and the poet. The
color of his instrument sets the player off from his critics;
Stevens here identifies blue with the imagination.
Although at times he seems to assign colors certain consist-

ent powers, [7] he does not always do so. Sometimes, indeed, like Shem and Shaun in *Finnegans Wake*, blue and green exchange roles, and elsewhere they happen to be the colors of objects and nothing more. If a prismatic world revealed itself symbolically to everyone each day, every man would become a poet writing the same poem about things as they really are. To explicate the lines, "So that's life, then: things as they are? | It picks its way on the blue guitar," Professor Poggioli comments, "Alla mia domanda se 'it' si riferiva a 'life' il poeta rispose: 'Yes. But it also means things as they are. In this poem, reality changes into the imagination (under one's very eyes) as one experiences it, by reason of one's feelings about it.' " [175d] Equating twentieth-century science with its poetry often provides a meaningless analogy, but here Stevens does hint at a parallel with Heisenberg's Uncertainty Principle. Because poetry depends upon shifting qualities, "The Man with the Blue Guitar" may juggle its points a bit frantically. By the time it has gathered all the qualifications, it tends to have returned to the argument without having exhausted its possibilities, the incompleteness on which other poems have likewise ended.

When his poems employ two speakers, as this one sporadically does, either no common ground joins them or a violent recognition fuses them into a single individual, an enlargement of the anecdotal manner. Here the questioners soon fade, as does the player (both parts of "reality?") of the blue guitar intermittently himself, and an outside narrator assumes the role of declaiming the poem. Invoking this criterion may smack of applying to poetry Jamesian standards devised for prose fiction. If any author elects to set figurines in his landscape, however, he assumes some responsibility for their consistent behavior or metamorphosis. *The Waste Land* (or, to a lesser degree, "The Love Song of J. Alfred Prufrock") blurs individuals for certain effects; Stevens here seems bent upon outdoing the cubists, particularly Braque, in breaking up the continuity of surfaces. The opening altercation fades into a display of the working poet. With this faculty man can neither outstrip his human limits nor analyze himself fully. An enemy, who advocates a "super-reality" remains, "him whom none believes, | Whom all believe that all believe." Or, as Stevens propounds, "If we are to think of a supreme fiction, instead of creating it, as the Greeks did, for example in the form of a mythology, we might choose to create it in the image of a man: an agreed-on superman. He would not be the typical hero taking part in parades (columns red with red-fire, bells tolling, tin cans, confetti), in whom no one believes as a truly great man, but in whom everybody pretends to believe, someone completely outside of the intimacies of profound faith, a politician, a soldier, Harry Truman as god." [176d] (One might note here how Stevens' mind accumulates images and resemblances; he jotted down rapidly his typical hero's traits, and less polished transitions than in his published writings tie the features together.) The poet, qua poet, then emerges to defend the color of his instrument as a part of its surroundings, which affect him and which he, in turn, shapes, a concept encountered frequently in *Ideas of Order*.

The eleventh section contains one of the many passages to gloss what poetry does with resemblances.

> *Slowly the ivy on the stones*
> *Becomes the stones. Women become*
>
> *The cities, children become the fields*
> *And men in waves become the sea.*
>
> *It is the chord that falsifies.*
> *The sea returns upon the men,*
>
> *The fields entrap the children, brick*
> *Is a weed and all the flies are caught,*
>
> *Wingless and withered, but living alive.*
> *The discord merely magnifies.*
>
> *Deeper within the belly's dark*
> *Of time, time grows upon the rock.*

By thus accepting all aspects which ultimately merge, the poet pieces together his world, although it need obey

neither transitory resemblances nor fixed realities. Having
created a sphere beyond the actual, if based largely upon
it, the guitarist, in descending again to this one, condemns
what it accomplishes: "To improve the sewers in Jerusa-
lem, | To electrify the nimbuses." The guitar must relate
the segments, which partake, among others, of the poet
himself. Comparable with this interchange, in the quoted
passages, the poet assumes the mob's attributes while the
guitar welds them. Just as the creation of an ideally poetic
world reached too high, this violent one, based on Picasso's
"hoard | Of destructions" sinks too low; an ordinary sim-
plicity comes back to the musician and his instrument.
"The person has a mould. But not | Its animal," as ampli-
fied by Stevens, "Anima = animal = soul. The body has a
shape, the soul does not. The soul is the animal of the
body. Art deceives itself in thinking that it can give final
shape to the soul." [179d] The body certainly cannot quite
lose itself among other physical objects, as Stevens says
further.

> The monster = nature, wich [sic] I desire to reduce: master,
> subjugate, acquire complete control over and use freely
> for my own purpose, as poet. I want, as poet, to be that in
> nature, which constitutes nature [sic] very self. . . . I
> want to face nature the way two lions face one another—
> the lion in the lute facing the lion locked in stone. I
> want, as a man of the imagination, to write poetry with
> all the power of a monster equal in strength to that of the
> monster about whom I write. I want man's imagination
> to be completely adequate in the face of reality. [He
> goes on to assert] I apostrophize the air and call it friend,
> my only friend. But it is only air. What I need is a true
> belief, a true brother, friendlier than the air. The imagina-
> tion (poor pale guitar) is not that. But the air, the mere
> *joie de vivre*, may be. This stands for the search for a
> belief. [179d]

Poetry, then, becomes both principle and example, concept and image, the creative and the created, natura
naturans and natura naturata; as such, it demands much
attention in one of Stevens most famous assertions, which

has already engaged him and which will concern him increasingly.

> Poetry is the subject of the poem,
> From this the poem issues and
>
> To this returns. Between the two,
> Between issue and return, there is
>
> An absence in reality,
> Things as they are. Or so we say.
>
> But are these separate? Is it
> An absence for the poem, which acquires
>
> Its true appearances there, sun's green,
> Cloud's red, earth feeling, sky that thinks?
>
> From these it takes. Perhaps it gives,
> In the universal intercourse.

If poetry does mediate everywhere "in the universal intercourse" by its own improvised order—a view which Stevens, Valéry, and others share in this century—one must grant it exalted heights. Having thus defined the matter, the poet-player apparently finds a liberation for creating multiple chords as he wishes upon his harmonium, clavier, guitar, bells, and all other instruments.

Ensuing parts elaborate upon this concept, but, unfortunately, the first twenty-eight of the thirty-three sections contribute the major effects of the material. The rest returns to narrowing down the themes largely accounted for. In the statement on the jacket Stevens makes explicit that the poem falls into no absolute arrangement; indeed, the nature of the subject forbids a resounding climax. By a transition which scarcely pretends to establish necessary bridges, the scene moves inside a cathedral for a reprise upon the double aspect of man's grandeur and his evading its consequences. By a new route one returns to things as they are, the irreducible quality which Stevens may desperately wish to escape and which he honestly recognizes as undeniable. In creating a man ironically, he turns, it would seem, to the image of hollowness already devised for Crispin, the scarecrow, and heavier details mark how the clown, as such, assumes a new guise. "This is his essence: the old fantoche | Hanging his shawl upon the wind. . . . his eyes | A-cock at the cross-piece on a pole." It surely looks like a scarecrow, although Stevens' note glosses the image as a telephone lineman at work. Of course, once again, the one identity need not cancel the other. This worker resides in an industrial suburb called Oxidia. After fourteen lines of loathing for the jerry-built scrap, suddenly he closes on the affirmation, "Oxidia is the soot of fire, | Oxidia is Olympia." Significantly, he chose the comparative modesty of Olympia, rather than Olympus. Nor does he scoff at the old Olympia in his note. "The statements in the poem are all succinct, necessarily; and I am afraid you will find my exposition of them equally so. But if I am to 'evolve a man' in Oxidia and if Oxidia is the only possible Olympia, in any real sense, then Oxidia is what [sic] from which Olympia must come. Oxidia is both the seed and the amber-ember pod from which the seed of Olympia drops. This [sic] dingier the life, the more lustrous the paradise. But, if the only paradise must be here and now, Oxidia is Olympia." [183d] As usual, nothing so much resembles a swelling as a hollow, and he adds, "These are opposites. Oxidia is the antipodes of Olympia. Oxidia (from Oxide) is the typical industrial suburb, stained and grim." [183d] Presumably he abhors the modern community, but the ancient heroes, one has learned from other poems, have gone, and their houses stand in ruins. This violent yoking together heterogeneous ideas outdoes most metaphysical conceits and leads to a last statement, which describes what Stevens has done all along, "Throw away the lights, the definitions, | And say of what you see in the dark."

Poetry in all its manifestations lives, mediates, justifies, and explains afresh. Roger Fry's observation that poet and scientist alone in this society jettison commercial symbols and grasp a reality describes what "The Man with the Blue

Guitar" builds upon. The seemingly false antitheses between things as they are and the imagination can thus result in a new order of reality, one neither so fanciful as Olympia nor so insipid as Oxidia. In daring "The moments when we choose to play | The imagined pine, the imagined jay," we neither invent nor discover, neither contrive nor depict. Instead, the exercise induces awareness of the real as the real is, not what to most minds glibly symbolizes something else or projects an adornment for private vanity. Reality itself must be imagined on the guitar. "Owl's Clover" and "The Man with the Blue Guitar" both expand the concepts treated in *Harmonium*, but the two long poems stay less aloof. Neither succeeds poetically throughout because the vocabulary cannot resist its accustomed wayward impudence. The struggle with a daily scene, apart from the blue guitar, continues, and an approach different from the one in "Owl's Clover" eventually gains the victory. "The Man with the Blue Guitar" does allow Stevens to recognize the imagination as the force he wished it to be all along and to rid himself of a certain squeamishness about it. That he continued still to prove his postulates and uncover greater ramifications keeps the next volume uneven with poems where all contributes to a unified design and others where everything falls apart between internal and external.

The most effective single poem in *The Man with the Blue Guitar* is also the shortest: "The Men That Are Falling." [187–88a] Unlike its ominous title, it speaks with an assurance and attains indisputable confidence. For the first time in his later manner a single subject, in a restricted compass, fastens to itself associations and through fragments presents a totality, combining methods and styles contrived earlier. It depicts with a slow, wonderfully modulated stroke, a desire beyond desire, which yet must be related to living and the earth itself. In his darkened room a man faces a head, an alter-ego, perhaps, or one of those presences which increasingly inform the poems. Not pleasant, "bodiless, a head | Thick-lipped from riot and rebellious cries," it belongs to one whom the title names. If the man cannot define his desire conceptually, neither can the other's martyred lips speak it. Unlike the roaring wind of *Harmonium,* this silence does not move in a vacuum. "This death was his belief though death is a stone. | This man loved earth, not heaven, enough to die." Facing consequences of death beyond the denials in "Sunday Morning," Stevens reaches hardships exceeding a transitory economic depression. The verse must, at times, look more austere, and the gnomic phrases compress highly involved concepts. "The Men That Are Falling" makes less of a statement than "Owl's Clover" and "The Man with the Blue Guitar," but the mode which will shape later works advances here upon the style of "A Postcard from the Volcano." No more than any other artist could Stevens overcome all difficulties at once, and the next volume struggles very hard without realigning all aspects.

vii

Parts of a World, with its defiant reference to fragments, will remain his most widely uneven volume. The title, as though the book prints a tattered atlas, which charts a single sphere, implies likewise a coherent tracing of demarcations. Just as the world contains many, many orders (what else have nearly all the poems been about?), so must its arts; indexing the full hierarchy proves too arduous for a reader and, intermittently, the poet himself. The principle, as in "The Man with the Blue Guitar," turns on the ultimate belief that the poet's world must share the climate of poetry as well as the nature of reality. Because the borders of these quantities enlarge constantly, the expression veers toward the elliptical, and the structure toward the fortuitous. The newly mastered control of intensity somewhat restricts the range of subjects, but even familiar categories turn up bafflingly altered. The Imagistic habits persist with enigmatic statements. Unabashedly satiric verse declines, while its petulant tone takes over in many poems for several lines. Anecdotes suspend fewer judgments. The incongruity between objects as well as between the beholder and his surroundings clashes with the violence of armed conflict itself. A heavy ingenuity among poems that undisguisedly philosophize relegates them to Stevens' least effective trials of this sort. They become jottings from which one pieces together a wisdom only sketched. Although imposing too stern an order on Stevens always runs risks, this volume, particularly, defies precise labels, and the ones below can, at best, trace major tendencies.

Poems which exemplify the older modes occur at random throughout *Parts of a World*. "Parochial Theme" [191–92a], leading off the volume, asserts in freely shifting figures that life continues beyond any single man or culture; its incisive strokes resemble Imagism, if a few too many statements accompany them. The advice for the volume, although curiously brusque here, "Piece the world together, boys, but not with your hands," sets the note for what follows. "Arrival at the Waldorf" [240–41a] keeps a satiric irony as vers de société with the bored opening, "Home from Guatemala, back at the Waldorf"; the poised ennui in New York makes the hotel phantasmagorial and contrasts with a memory of "that alien, point-blank, green and actual Guatemala." Although not quite a fair comparison, a reading of "Farewell to Florida" and this one together demonstrates the dangers of patching up a world in verse: flatness, explanation, discontinuity, and rambling. From this pattern, nevertheless, a mellowness lights single lines because the older training continues as assured as ever: "The fire eye in the clouds survives the gods. | To think of a dove with an eye of grenadine." [222a] In some poems, "The Man on the Dump" [201–3a], for example, a new directness enters the bemused anecdotes: "The sun is a corbeil of flowers the moon Blanche | Places there, a bouquet." Time then examines "the janitor's poems | Of every day." The tedium becomes the world, the discarded heap itself, but the moon may momentarily purge the dump and life. Without a blue guitar, the poet must arrange fragments or, at least, try to rid himself of habitual complacency. Whether one should regard the catalogued refuse as symbolic or actual the poem does not confirm. At

the end with his images and phrases, he asks in a suspended
series what the dump implies:

> *is it to eject, to pull*
> *The day to pieces and cry stanza my stone?*
> *Where was it one first heard of the truth? The the.*

Any one of these three poems could probably date from
an earlier period. In context, with the rest composing *Parts
of a World*, they help shape and sustain its different tone,
in spots more querulous, in others more conversational.
The faults derive not from any single taint so much as the
failure to modulate attitudes convincingly. As Stevens
himself said in "Agenda" [41–42b], not approved for a
book and published in 1935 at the time of the more
frankly bitter works:

> *Whipped creams and the Blue Danube,*
> *The lin-lan-lone of Babson,*
> *And yet the damned thing doesn't come right.*
>
> *Boston should be in the Keys*
> *Painting the saints among the palms.*
> *Charleston should be New York.*

One poem in this volume, excluded from the *Collected
Poems*, fully exemplifies his troubles when he shows the
mind overreaching itself. The tone surely invokes satire
and not, as one reviewer made it, a sketch of the emerging
hero. "When this figure, or its prototype, first appeared in
A *Duck for Dinner* . . . he bore some suspicion of resemblance to a sort of *fuehrer*. Things in the present collection
like *Life on a Battleship* don't quite clear him of it." [8]
Its philosophizing does bog down fuzzily into a series of
false postulates which the verse cannot exemplify. Even
the title sounds unpromising, "Life on a Battleship." [77–
81b] It shows vaguely what might occur had Claggart re-
placed Captain Vere in a versified version of *Billy Budd*.
"The rape of the bourgeoisie accomplished, the men | Re-
turned on board *The Masculine*." Afterwards, the captain
schemes to erect his battleship as the center of the world,
which he will rule as dictator. A plot so inflated must be

doomed to even an allegorical failure, which the final
refutation dispatches too glibly. On the other hand, the
poem following it in *Parts of a World*, likewise rejected for
the *Collected Poems*, represents one of the more sustained
pieces in this volume. In its own way the title, "The
Woman That Had More Babies than That" [81–83b], is
as right as "Life on a Battleship" is wrong. The beginning
evokes one of Picasso's powerful, pensive clown-saltim-
banques on a beach:

> An acrobat on the border of the sea
> Observed the waves, the rising and the swell
> And the first line spreading up the beach; again,
> The rising and the swell, the preparation
> And the first line foaming over the sand; again,
> The rising and the swell, the first line's glitter,
> Like a dancer's skirt, flung round and settling down.
> This was repeated day by day. The waves
> Were mechanical, muscular. They never changed,
> They never stopped, a repetition repeated
> Continually— There is a woman has had
> More babies than that.

The theme represents the universal flux, never quite fixed,
never quite identical, but everywhere present, which imparts knowledge of the world as more than a mechanism.
The ocean frequently, but not always, stands for the un-
thinking, the regimented, as to a degree it does here. The
woman, as a pervasive force, and the playful title combine
to warn that the male-female, water-earth form no dichoto-
mies. The pictures of her presences gather together some
of Stevens' softest images. They form a counterpart to the
ruthlessness aimed at, if not reached, in "Life on a Battleship." Although a conjecture would be rash—and probably
no reasoning exclusively dictated the principle—the dele-
tion of the first poem may have prompted omitting the
second. They form a complementary pair of unequal parts:
"Life on a Battleship" masculine, logical, monolithic, and
Cartesian, "The Woman That Had More Babies than
That," feminine, intuitive, multiple, and belonging to
"Children and old men and philosophers, | Bald heads

with their mother's voice still in their ears." From the evidence which these two poems offer, one notices how Stevens fails to clamp together a wholeness to which he can fully assent.

viii

Observations about the social crises of the world sometimes terminate in a remote shelter, and the grudging hauteur which marked "Owl's Clover" persists. "The Common Life" [221a] reduces a town like Oxidia and its inhabitants to Euclidian shapes without depth or life, "The men have no shadows | And the women have only one side." The determinedly macabre "Cuisine Bourgeoise" [227–28a] depicts once again those who permit their private anxieties to engulf them and everything else. "These days of disinheritance, we feast | On human heads." All else goes on as it generally does, except for the final twist, "Is the table a mirror in which they sit and look? | Are they men eating reflections of themselves?" One may feel that the autophagia belongs by rights to Dante, who can manage it, or to Stephen Crane, who gets it out of the way with dispatch. Unlike the satiric poems of the 'thirties, here a personal concern often links poet and scene. If Stevens does not identify himself with its partial poverty, knowledge of a lack in himself allows more charity. "I heard two workers say, 'This chaos | Will soon be ended'" joined with the confession, "I am the poorest of all. | I know that I cannot be mended," does not dismiss ironically the actual "Idiom of the Hero" [200–201a], although it favors a tentative insight and relies on slight faith. If a franker despair expels practical matters from *Parts of a World*, in many landscapes a delicate nuance pervades externals and shapes them. "Like Decorations in a Nigger Cemetery" centered disassociated images in autumn; "Variations on a Summer Day," if shorter and less vivid, brings together under a comparable looseness what the summer may suggest by vistas and their present or fancied adjuncts. It helps prepare the way for the next volume as a deliberate transport to summer. Even the incantatory tones manage a unity, as though they now addressed themselves to a valid force and did not represent seeking power through magic spells by verse. The haunted "The Candle a Saint" [223a] weaves from its controlling image "Green is the night" stunning improvisations. Here merely circulating becomes pleasurable because a living force holds the world together but not in terms of a divorced belief which places a red votive light before a stilted figure. Liberation comes from a fecundating force as "The abstract, the archaic queen" towers above her creatures, astronomers, man, "The topaz rabbit and the emerald cat," as a power more immediate than the Belle Étoile or the singer at Key West. Everwhere the way of seeing, which by implication made poems possible, now must grow conscious of how it sees.

The new concept, centered not only in "The Woman That Had More Babies than That" and "The Candle a Saint," becomes without any apology whatsoever, poetry, which any topic can accommodate; the richness of the results justifies its prerogatives. Lacking some of the delicacy in earlier embodiments, it grows vigorous, indeed dangerous, as its sway becomes autonomous. "Poetry Is a Destructive Force" shows through creatures of primitive power, lion, ox, dog, and bear, the strength which poetry can summon, comparable with the two lions about which Stevens commented in "The Man with the Blue Guitar" and considerably more forceful than the "Lions in Sweden." A poem like "The Latest Freed Man," when poetry does not enter directly, employs the same pattern with the sun as an ox, transferring the strength to man, who in turn transforms the world about him and summons similar daring. Whereas *Harmonium* rejected sheer animal force, here, when allied with poetry, it nearly connotes grandeur. In an opposite manner, "On the Adequacy of Landscape," the pettiness of those who can accept neither the red bird of day nor the little owl flying through the night stands for a shrinking from any imaginative experience as well. The settings throughout vibrate with deeper intensity and less lush assurances than in *Harmonium*. The art of poetry makes increasingly harsh demands. Both these aspects occur with greatest clarity in "On the Road Home" [203–4a] and "Add This to Rhetoric," the former with the striking:

> It was when I said,
> "There is no such thing as the truth,"
> That the grapes seemed fatter.
> The fox ran out of his hole.

Denying absolutes may uncover a partial truth; and, yet, the insight might ultimately turn out illusory and, nevertheless, must in such an extremity suffice. Likewise, "Add This to Rhetoric" [198–99a] triumphs not in what thing exists but in how one observes it. "This is the figure and not | An evading metaphor." Thus, the function of rhetoric becomes, "Add this. It is to add." In the poems themselves the theories might frequently look cryptic or fragmentary. Against the background of the main drift, allowing divergencies and ellipses as required, the belief comes through with remarkable precision. One grasps more confidently the point of an ideal interchange between concept and image. The very approach may entail finicky qualifications, the sort of faltering which often disturbs *Parts of a World*.

ix

The longer reflective poems in this volume unsurely blend questioning and overconfidence, with some postulates pushed not doggedly enough and others snapped up too eagerly. "Connoisseur of Chaos" [215–16a] begins promisingly with an ambiguous assertion which Stevens, despite its paradoxes, can sometimes resolve. "A. A violent order is disorder; and | B. A great disorder is an order." The dictum applies to both the organization of these poems and what they say. After toying with the opposites, and bringing them round to a nearly perfect wholeness based on acceptance of what is, it concludes, "The pensive man . . . He sees that eagle float | For which the intricate Alps are a single nest." By themselves the lines prompt one to speculate, and order's breeding disorder has intrigued other philosophers. For example, a comment by Confucius on the twelfth oracle in *I Ching* notes, "Danger arises when a man feels secure in his position. Destruction threatens when a man seeks to preserve his worldly estate. Confusion develops when a man has put everything in order." [9] The "Connoisseur of Chaos" makes his ironic point that his very quest for ideas of order keeps him alert for all inflexibility which becomes mere dogma, a subjective disorder. The poem following next in the arrangement, "The Blue Buildings in the Summer Air" [216–17b], contrasts Cotton Mather's rigorous pursuit of impossible assurances against mockery by a gnawing mouse, whose function continues from "Dance of the Macabre Mice." "Go, mouse, go nibble at Lenin in his tomb. | Are you not le plus pur, you ancient one?" Cotton Mather, who scorned as ascetically as fatalistic Africa of "Owl's Clover" the "honey-comb of the seeing man," presumably has not entered the permanent heaven he preached (a violent old order), whereas the mouse continues its busy scamper (a great disorder which persists). A similarity in difference also links the two passing figures, a "Mrs. Alfred Uruguay" [248–50a] of the title and an unnamed man; it summons back the tested polarities: moon-sun, female-male, donkey-horse, wealth of dress-poverty in dress, anabasis-katabasis, and "I fear that elegance | Must struggle like the rest" with

> And, capable, created in his mind,
> Eventual victor, out of the martyrs' bones,
> The ultimate elegance: the imagined land.

Judgment hangs suspended, but the points narrow down according to the parallels, an enlargement of the anecdotal mode.

Prolifically as resemblances exfoliate, how determinedly to push the parts into a whole remains an unsolved enigma, which threatens rigidity or shambles. The most impressive poem in the volume reviews the patterns throughout the whole work. "Extracts from Addresses to the Academy of Fine Ideas" [252–59a] begins with another opposition between "The wrinkled roses tinkle, the paper ones" and "the blood-rose living in its smell." Each object belongs to the world, which composes it, and judgments still entail recklessness; one dares scarcely name a preference. Because Stevens wastes no time on perfect parallels, which exist in neither reality nor the volatile imagination, he consequently contributes to the uncertainties about his poems. All factions may meet eventually, even, as here "The false and true are one . . . [but] The good is evil's last invention." From an insight into patience arises the start of wisdom: "Be tranquil in your wounds. It is good death | That puts an end to evil death and dies." As in "Connoisseur of Chaos," if everything eventually blends, to aver that one view serves as well as any other does not necessarily follow. With a glimpse of the whole, but caught among the deceptive parts, the poem revives the old chaos of the sun from "Sunday Morning" as a necessary part of life. No easy statement, a single credo or denial, will rescue disturbing times from their troubles, and religion has the chaos of Cotton Mather's violent order. The fourth section withdraws into one of those luminous realms which glow so resplendently by themselves that frequently they say enough, and further discourse darkens without deepening them. Spring arrives on an early April Sunday to induce the awareness, "There was that difference between the and an, | The difference between himself and no man." Here the observer can accept himself in terms of the world.

From the fourth section no bridge links with the fifth, which consists of freely unrhymed couplets like those of "The Man with the Blue Guitar" and equally bold in their assertions. Here, chaos means any arbitrary limitation, the figures identical with those of "Life on a Battleship"; "In the end, these philosophic assassins pull | Revolvers and shoot each other. One remains." The function of the survivor, unlike the fighters sprung from Cadmus' dragon's teeth, resembles that of the singer at Key West and the blue guitarist. If all parts return to one, then the one begins redistributing its component elements from limbo. Both the imaginary player and ordered system elude the human mind; "It cannot be half earth, half mind; half sun, | Half thinking; until the mind has been satisfied." Reconciliation celebrates the vividness of the earth, apprehending it for a moment as a whole created by one observer.

> What
> One believes is what matters. Ecstatic identities.
> Between one's self and the weather and the things
> Of the weather are the belief in one's element,
> The casual reunions, the long-pondered
> Surrenders, the repeated sayings that
> There is nothing more and that it is enough
> To believe in the weather and in the things and men
> Of the weather and in one's self, as part of that
> And nothing more.

Virginia Woolf gives Mrs. Ramsey a strikingly similar reflection in *To the Lighthouse*. Stevens, of course, did not versify the novel, but the correspondence indicates a coherence of temperament and concepts which engaged artists of their generation.

> With some irony in her interrogation, for when one woke at all, one's relations changed, she looked at the steady light, the pitiless, and remorseless, which was so much her, yet so little her, which had her at its beck and call (she woke in the night and saw it bent across their bed, stroking the floor), but for all that she thought, watching it with fascination, hypnotised, as if it were stroking with its silver fingers some sealed vessel in her brain whose bursting would flood her with delight, she had known happiness, exquisite happiness, intense happiness, and it silvered the rough waves a little more brightly, as daylight faded, and the blue went out of the sea and it rolled in waves of pure lemon which curved and swelled and broke upon the beach and the ecstasy burst in her eyes and waves of pure delight raced over the floor of her mind and she felt, It is enough! It is enough! [10]

Just as, for different reasons, Mrs. Woolf with all her rapture escapes the charge of hedonism lodged sometimes against her, so does Stevens. The close of his poem puts a limit on limitations; there is enough even of enough. This address will consist only of extracts; the academy has no peristyle. One rejoices neither in nirvana nor renewal but rather in the partial earth: "one line in which | The vital music formulates the words."

Stevens' attitude toward "reality" shares further affinities with Mrs. Woolf's, as described by E. M. Forster. "The epitaph of such an artist cannot be written by the vulgar-minded or by the lugubrious. They will try, indeed they have already tried, but their words make no sense. . . . And sometimes it is as a row of little silver cups that I see her work gleaming. 'These trophies,' the inscription runs, 'were won by the mind from matter, its enemy and its friend.' " [11] Stevens in a similar vein noted, "The highest pursuit is the pursuit of happiness on earth." [157b] At the same time, conscious of how very fragile the prizes in the pursuit can be, except as the trophies exemplified by books, he noted, "Poetry is a purging of the world's poverty and change and evil and death. It is a present perfecting, a satisfaction in the irremediable poverty of life." [167b] These contradictory views get at the center of the conflict in *Parts of a World*. Oversimplifying a bit, one can see *Harmonium* as chiefly a delighted praise of "matter" undercut by the knowledge that, as refined by a reasonable imagination, it had to be enough. The two intervening volumes regard it suspiciously as an enemy, or potential traitor, yet without quite abandoning the earlier beliefs, while poetry itself gains sway. *Parts of a World* begins an acceptance of matter as foe and ally, not as alternating rhythms nor as life's dual masks but as a necessary concomitant of human existence. The two depend on each other, and Stevens revels in reconciling such opposites. The admixture, consequently, becomes enriched; the repetitions can celebrate variety, and a single image no longer quite suffices. One must bring the world wholly round until Boston and the Keys join, until the dump does contain actual poems, until chaos and order intertwine, until one says freely to this plenum: it is enough.

In spite of the gain in profundity, a questioning sagacity keeps Stevens from fully celebrating actualities; nor does he forget that one always hankers after imperishable bliss which by its nature cannot endure. When such joy is falsely contrived by the imagination itself one must probe scrupulously to recognize and reject it. The attitude could, in less assured hands, lead only to a maudlin confusion bordering on schizophrenia. With someone as painstaking as Stevens, it culminates in strikingly new insights about the unknown and the familiar, another of the changes which poetry can bring about through ways which Wordsworth and Coleridge did not fully grasp.

x

Granted this degree of intricacy, the conclusion that no ready symbolic system will codify his work must inevitably follow. He seeks ever to draw closer to what he considers actuality, not flee from it. In an age which still counts itself dispossessed, esoteric symbols speciously establish an elevated claim for literature amid the instability of all dogma. Symbols have, of course, protean functions. They may exist as the clichés of wealth to which Roger Fry alludes. When Stevens describes his "Arrival at the Waldorf," he draws tentatively upon this kind of substitute. One cannot deny that the hotel connotes a way of life beyond its single name. Had he wished only a popular tag, however, he might have chosen the Ritz as having a wider currency at that time. Moreover, the outside associations by themselves contribute so little to the poem that making the Waldorf stand for a definite way of life contributes nothing. He might have taken one step beyond current clichés and offered merely external objects, like decorations on a Christmas tree, which he twined around his private doubts. One dare hardly employ the term Objective Correlative any longer, but it pins down this process most readily. Were such his aim, the poems would have long since opened themselves to an unequivocal analysis and, like troops across a drill field, have presented themselves for a review and awards. Nor does he seek to bring to earth the invisible through an observed cypher, either with a known theology or a provincial concoction of his manufacture. Finally, another definition for poetic symbols runs, "Any unit of any work of literature which can be isolated for critical attention. In general usage restricted to the smaller units, such as words, phrases, images, etc." [12] In this sense Stevens may rank among symbolists, but so can any writer who makes a house a home.

He more closely resembles, in one sense of the term, a nominalist. Yvor Winters has pejoratively described him with this term, but, clearly, in their works the two differ almost as much as two master craftsmen can. For Stevens a word does not function as an automatic counter but poetically exists as itself in a somewhat neutral ground, neither good nor bad, high nor low on any scale of values. The poetic atmosphere gives words life, but, of course, they themselves comprise the topography. Words and their world resemble man and his world. If, like the gods, they spring from man, also like gods they enjoy their own mythology. The imagination can deck out peoples and places as it chooses, aware, always, of the limits which it dare not cross without turning into sheer whim and phantasy. Comparably, words create their context which in turn shapes them. For this reason no single code will muster all items into a violence with a pattern or an order resembling chaos. Moon does not always equal imagination which goes on to equal the transubstantial. Sun does not always equal actuality which then equals subman. Nor do seasons, places, peoples, and ideas present a permanent aspect: ideas of order do not catalogue an inflexible paradigm. All may delight; anything may appall. The sole abiding anathema centers on the man of a single principle, the heedless dictator. Even he might have a function, just as the antipoetic, in its way, sets off the truly imagined, especially for comedy. Good and evil, as conventionally defined, may exchange roles because both can, when misunderstood, represent absolutes. By this time, then, the attributes listed in the first chapter should reveal more fully why Stevens inhabits his kind of aesthetic atmosphere and why it so little resembles the more common ones. An odd twist in the poetry of his contemporaries led them from shunning the tired Victorian symbols to importing their own. As John Peale Bishop, who shares in some traits as much with Stevens as anyone does, observed, "Symbols do not die. They become innocuous, useless and at last ornamental, like an antiquated bronze cannon in a park where children and pigeons play." [13]

If Stevens has progressed a certain distance by the end of *Parts of a World*, he has not won all battles, and no perfect serenity prevails. In his "Adagia" he quotes one of Braque's aphorisms; he might also have approved of another one, published in a later issue of the journal which printed the other: "L'art est fait pour troubler. La science pour rassurer." [14] No single idea suffices and no assured system will write poems. Applied science, however frightening or beneficial its contrivances, can duplicate them in reality as long as the postulates hold. Otherwise, such objects would be unscientific and decidedly more disturbing than they are. To this degree they reassure. Each new poem must incorporate its own land and laws, and any one may change slightly at every reading: in a sense nominalistic. With such uncertainties as a principle, disturbing doubts will continue to trouble many lines; new concepts will enter and purify the older ones. Oddly enough, a striking, hostile aspect of reality prompts a significant advance in *Parts of a World*. It derives from the Second World War. Even the assured "Extracts from Addresses to the Academy of Fine Ideas" takes exit on a jarring note: "Behold the men in helmets borne on steel, | Discolored, how they are going to defeat." To quite appreciate the force of this line one must consider a concern which intrudes into a number of poems in *Parts of a World* and forms its main link with *Transport to Summer*. It appears, oddly enough, to have led Stevens to his ultimate counters for resolving various dilemmas. Without the evidence no one could have predicted the uses to which he would have put the Second World War and its soldiers. Yet, during the First World War he had regarded it with a novel serenity, and, incidentally, quite beyond easy symbols: "The Death of a Soldier" [97a]—

> Life contracts and death is expected,
> As in a season of autumn.
> The soldier falls.
>
> He does not become a three-day personage,
> Imposing his separation,
> Calling for pomp.
>
> Death is absolute and without memorial,
> As in a season of autumn,
> When the wind stops,
>
> When the wind stops and, over the heavens,
> The clouds go, nevertheless,
> In their direction.

Poetry is not the same thing as the imagination taken alone.
Nothing is itself taken alone. Things are because of inter-
relations or interactions.

WALLACE STEVENS [163b]

Ἔστιν δὲ μέγα μὲν τὸ ἑκάστῳ τῶν εἰρημένων πρεπόντως
χρῆσθαι, καὶ διπλοῖς ὀνόμασι καὶ γλώτταις, πολὺ δὲ μέγισ-
τον τὸ μεταφορικὸν εἶναι. μόνον γὰρ τοῦτο οὔτε παρ᾽ ἄλλου
ἔστι λαβεῖν εὐφυίας τε σημεῖόν ἐστι· τὸ γὰρ εὖ μεταφέρειν
τὸ τὸ ὅμοιον θεωρεῖν ἐστιν.

ARISTOTLE [1]

THE WORK OF LITERARY HISTORIANS never ends, and they
recognize the challenge with alacrity. In rushing to honor
their debts to the past, they presently make enough mis-
takes so that Stevens' belief about their getting it straight
one day at the Sorbonne sounds like the rankest optimism.
The inevitable revisions guarantee that the rewriting of
literary history will go on. Eventually, then, someone may
set down an orderly account tracing what impacts the
Second World War made not upon the children of the
lost generation but rather upon that group itself. A cursory
review indicates, surprisingly, that on the whole it supplied
them fresh material and impetus whether for the gascon-
ade of *Across the River and into the Trees* or the humility
of "Little Gidding." Having seized their experiences of the
First World War as the license for doubting everything, in
an era of numbness they claimed a further prerogative and
believed something. The actual faiths varied, but the effort

to fit belief into a mold designed for angst may explain a falling off. One should not, obviously, rule out the possibility that once again history may have failed, so far, to catch up with its subject. As a generalization about these writers, and consequently their development, this conjecture admits disagreement; undoubtedly Stevens himself felt an urgency in the Second World War. Moreover, unable to retreat into a prefabricated, official myth, he had to rely upon the standards he already had constructed. He could never have expressed himself in the patriot's patois.

i

To guess about motives, especially with a poet of Stevens' reticence, must sound impertinent. While he never celebrated a war, neither did he shrink from it as a public actuality. In a manner, it represents the ultimate test for the imagination set by the world. What a sensibility can make from this violent blank, which denies the creative mind, intrigued him: "war is the periodical failure of politics." [164b] In *Poetry* for November, 1914, "Phases," four short pieces all treating themes from the war, helped break the silence he had maintained since his undergraduate verse broke off in 1900. Later, in 1918, nine poems under the title "Lettres d'un Soldat" borrow phrases from a book with that name as epigraphs, of which "The Death of a Soldier" comes last. He published on other subjects between 1914 and 1918, of course, and during the two decades from 1918 to 1939 military matters seldom interested him. The mocking "The Revolutionists Stop for Orangeade" [102–3a] contains no seeds of a final decadence, however much it distresses Yvor Winters. "Since the poet . . . is not to abandon his art, there remains only the possibility that he seek variety of experience in the increasingly perverse and strange; that he seek it, moreover, with no feeling of respect toward the art which serves as his only instrument and medium. In the poem entitled *The Revolutionists Stop for Orangeade*, we are given the theory of this type of poetry. . . . And from this point onward there remains little but the sly look of a perverse ingenuity

in confusing the statement of essentially simple themes." [2]
On the contrary, it evades nothing and ridicules those who
enlist themselves under fanatical slogans in politics or art,
or a militant alliance of both, and those who subscribe to
their own absolutes. The rebels resemble realists whom
Stevens cannot challenge on their own blind terms.

> *Hang a feather by your eye,*
> *Nod and look a little sly.*
> *This must be the vent of pity,*
> *Deeper than a truer ditty*
> *Of the real that wrenches.*
> *Of the quick that's wry.*

Properly understood, the same attitude belongs to Crispin.
In the main, throughout *Harmonium* and sporadically
afterwards, Stevens saw—or wished to see—the world as
providing materials for the imagination. Whatever passes
as "perverse and strange" by itself should become less
outré, without diminishing its powers, through poetry.
Strife, riot, revolt, and war would appear to engulf and
destroy his chosen subjects. He could, obviously, have
skirted the matter entirely, thus justifying somewhat Yvor
Winters' charges, made before the later poems became
available. That Stevens elected to investigate the problems
in a characteristic style speaks well of his integrity and
surely exculpates him, although the verses he wrought do
not always equal the claims which they advance.

Parts of a World and the Cummington Press edition of
Notes toward a Supreme Fiction, both dated 1942, conclude elaborately with thoughts about war, a poem in the
latter lending its opening and closing lines, slightly modified, for a border around the back on the binding of the
limited edition. "Soldier, there is a war between
the mind | And sky, between thought and day and night.
It never ends. . . . How gladly with proper words the
soldier dies, | If he must, or lives on the bread of faithful
speech." [408a] In the *Collected Poems* it has become a
permanent part of that work, and, fine as the expression
may be, it looks slightly quaint there decades later. The

prose which comprises the tailpiece, *Parts of a World,* a more peculiar document, has vanished.

> The immense poetry of war and the poetry of a work of the imagination are two different things. In the presence of the violent reality of war, consciousness takes the place of the imagination. And consciousness of an immense war is a consciousness of fact. If that is true, it follows that the poetry of war as a consciousness of the victories and defeats of nations, is a consciousness of fact, but of heroic fact, of fact on such a scale that the mere consciousness of it affects the scale of one's thinking and constitutes a participating in the heroic.
>
> It has been easy to say in recent times that everything tends to become real, or, rather, that everything moves in the direction of reality, that is to say, in the direction of fact. We leave fact and come back to it, come back to what we wanted fact to be, not to what it was, not to what it has too often remained. The poetry of a work of the imagination constantly illustrates the fundamental and endless struggle with fact. It goes on everywhere, even in the periods we call peace. But in war, the desire to move in the direction of fact as we want it to be and to move quickly is overwhelming.
>
> Nothing will ever appease this desire except a consciousness of fact as everyone is at least satisfied to have it be.[3]

A passage composed sometime before the Second World War clarifies aspects of this outlook. It restates succinctly what the poems discussed in the previous chapter considered. "The pressure of the contemporaneous from the time of the beginning of the [First] World War to the present time has been constant and extreme. No one can have lived apart in a happy oblivion. For a long time before the war nothing was more common. In those days the sea was full of yachts and the yachts were full of millionaries. It was a time when only maniacs had disturbing things to say. The period was like a stage-setting that since then has been taken down and trucked away." [224b] The comments turn on the approaching clash and to the impoverished life in Russia under Communism and Germany under the Nazis. But, he argues—and here lies the crux—that if contemporary events force themselves upon awareness so, concurrently, does poetry. "Does anyone suppose that the vast mass of people in this country was moved at the last election by rational considerations? Giving reason as much credit as the radio, there still remains the certainty that so great a movement was emotional and, if emotional, irrational." [225b] In this manner he establishes that poetry and events both spring from an anti-logic, which one almost instinctively resists. "Resistance is the opposite of escape. The poet who wishes to contemplate the good in the midst of confusion is like the mystic who wishes to contemplate God in the midst of evil. There can be no thought of escape. Both the poet and the mystic may establish themselves on herrings and apples. The painter may establish himself on a guitar, a copy of *Figaro* and a dish of melons. These are fortifyings, although irrational ones." [225b] In a sense, then, poetry provides not a timorous escape but a transfer through awareness into a willed liberty. In this novel manner the war intensified the irrational stirrings and provided him with materials for exploring further the adjuncts of the realities which engaged him. Lacking a predetermined end, the tendency remains: to accept the present and abstract it into poetry.

Whatever the "realities" of the Second World War—and a plethora of eyewitnesses have distorted it beyond comprehending—it served Stevens to focus the drifting doubts which disrupted some poems after *Harmonium*. To argue that he entertained such responses may sound unfeeling both because one believes that war cannot engender these results and because of Stevens' reputation for immunity behind his supposed indifference to public events. His general concerns—about the individual's resisting the masses, with patterns despite impermanence, for the modern hero, and in choosing where few designated evils exist—here converge as parts of global skirmishes. Instances of disciplined feeling within a frame which reduces total war to an aspect: these exercises celebrate neither despair nor vengeance. "Dry Loaf" [199–200a], for example, captures once again the sensitive reciprocity between a people and a place in its quiet, "It is equal to living in a tragic land | To live in a tragic time," then sketches a countryside which corresponds with the well-known beginning of *A Farewell to Arms*. In "The Death of a Soldier" the clouds go on their way, and here, amid want and war, the "Birds that came like dirty water in waves" also arrive because they must. It concludes:

> It was soldiers went marching over the rocks
> And still the birds came, came in watery flocks,
> Because it was spring and the birds had to come.
> No doubt the soldiers had to be marching
> And that drums had to be rolling, rolling, rolling.

The same double glance joins two poems called "Contrary Theses." [266–67a, 270a] The soldier in the first stands before a door and blackens the otherwise brilliant autumn. In the second nature continues, and a man with his son and a dog walk "From the bombastic intimations of winter | And the martyrs à la mode," until the man observes "The premiss from which all things were conclusions, | The noble, Alexandrine verve." Reflections upon the necessity of war enter many poems; for instance, "Asides on the Oboe" [250–51a] uses it in resolving its beliefs, although here, as elsewhere, other matters intrude. Extracting the single military image would disfigure both it and its context. However private the last figure," we know | The glass man, without external reference," it evolves from "That obsolete fiction of the wide river in | An empty land; the gods that Boucher killed." The old gods' disappearance has swollen into nearly a leitmotiv by this time; now a true hero, born of many battles, takes their place.

ii

More than a mere part in an aside, the theme of war and its soldiers fills complete poems from the titles themselves, such as "Martial Cadenza" [237–38a], on the surface of a reflectively quiet reverie, while the unhurried pace, nevertheless, produces an unemphatic grandeur. If it shades the gaudy colors in *Harmonium,* it can come to grips directly with its fierce subject, although any absolute knowledge must itself prove provisional. Despite its title an unwarlike poem, it evokes a feeling toward the evening star in a time of conflicts. Because the verse becomes "The vivid thing in the air that never changes, | Though the air change," no paraphrase will satisfy it. Far from evoking a Meredithian army of unalterable law, the star opposes slaughtering battalions with its dilating permanence. A flickering star may outlast a holocaust and Götter-dämmerung. The dichotomies between the world and its cosmos end with accepting actuality: "Not the symbol but that for which the symbol stands," a sentiment like the one which heads the preceding chapter. To transcend journalistic reporting taxes even Stevens' capacities for avoiding the banal; he does, nevertheless, speak more directly about war than on most other subjects. Before the concluding page of prose in *Parts of a World* stands a long work with the forbidding title, "Examination of the Hero in a Time of War." The ambiguities of the title do not explain themselves in the verse: would the hero become a hero without a war; if so, does he live unchanged beyond it; can this study also extend to peace; if so, what relevance does it have? Later, accumulated traits define more neatly the hero, who, if he resolves much, fits a bit uneasily into the rationale at first. Once again, Stevens attributes his subject a dual aspect, and his refusal to name both may avoid oversimplifying but also cloaks the hero ambiguously. In *Harmonium* the immense powers of poetry often had to withstand the test of exaggeration. The soldier, as well, and his war must resist grandiloquence. Often Stevens probes his values by rhetoric, and, if they can keep their pedestals when decked in the highest flattery, then, presumably, he judges them companionable for the hearth.

The chosen form for "Examination of the Hero in a Time of War" [273–81a] exhibits sixteen parts of about equal length in the increasingly favored blank verse, loosely constructed. A wintry European landscape establishes the mood suitable for seeing culture decline. After "the psalter of their sybils," a more puzzling line begins the next

section, "The Got whome we serve is able to de-
liver | Us." The false archaizing, or dialect, occurs al-
most nowhere else in these pages; here it suggests that
clinging to an outmoded belief cannot save. A bit more of
it as a Miltonic echo enters some rejected stanzas, but the
"star-yplaited" [83b] profits little when compared with "a
Star-ypointing" in Milton's sonnet "On Shakespeare." In
contrast with outmoded diction, lines like "good commom
man, what | Of that angelic sword?" sound especially flat,
no matter what satiric animus they bear. The angels with
machine guns fail to colonize the Africa of "Owl's Clover,"
and modern man begs an old grace, forgetful of the pride
which led him to contrive weapons. The hero enters the
warriors' company as a virtuoso, but irony undercuts his
posturing when submarine warfare becomes in yet another
inexplicable—and not wholly beguiling—expression, which
concludes this part, "Chopiniana." In the first edition an
experiment with typography throughout *Parts of a
World* set off certain words by added spaces, a practice
wisely dropped from the *Collected Poems*. Now and then
it helps a reader, but that word dangling by itself stresses a
looseness which no poet can afford to underline. The fifth
section begins with another recourse to the chopped logic
which intrigues Stevens but which he cannot always
express quite satisfactorily: "The common man is the
common hero. | The common hero is the hero." With
this very point, where conjecture hovers at the final turning
in upon itself to dissolve all opposites by a blind affirmation, one of those passages arises which succeeds so mag-
nificently as poetry that it nearly convinces one about its
theories, too. Commonness dissolves, because it must, into
nothing, or mere change, perhaps the cast of the dice
which Mallarmé envisaged in *Un Coup de dés*, the eternal game where repetition reaches no finale except the
prelude to another gaming hazard.

> Soldier, think, in the darkness,
> Repeating your appointed paces
> Between two neatly measured stations,
> Of less neatly measured common-places.

The hero then becomes a statue, comparable with the one in "Owl's Clover," but his being, also, exceeds a public monument. Just as the winged horses made their landscape, which, in turn, altered them, so the hero does not correspond with Carlyle's giants but, rather, draws upon circumstances as much as he shapes them. Stevens' figure lives through war into peace, endures journalists, fulfills a role for the bourgeois epics: one ends with no simple, public hero but a variety of them, all contributing to the ideal. Nor does he impart his qualities to memorabilia; the insistence on a usable past again appears. An effort to parade the hero in all his multiple trappings becomes, in contrast, excessive. The instance of Xenophon shows him as himself only in active principle, not in any stylized icon.

> If the hero is not a person, the emblem
> Of him, even if Xenophon, seems
> To stand taller than a person stands, has
> A wider brow, large and less human
> Eyes and bruted ears: the man-like body
> Of a primitive. He walks with a defter
> And lither stride. His arms are heavy
> And his breast is greatness.

Probably a hero, like Xenophon, of marginal reputation at present was selected for his very ambiguity as commander-author-philosopher. Curiously enough, the conjunction of Xenophon as man rather than abstract statue echoes Spenser's letter to Raleigh outlining his standards for *The Faerie Queene*, a poem to which Stevens alludes several times in his prose without betraying any opinions about it. He would seem, however, to reverse the epic values attributed the two men by the sixteenth-century poet.

To some, I know, this methode will seeme displeasaunt, which had rather have good discipline delivered plainly in way of precepts, or sermoned at large, as they use, then thus clowdily enwrapped in allegoricall devises. But such, me seeme, should be satisfide with the use of these dayes, seeing all things accounted by their showes, and nothing esteemed of, that is not delightfull and pleasing to commune sence. For this cause is Xenophon preferred before Plato, for that the one, in the exquisite depth of his judgement, formed a commune welth such as it should be, but the other in the person of Cyrus and the Persians fashioned a governement, such as might best be: so much more profitable and gratious is doctrine by ensample, then by rule.[4]

However varied his attributes, a hero, who for Stevens shares affinities with the poet, misleads when made to act as a substitute for bread and circuses. At the same time, he does not dwell apart from daily matters. Just as Stevens seems to have glanced at Milton, so he rejects Dante's phenomenon of a single divine will: "Further magnified, sua voluntate. | Beyond his circumstances." If the hero does not swerve into the twentieth-century company of anti-heroes, neither does he belong to a standard epic. Stevens' hero, for all his might, exists in this world, not Platonic clouds, and embodies what might best be. He expresses the aspects by which Yeats designated a saint: "If he possess intellect he will use it but to serve perception and renunciation. His joy is to be nothing, to do nothing, to think nothing; but to permit the total life, expressed in its humanity, to flow in upon him and to express itself through his acts and thoughts."[5] "Instead of allegory, | We have and are the man," as Stevens' hero takes living minds for his residence and emerges again from there and from no place else, an enlargement upon Peter Quince's awareness of beauty. So composite an entity goes beyond heroics, and by the very nature of its being scarcely exists—not an original paradox—although the essence has seldom had such a tantalizing simplicity as "This actor | Is anonymous and cannot help it." Consequently, the hero, being man supremely created by man, draws to himself all aspects and looms as a sun god; the theme of "Sunday Morning" sounds again but with a new and, dependent upon one's prejudices, a somewhat enforced greatness. If the one of fictive music outdid the imagination, the created hero towers above simple reality, but the newer figure, less remote, more understandable, inhabits a part of the world. Both can be truly imagined, therefore both exist, although both vanish, properly, in the mixtures of daily life. The poem ends on autumnal ambiguites: "After the hero, the familiar | Man makes the hero artificial." Crispin, although something of a hero and a saint himself—to adapt Santayana's phrase—lacked the stature for such powers; the hero, never a comedian of Crispin's stamp, represents Stevens' final forging of a superior being.

If he does not endow war with a glamor which automatically elevates the participants by nobility, neither does he shrink from recognizing its battles nor congratulate himself for heeding a Voice of Duty. His concern extends to whatever is, and he risks judgments on events only after examining the images for understanding them. Nothing in his world occurs wholly by itself, and all that one observes with care contributes to awareness. He seeks the child's private, immediate response uncorrupted by the symbolic stereotypes which pass for reality and progresses to an adult scale by trenchantly probing all values. Total war embodies immensity; in how many ways—thirteen or more?—does the vastness impinge upon the world? What armed conflict in the abstract and by its actual soldiers means sets a test for the imagination. The final discovery says that the individual—soldier or poet—must partake of hostilities but that their behavior wins laurels only by transcending what would negate them. An equally hard struggle faces both; acceptance proves defeat, but triumph over a political rival or recalcitrant words may itself corrupt by settling for arbitrary limits. War aims do not bother Stevens; he seldom worries about ends, only means, or, rather, every gesture merits the respect accorded an end. His stability allows him to believe that evil, if nothing can quite redeem it, remains sufficient unto each day. This same burden of reconciliation sounds in the "coda" which ends "Notes toward a Supreme Fiction," the final poem in *Transport to Summer*. Here the poet and soldier both carry out their war. The poet must always continue his struggle; the soldier returns, somewhat dependent upon

the poet, who has relied upon him: "How simply the
fictive hero becomes the real." [408a]

iii

If, however, affinities link *Parts of a World* and
Transport to Summer, the latter book succeeds beyond any
other. With the technical inventiveness which distinguishes *Harmonium* and with the increased scope of the
other three volumes, it merits the calmly vibrant title. For
the first time the order of the printed poems follows the
chronology of composition, save for "Notes toward
a Supreme Fiction," the earliest work, appearing last. This
very reversal demonstrates the mastery which permitted
Stevens to sketch out the areas he expected to explore.
Here, then, all the values, while not precisely repetitious,
have, after being named, an easy commerce among each
other. His genius for recognizing resemblances, the gift
which Aristotle ranked indispensable for the poet, flourishes with a neat assurance while object after object enters
the poems, keeps its own identity, and prepares the way for
another. "There is no such thing as a metaphor of a
metaphor. One does not progress through metaphors. Thus
reality is the indispensable element of each metaphor.
When I say that man is a god it is very easy to see that if
I also say that a god is something else, god has become
reality." [179b] The subjects which he selects maintain
their own rights in the architectonics of every work. The
flexible lines of blank verse can by this time accommodate
everything. Claiming this much does not mean that every
poem fully succeeds or that no problems remain. Perhaps,
too, the very finish contributes its own share of difficulties
for readers: no façade betrays rents; disparate materials
dovetail smoothly.

As an example of the newly acquired assurances,
"Repetitions of a Young Captain" [306–10a] expatriates
upon the war and relates it to older themes and sounds,
both moderately elusive only when considered in a vacuum. With a confident vocabulary and elevated serenity,
the form utilizes the arrangement which Stevens now

handles assuredly: groups of three unrhymed lines, each having ten or eleven syllables with, generally, four stresses. A sort of characterization, although drawn in only a glancing manner, presents the figure of the title, who probes a calamity during a foreign war. From a ruined theater his thoughts shift to the audience, then to an actor and "faintly encrusted, a tissue of the moon | Walked toward him on the stage and they embraced." So much may exemplify the passing of peace, but a dichotomy continues in war between the individual and his world, the actor comparable with the player of the blue guitar. War, thus, does not unite the fragments it creates; opposing armies composed of single men cannot bestow soldierly, or any other desirable, traits on its members. Anyone's effort to gain stature by identifying himself with the group must prove deluded. To a degree the captain's martial experiences have altered him, and he cannot return to an older past, changed as he is and destroyed as it has been. Inured to war, his being must now derive from actualities, and the theater, actor, and moon reappear in a new guise. With them now comes a speaker who surmounts all the fragments, which help compose him. The poem commands a new outlook:

> Discover
> A civil nakedness in which to be,
>
> In which to bear with the exactest force
> The precisions of fate, nothing fobbed off, nor changed
> In a beau language without a drop of blood.

"Repetitions of a Young Captain," while a thoroughly original work, turns from strife to peace and gathers around itself former theories observed in a new way.

Soldiers stalk elsewhere in *Transport to Summer* but usually within the confines of a context to which they contribute without dominating it. They do not become summer soldiers in the common sense of that pejorative phrase, although generally sunshine rules the land to which they pledge their allegiance. Their continuing presence says that one duty need not eclipse all life to darken the world. Likewise, references to the hero and the heroic recur frequently, but organized conflict gradually subsides into daily routines. Just as the peaceful man, Crispin, had to come to terms with his climate, so does the soldier, but the latter can perpetuate a grandeur denied the poet manqué. War offers both a violent order through military precision and a greater disorder in battles with their aftermath; the combatants proceed, "Under the arches, over the arches, in arcs | Of a chaos composed in more than order." [293a] At the heart of the impersonal machine, despite all, an individual may survive. The victory over the alternatives of either decrying controversy or shrugging it off has not come about easily, but ultimately Stevens' confronting war deepens many passages and can impinge upon the most casual lines. In this book the sun rules, but it presides over the variable air, as in "Martial Cadenza" the evening star does. Actualities, such as the young captain whose broken visions partake of the extreme reality, inhabit this atmosphere. Its hero, sun or fictive, exists nowhere and everywhere. The volume unfolds almost a lexicon of Stevens' methods made uniform by less glaringly individual touches. A rapid survey of the categories in *Transport to Summer* under the rubrics devised for *Harmonium* will show how he developed his initial styles through the intervening volumes.

"God Is Good. It Is a Beautiful Night" repeats an evolved Imagistic exercise by presenting the aspects of the moon as it rises. The usual accouterments deck the night: zither, the book, the scholar, thin music, and reddest fragrance; the moon through an observer lends them meaning. To show a lack in the external world "No Possum, No Sop, No Taters" once again draws a dreary winter, complete with its blackbird, as a focus of austerity. In spite of all its assurances, "The Snow Man," a comparable poem, bore traces of a brittleness, like thin ice which held just long enough. Here the same barrenness sweeps across a wider setting and conveys a greater vacancy. The anecdotes, to extend that approximate term, suspend their judgments more aggressively as the world grows more neatly round. The final positions sometimes elude one; perhaps the last syllable of meaning does not lie on the page or perhaps one has failed to examine the poem fully. "Man Carrying Thing" [350–51a], for example, declares at once, "The poem must resist the intelligence | Almost successfully. Illustration." So many critics, particularly those unsympathetic, have taken this gnomic phrase to summarize Stevens' entire output that one wishes, in defiance of his methods, for a fuller proof. His vision depends upon pitting the precise against the general, upon making claims casually. Here the "illustration," with a long parenthesis, enlists the same maddening catalogue toward no total which Gertrude Stein frequently presents, for example in "A Valentine to Sherwood Anderson." The crux depends on the word *poem*, which submits to Procrustean handling in *Transport to Summer*. At first the point of "Man Carrying Thing" could not be more patent: to meet objects head-on misses them, but, once they fully reveal themselves, they have lost their essential power. Trouble begins when one tries to distinguish what a "storm of secondary things" contributes to this poem and how it relates to any context outside it. Likewise, "Pieces" [351–52a] offers bits: "Snow glistens in its instant in the air, | Instant of millefiori bluely magnified," but here title and subject bolster the nuance, "There is a sense in sounds beyond their meaning," to connect parts of what otherwise might not exceed a snow tempest in a paperweight.

A controlled satiric tone, after the frequently strident or petulant distress of preceding volumes, can confront the ridiculous without fearing it. "The Creations of Sound" [310–11a] speaks with a direct disdain and includes a brilliant rebuff:

> *Tell X that speech is not dirty silence*
> *Clarified. It is silence made still dirtier.*
> *It is more than an imitation for the ear.*
>
> *He lacks this venerable complication.*
> *His poems are not of the second part of life.*

Although no single poem wholly sums up Stevens' mature craft, this one serves well as a map of what he shuns in continuing:

> They do not make the visible a little hard
>
> To see nor, reverberating, eke out the mind
> On peculiar horns, themselves eked out
> By spontaneous particulars of sound.

The scorn for those lacking imagination, likewise, looks more steadily at its sources, the negative aspect of the positive content which distinguishes this volume. Often, however, the strident tone softens to encompass values along with their parodies. "So-and-So Reclining on Her Couch" [295–96a] crowns a vapid model, "This mechanism, this apparition," with a fantastic Gothic coronet. Relating the two produces an overly ornate arrangement, and the poet gives up in playful despair with, "Good-bye, | Mrs. Pappadopoulos, and thanks." At times, on the other hand, contempt for those who counterfeit emotions and scorn for those who yield to spleen no longer mocks so curtly. "Jouga" [337a], a title presumably hit upon for an onomatopoetic effect, depicts another man with a different guitar. "Ha-eé-me, who sits | And plays his guitar. Ha-eé-me is a beast." Although the diction always fits the lengths of the periods, another departure in *Transport to Summer* is the short, declarative sentence whose assertions tell less of the blunt fact than they laconically imply. Ha-eé-me also sings his world, a crude, misshapen one, a fault in part his. In "Jouga" the man who must limit himself to his own malice repeats that most suspect figure, the one who compulsively projects himself into the physical objects around him. "Crude Foyer" [305a] gets to the same point as "Jouga," but it takes an opposite tack. It consists of one long period, through twenty lines, whose repetitions halt as though testing their own overconfidence: "Thought is false happiness," it begins, although properly instructed, thought must turn back on itself. *Transport to Summer* presents, then, the defeat of varied threats and celebrates victories, but the struggle with some topics does not lessen.

iv

Problems about reality and how it functions for poetry involve many forays which lead somewhere beyond logic. *Transport to Summer* abounds in longer poems, all attaining a high order of complexity. Probably "Esthétique du Mal" will ultimately emerge as Stevens' finest single achievement; its main subject traces out strands less emphasized elsewhere, but in itself it exhibits both completeness and unity. Because it offers so many facets, an analysis fits more suitably in the last chapter. "Notes toward a Supreme Fiction," if a degree less satisfying as an independent work, comes closest to an exhaustive catalogue of the major themes on poetry. A finicky attention to all parallels never distinguishes these musings which dismiss the severely symmetrical as a dangerous idol: a violent order remains disorder. While never slipshod, they threaten constantly to break apart into a series of short images. At their best the whole coheres firmly, and the informality contributes its own charm in the process. What the poems say by its very nature cannot bear superimposed forms, but the act of improvising meets deliberate dangers. The results alone vindicate the daring. All poetry other than brief lyrics or Imagistic pieces may find itself confronting the choice between sacrificing fine touches for the sake of structure and risking dull passages to finish a pattern. *Le Cimetière marin* stays close to the congeries of musical lines from which it took its origin, in spite of the ingenuity spent on reconstructing it by others and Valéry himself. Presumably some of W. H. Auden's undergraduate verse owes its obscurity to his rejecting phrases, without replacements, of which friends disapproved. Brood upon a Weltanschauung as he might, W. B. Yeats ultimately transcends the rubrics propounded in *A Vision*. Not afraid of occasional looseness, "Notes toward a Supreme Fiction" flaunts epithets, insights, metaphors, and images garnered from the whole catalogue of past effects. Every section offers at least one delight of sound, insight, color, or phrase. More than "Like Decorations in a Nigger Cemetery," it weaves singleness from multiplicity. Whether without the titles and examples from other works one would light upon the ensuing generalizations as the most significant remains problematic.

The closest link with Stevens' other poetry brings back, over twenty years later, the first remark to "A High-Toned Old Christian Woman" [59a], "Poetry is the supreme fiction, madame," made now in another accent. These further enlargements explore it under three headings: "It Must Be Abstract," "It Must Change," "It Must Give Pleasure." Although the phrase supreme fiction remains the same, the concepts it extends to include much more. After its lines of dedication the discourse unfolds with a nobly assured authority, as though no jibbing at premises and examples could ruffle it. The ghost of abstraction has haunted Stevens and his critics a bit too persistently. No poet has set before himself more steadily the outside world, both what strikes the eye immediately and resemblances later promulgated from the data. On the other hand, the problem of holding together such objects, going back to their initial selection and forward for their final arrangement, has rarely troubled anyone so repeatedly. Contradictorily, abstraction requires getting the essential qualities of an object and, simultaneously with grasping the very thing itself, its own "secondary" qualities in all their jumbled aspects. "It Must Be Abstract" [380–89a] recommends in lines which should strike a less bizarre note here than they did at the outset of this book:

> Begin, ephebe, by perceiving the idea
> Of this invention, this invented world,
> The inconceivable idea of the sun.
>
> You must become an ignorant man again
> And see the sun again with an ignorant eye
> And see it clearly in the idea of it.
>
> Never suppose an inventing mind as source
> Of this idea nor for that mind compose
> A voluminous master folded in his fire.

How clear the sun when seen in its idea,
Washed in the remotest cleanliness of a heaven
That has expelled us and our images . . .

The death of one god is the death of all.

From this it appears that an "idea" or "idealization"
corresponds with the dramatis personae in a neo-classical
play; they surely do not lack traits but need generalized
features. To define the sunniness of the sun proposes a
nudity which, after centuries of poetry, may appear either
superfluous or naive. One may chant Yvor Winters' one-
line poem "Noon," "Did you move, in the sun?" [6] as a
scarab, but sun is a sun is a sun ad infinitum does not
amount to identical knowledge. In the process of sloughing
off associations, inevitably, one uncovers new ties between
the sun and everything else.

The concept again takes up where "Sunday Morning"
stopped with the sun as a force cut off from false poetizing.
The verse here further seeks by the denial of an overly
human god to arrive at what the sun must "be | In the
difficulty of what it is to be." The task defies any definite
end, but an alarmingly understated line reveals the invention for study: "It is the celestial ennui of apartments
| That sends us back to the first idea," the source of
comfortable symbols and myths which dispel any chances
for a true understanding. Poetry alone can revive the first
idea (of elephant? or tortoise? of what?) from its stained
condition. "Life's nonsense pierces us with strange relation"; some primitive energy, akin to the unidentified solar
source, sends one's mind into all kinds of "reality," little
better than formlessness. In trying to arrive at any conclusion, save the sudden insight, one indulges in the search
for a false unity, inevitable though the pursuit may be.
"The first idea was not our own. Adam | In Eden was the
father of Descartes"—so many others would have written
Darwin. Nevertheless, "There was a myth before the myth
began"; in spite of his ridiculing first causes, Stevens, along
with Descartes, must draw up short before them and
concede the primacy of the cogito. Because, then, life

exists neither at a matrix nor in its ultimate emanations, man briefly becomes Crispin, a comedian trying to express an individuality through language drawn from an indifferent universe and hoping to grow a new-world beauty from the old-world turnip. Yet, comedian and hero merge when the fifth section praises man with a delightfully modest compliment. The anti-Cartesian lion, elephant, and bear, like men of earlier poems who compulsively projected themselves into all their surroundings, make their environment themselves: man, as poet, has only art from which to fashion his world, for, otherwise, he may quaintly "lash the lion, | Caparison elephants, teach bears to juggle." Having proposed an abstraction, then gone to man's general nature, the poem turns to the daily weather and what it unites. If a giant arises, it must seem "An abstraction blooded."

Yet, with the deposing of distant gods, the near-at-hand tinkles in mere gemütlichkeit; "It feels good as it is without the giant, | A thinker of the first idea." The fortuitous event, the unexpected revelation which Stevens prizes, the sort which often resolves the poems, accounts for meaning, one capable of analogies but not proof. Having posited a general abstraction rather than a principle, having found that this quality inhabits the specific, the concept now destroys the habitual actualities, reassure though they may.

> Can we compose a castle-fortress-home,
> Even with the help of Viollet le-Duc,
> And set the MacCullough there as major man?

The question sounds prejudicial; who can restore an inevitable ruin?—demonstrably not Viollet-le-Duc, villain of nineteenth-century restoration in France. The major man MacCullough, a figure unlike the army captain, stalks onto the scene. Stevens again depicts two kinds of heroes, as he said in his note on "The Man with the Blue Guitar": the true, timeless, anonymous, abstract, and imagined one, and the false, historical, public, perhaps literally concrete icon, here MacCullough. In this welter man remains wavering between the difficult and facile concepts; nothing comes ready-made but must be pieced together imaginatively. One seeks the ideal, but not idealized, possibility, related to the scarecrow, yet worthy of a poet.

> *The man*
> *In that old coat, those sagging pantaloons,*
>
> *It is of him, ephebe, to make, to confect*
> *The final elegance, not to console*
> *Nor sanctify, but plainly to propound.*

By necessity poetry addresses not this man nor depicts that concept but fuses the subject it shows and the subject it speaks to: between them it must seek the abstract.

This grandeur, in simplicity, partakes of the heroic as Stevens now conceives it, but its nature stays as humble as blackbirds, if one views them steadily and variously. Even statues, unless they resemble the impossible one of General Jackson, shift their qualities, as do the horses in "Owl's Clover." Otherwise, they fade as nearly an autumnal souvenir, a bit of private sentimentality. Steven's harping upon the necessity for change has permeated many poems, and it here becomes a token of survival: death alone houses absolute invariability. As a theory, the second part, "It Must Change" [389–98a], fits more gracefully the suppleness of poetry than does the permanence of bronze, which has often accompanied it before. Also, the many tests to which Stevens has subjected flux contribute to the ease. After a scene with flowers, birds, girls, and bees, the conclusion follows that these instances "Are inconstant objects of inconstant cause | In a universe of inconstancy." Alterability does not imply irrevocable change because the rhythm which brought it forth endures. "The seraph | Is satyr in Saturn, according to his thoughts." The first section treated transcendency of the minute; a less distant area continues the example with the fantastic:

> *The President ordains the bee to be*
> *Immortal. The President ordains. But does*
> *The body lift its heavy wing, take up*

> *Again, an inexhaustible being, rise*
> *Over the loftiest antagonist*
> *To drive the green phrases of its juvenal?*

Change comes without proclamations, and to issue a ukase for immortality exceeds man's power, as when General Du Puy, the equestrian figure more pompous than MacCullough, rides his horse through a setting appropriate only for geraniums; the mounted rulers, General Du Puy and the Monsieur of "Dance of the Macabre Mice," must fall. If, then, the abstract draws nourishment from outside time, change must exercise in space. Endless dependence influences everything in the world, and life proliferates a series of yin-yangs of linked associations; "Two things of opposite nature seem to depend | On one another." If, however, man's decrees cannot induce change or permanence, the principles of alternation must obey their own dictates. Man can only observe, accept, add to, and leave his general inheritance. A passage which complements the presidential proclamation has nature vainly exhorting man, an enlargement of "Bantams in Pine-Woods":

> *Bethou me, said sparrow, to the crackled blade,*
> *And you, and you, bethou me as you blow,*
> *While in my coppice you behold me be.*

Just as abstraction, for a while in the first part, yields to quotidian enchantments, so change, for an ironic moment, soars beyond time: "We encounter in the dead middle of the night | The purple odor, the abundant bloom," but love, likewise, must perish. The bizarre encounter between Nanzia Nunzio and Ozymandias reinforces the search for a supernatural endurance when all that motivates it must depend upon impermanence. Ozymandias as a statue lies in ruins as does General Du Puy; the woman, dedicated to passion, as her name implies, seeks an absolute, impossibly "standing before an inflexible | Order, saying I am the contemplated spouse." Nanzia Nunzio, "stripped more nakedly | Than nakedness," unlike the Susanna on whom Peter Quince broods, has faded. (It seems, at the moment, profitless to speculate about the echoes from Shel-

ley—"Bethou me" and Ozymandias—beyond their obvious
satire on an extreme romanticism which would enshrine
poetry beyond the limits of sight and human knowledge.)
Just as the abstract moved between poles without residing
there, so "The poem goes from the poet's gibberish to
| The gibberish of the vulgate and back again." Only
through transit can it reside anywhere in its fullness. One
might feel that "It Must Change" could well end here,
that a gesture for false unity to correspond with the other
two parts dictated the tenth section. It illustrates freshly
how, within a constant pattern, all that the poet observes
or has observed reinforces his sway over an order a bit beyond the total of experience: "Of these beginnings, gay
and green, propose | The suitable amours. Time will write
them down."

The third section, "It Must Give Pleasure" [398-407a]
poses more difficult questions: abstractness and change
depend upon a somewhat objective measure, as the examples adequately showed. Pleasure must stem from subjective reactions, and, consequently, the language tends toward greater density. Although beginning with rumbles of
exulting, such "jubilas" cannot define it. The next part
reiterates joy in the transitory as enough, for it gives all
that one may expect, and takes the guise of a random
catalogue, similar to the one envisaged by the pondering
woman of "Sunday Morning." Pleasure assumes a nearly
existential sense of being a totality in itself, quite apart
from what precedes or follows it. As an actuality, not the
posturing of an Ozymandias and Nanzia Nunzio, the
"mystic marriage" of a great captain and Bawda should
incorporate the thesis; in verse the nuptials bounce along so
merrily that the poem almost breaks apart. "The great
captain loved the ever-hill Catawba | And therefore mar-
ried Bawda, whom he found there." Their romance does
not spring from a sudden rapture between people but out
of a liking for general harmony. At another extreme, as the
setting changes, "We drank Meursault, ate lobster Bombay
with mango | Chutney. Then the Canon Aspirin de-
claimed." His discourse, presented with some irony at his

condescending tone, describes his widowed sister and her two small daughters, her contentment in their way of life, simple as it is. This pleasure, suitable for earth, at night dissolves into a dream which surpasses without negating day. "He imposes orders as he thinks of them, | As the fox and snake do. It is a brave affair." One must differentiate between the exclusiveness which imposes an order and the nonchalance which uncovers affinities already existing. Consequently, the essential moment, in spite of all one's exploration, at last simply presents itself. In such is pleasure: "Whistle aloud, too weedy wren. I can | Do all that angels can" again harks back to "Bantams in Pine-Woods" but with a fuller detachment. The theme of several other poems, especially "Sailing after Lunch," centers in circulating "Until merely going round is a final good, | The way wine comes at a table in a wood." Pleasure, then, takes its being from the rediscovery of casual moments never quite identical. The poem works out to its conclusions:

> That's it: the more than rational distortion,
> The fiction that results from feeling. Yes, that.
>
> They will get it straight one day at the Sorbonne.
> We shall return at twilight from the lecture
> Pleased that the irrational is rational.

These notes toward a supreme fiction provide neither program nor blueprint; rather, they indicate the needed proportions and harmonies. Nevertheless, they fully express the theory toward which nearly all these poems have so far pointed and to which later ones look back. The exercise itself obeys laws of the strictest poetic. The practice is hardly new: Horace, Pope, Goethe, and Baudelaire have incorporated philosophic aspirations differently with their verse, and philosophers have ventured into what looks like poetry: Lucretius and Nietzsche, although Stevens did not fully approve of their efforts. In the earlier literature the discourses departed from and returned toward externals. Here, the work embodies its own belief so that the poem, as poetry, becomes both subject and object. The work illustrates itself. Regretting the fragmentary nature of his notes on poetry and, particularly, the essays, Stevens said in presenting the collected prose pieces, "The theory of poetry, as a subject of study, was something with respect to which I had nothing but the most ardent ambitions. It seemed to me to be one of the great subjects of study. I do not mean one more *Ars Poetica* having to do, say, with the techniques of poetry and perhaps with its history. I mean poetry itself, the naked poem, the imaginative manifesting itself in its domination of words. The few pages that follow are, now, alas! the only realization possible to me of those excited ambitions." [vii–viii c] Taking all his books together gives one an outline for this unwritten tome more effectively than any single tract could do. For him the essence of poetry derives from inherent aspects and so defies a glossary or jargon. Intriguing as his own ventures into philosophy may appear, they do not come to grips with metaphysical problems.

v

The very impossibility of finishing one work to encompass his entire poetic forces the titles before "Notes toward a Supreme Fiction" in *Transport to Summer* both to predict and fulfill it. "Chocorua to Its Neighbor" [296–302a], as so many of his poems will, suggests a passage in an earlier one. A segment of "The Man with the Blue Guitar," one of the more loosely inserted, depicts the singular New Hampshire mountain [176a]:

> *A substitute for all the gods:*
> *This self, not that gold self aloft,*
>
> *Alone, one's shadow magnified,*
> *Lord of the body, looking down,*
>
> *As now and called most high,*
> *The shadow of Chocorua*
>
> *In an immenser heaven, aloft,*
> *Alone, lord of the land and lord*
>
> *Of the men that live in the land, high lord.*
> *One's self and the mountains of one's land,*

> *Without shadows, without magnificence,*
> *The flesh, the bone, the dirt, and stone.*

Stevens glossed "the dirt" as "It means the physical earth: the very ground. The anthropomorphic can only yield in the end to anthropos: God must in the end, in the life of the mind, yield to men." [180d] Chocorua becomes similar to a poetic source, in the title of a later one, "The Poem That Took the Place of a Mountain." "Chocorua to Its Neighbor" itself names the ideal at once: "To perceive men without reference to their form," as the poet addresses the mountain. The chaos of war, with overtones from "Metaphors of a Magnifico," follows: "A swarming of number over number, not | One foot approaching, one up-lifted arm." The abiding takes again the shape of a star which endures in air, as in "Martial Cadenza."

So much prepares the way for an anonymous hero, the true figure, whom the next several lines describe. This elusive creature, almost identical with the one in "Repetitions of a Young Captain," imparts to the mountain vitality, and his monologue expands upon man's role:

> *The moments of enlargement overlook*
> *The enlarging of the simplest soldier's cry*
> *In what I am, as he falls. Of what I am,*

XI

> *The cry is part. My solitaria*
> *Are the meditations of a central mind.*
> *I hear the motions of the spirit and the sound*
> *Of what is secret becomes, for me, a voice*
> *That is my own voice speaking in my ear.*

XII

> *There lies the misery, the coldest coil*
> *That grips the centre, the actual bite, that life*
> *Itself is like a poverty in the space of life,*
> *So that the flapping of wind around me here*
> *Is something in tatters that I cannot hold.*

As near a mystic vision as Stevens ventured, this commentary between nature and a central being may suggest affinities with Blake. The speaker, almost Chocorua's alter ego, resembles an anthropomorphic being summoned up by mankind. The surprising effect here derives from Stevens' independence of all systems. While "Chocorua to Its Neighbor" alludes to "The Man with the Blue Guitar," the war poems, and others, it, likewise, incorporates its own valid references, exotic as they sound. As Dr. Johnson knew, one may always find the marvelous by forsaking the probable, but few poets have managed to keep wonder and likelihood steadily within a single, coherent view. This collective imago, then, belongs to all men, and the catalogue of personae, already quoted out of context in section viii, Chapter 1, where it may have sounded decidedly quaint, both contains and extends its subject. Man cannot inhabit the tops of mountains, and the nineteenth stanza reiterates the theory of limits which Stevens likes to propound.

> To say more than human things with human voice,
> That cannot be; to say human things with more
> Than human voice, that, also, cannot be;
> To speak humanly from the height or from the depth
> Of human things, that is acutest speech.

The remarkable figure instills in the mountain itself an awe with his simplicity. Although no one can identify his nature, he distills a living immanence which may vanish but which, when felt, dwarfs, even as a mountain dwarfs man, that mountain. The theme, the ultimate realization of a view which the earlier poems predicted but which their restricted measures could not contain, flows forth with quickening clarity. The figure itself speaks outright in the assured "Angel Surrounded by Paysans" [496–97a], in which the elusive spirit, as subtle as one of an annunciation, arrives to inform the countrymen of its purpose, then depart: "the necessary angel of earth," who appears in the title of the collected essays. If contemplating the war gave Stevens the discipline to confront all aspects of worldly change, translated into his own idiom, the hero has, by this poem, left off being a mere soldier and grown into the most human abstraction. By rejecting both inherited myths and trumped-up symbols, then by working with general qualities based on his own views, he created a world at once consistent with *Harmonium* and more spacious. For this very reason, he does not need to traffic with the portentous mouthings which appeal to self-conscious artists and many critics. Consequently, one dare not overpraise the hero. Certainly "The Comedian as the Letter C," if having little to do with fictional or dramatic comedy, makes Crispin, as a clown, express the pathos associated with that figure because the world does not share his pleasure in poetry. Comparably, compassion for Stevens' hero falls as wide of the mark as does laughing at Crispin. Having discarded the comedian and having substituted the hero, he affirms that man always confronts limits, which he may cautiously but not infinitely exceed. The hero is never an American *superman* in any sense of that tired, overworked term, although concepts in *Also Sprach Zarathustra* may have lodged in Stevens' mind.

The fictive hero, descended from the anonymous warrior, more persuasive than the one of fictive music, not a publicized personage, and unlike a god, roams beyond man, although as a greater than ghostly part of him. In *Transport to Summer* stronger ties link each living individual with his landscape, here often one of warmth. Because Stevens cares poetically only by fits and starts about people as such but always with intensity for the eye and what it sees, the long "Description without Place" [339–46a] manages to range widely over nuances and to bring off that favorite trick of getting at an abstraction without naming it. "It is possible that to seem—it is to be, | As the sun is something seeming and it is." These two concepts, which keep flowing into one another, suggest not just whether to judge by primary or secondary characteristics but whether to separate two categories by their functions at all. Unlike a logician, he delights in a continual hopping, without inductive leaps, between things and what may tentatively be termed things-by-themselves. The universal poetic faculty resembles a central diamond

which emits its own rays. Seen from a distance great
enough, the separate beams will not equal the stone, but
the gem enchants the eye and exists for it only in terms of
the refracted light; the shifting interstices bestow significance on the turning gem. Only a momentary despair
dictates the view, "Life is a bitter aspic. We are not | At
the centre of a diamond." [322a] Generally he agrees with
Valéry's comparable pensée: *"Diamant.*—Sa beauté
résulte, me dit-on, de la petitesse de l'angle de réflexion
totale . . . [sic] Le tailleur de diamant en façonne les
facettes de manière que le rayon qui pénètre dans la
gemme par l'une d'elles ne peut en sortir que par la
même—D'où le feu et l'éclat. Belle image de ce que je
pense sur la poésie: retour du rayon spirituel aux mots
d'entrée." [7] The sun becomes "What it seems | It is and in
such seeming all things are." The lines embrace all primary
phenomena, man or summer. (For a further understanding
of "Description without Place" and for an instance of how
the later poems constantly enlarge upon themselves, one
might consider two poems rather elusive in isolation,
"Ghosts as Cocoons" and "The Candle a Saint," against
the second section of this one. Although they do not
"explain" each other, they indicate how Stevens observes
and expresses.) A similar harmony binds together an age
or the abilities of those who observe it, the poet, musician,
painter, and "ordinary man." This rehearsal of the familiar
leads up to a question which Stevens generally prefers to
brush past: if any man's world equals another's, what
determines one preferable? Justifying the ways of A to B
clamps an icy hand over the most flourishing verse, and
one frequently wishes poets pushed less hotly after improbable certitudes. Multiple as his references to philosophic
creeds may be, rarely does he set out to demonstrate their
validity. Starting in the fourth section of "Description
without Place," he undertakes what comes as close to
arguing as he ventures.

A contrast between Nietzsche and Lenin pushes his
assumptions further into the open than usual. The actual
Lenin counts for little, although Nietzsche as a personality

and thinker seems to have impressed Stevens uneasily. The Russian and German offer their distinctive aspects: Nietzsche in creating the übermensch sought a single principle of the vertical; Lenin would have reduced all to identical flatness. Nietzsche loses himself too personally in a logical Swiss pool and becomes, with one of those acts untranslatable into any language, including English, "The sun of Nietzsche gildering the pool," the man who boastfully imposes himself as a single reflector. Lenin cannot appreciate the pool at all and contemplates it: "reaches, beaches, tomorrow's regions became | One thinking of apocalyptic legions." Looking too deeply or too broadly with a single eye will likewise deceive. "Description is revelation. It is not | The thing described, nor false facsimile," as words compose a subject which is itself and not a symbol. Far from being an exercise, the poem convinces that knowledge of past and future must interact each moment as a description without place. The goal seeks poetry as pure as possible. To avoid inflexibility one must practice at all times this multiple vision without an arid singularity of purpose, neither Nietzsche's nor Lenin's. Stevens cannot exhort and limits himself to the demonstrations. He strives to overcome the pitfalls in a secular learned ignorance and sees not as a primitive but simply as an intelligence freed from personal anxiety about past or future, the present washed of impurities, brought continually up to date. In the constant interchange among these aspects poetry serves as mediator; the future, like a gem, must "Be alive with its own seemings, seeming to be | Like rubies reddened by rubies reddening." That line, decidedly idiosyncratic out of context in section iv, Chapter 1, concludes the poem inevitably as it gathers together the concepts of jewels, past-future, Lenin-Nietzsche, and the wish to come as close as possible to the pure and abstract.

The images have now taken on a new significance, although still resembling those in "Metaphors of a Magnifico." The many becoming the one and the one which assumes a different guise for the many: these concepts have expanded until they subsume nearly all Stevens' preoccupations. The patterns exfoliate through so many permutations that they almost tolerate the massive burdens put upon them. Nowhere does a symbolic counter parasitically cover up the concrete; the actualities—as species rather than isolated instances—count for most. Similarly, the parallels with areas on a canvas continue in effect. When he concentrates on bits of broken surfaces, nearly like a pointillist, as some lines already quoted have shown and as many others needing no separate discussion reinforce, their interdependence with a context draws them back from a striking foreground. His interest in glittering jewels and their shifting luster does not amount to a fascination with kaleidoscopic colors and oddly shaped bits. Presenting phantasmagorial surfaces accompanies an effort to push ever further toward a freely depicted order. The quest always concedes the impossibility of an ultimate conquest, and thus never disappears into the uncharted regions of myth. For this dual purpose summer is the most congenial season. As a reality it unites external and internal; unlike winter, which excludes man, or spring, which fosters introspection, or autumn which often predicts a rude austerity. The positive colorings of summer derive from the sun, which exemplifies abstraction. Dazzling as Stevens' vistas may look, they soon become actual, comparable with the effect of stepping from a darkened room into a July afternoon. Nevertheless, nothing stands by itself, and the year must have a second solstice, June and its nights however short notwithstanding. Poetry, too, must change.

Particularly in the poem "Credences of Summer" [372–78a] the rays congregate and offer almost a summary of the volume. The first part establishes by language the positive stillness of the harvest air; nothing happens. Time, like the ocean in "Sea Surface Full of Clouds," momentarily ceases so that one can attempt to arrive at the essence of the season. A comparable serenity, perhaps the single one, occurs in *Ondine* when Giraudoux describes a day on which all spirits quit Earth briefly. The next portion fixes on the sun itself for another remarkable study like little else in experience or poetry, not like staring at the July sun but rather the sensation of having gazed into the sun steadily, were such endurance poetically possible. It becomes "This is the barrenness | Of the fertile thing that can attain no more." From here, much like the jar in Tennessee, the world is gathered up, but the vocabulary again mocks what supposedly it shows, "A point of survey squatting like a throne." The very air transfigures Oley, its fields and hay, as "Pure rhetoric of a language without words," a concept allied with musica ficta. After the survey of this lushness, the question inevitably arises whether this day extends to make the rest richer or whether the others have not contributed this one, a metaphoric ambiguity comparable with the major man's role and with other movements from centrality to multiplicity: all summer in a day or a day stretching over a season? In general Stevens seldom quarrels with this world as it is, and he here asserts—and one assents—"we accept what is | As good. The utmost must be good and is." In turning for an illustration once again to the soldier, he proves his deeper assurance by the bookish adjective compounded with the out-of-doors: another threatening force has been met and assimilated:

> The bristling soldier, weather-foxed, who looms
> In the sunshine is a filial form and one
> Of the land's children, easily born, its flesh,
> Not fustian.

Summer retains its grandeur not in sovereign isolation but as an apogee defining its own height. In the sixth section the concept of the rock appears, not for the first time but somewhat more fully defined. It represents Stevens' ultimate assertion about imagination and reality. For "Credences of Summer," of course, one can understand its significance without alluding to its permutations. In the final suite of poems its importance increases. Here, through being completely itself, brilliance would solidify into changeless statuary; the rock subsumes other quantities which can shift. The final qualification humbly depicts a

cock perched in a garden deserted from the previous season; emptiness does not negate present brightness. By such
half-stages the poem refers back to the vastness of summer,
whose chief condition rests on the human knowledge of its
being transitory and forging strength for a qualified sur-
vival and whole renewal.

vi

Granted that Stevens would never prescribe a
single remedy to dissolve all the maladies which he diagno-
ses, one force which stabilizes many segments in the late
poems springs from a native soil. In *Harmonium* the group
"Primordia," particularly, regarded indigenous cultural elements at times with a disdain for their indigence. He never
refused to acknowledge these, and touches almost colloquial recur throughout, but later not just for satiric whimsey. Beginning in *Transport to Summer,* an unforced acceptance of his native landscapes, Pennsylvania, where he
grew up, and Connecticut, where he lived, brings his world
partly round without piecing and patching. "Dutch Graves
in Bucks County" [290–93a] has the naturalness of the
syllables which its title joins together. It stems from the
war poems and contrasts the furious activity of battles
against dead ancestors, "my semblables," who in their
diminished way throb with a vitality still forceful. Through
juxtaposing contemporary warriors and conjectures about
a dead, unknowable past, the contrary theses build up the
consciousness that the poet bears the burden of two realities, equally great. An instance, again, of how little Stevens'
obvious borrowings matter: the repeated tag "my semblables" must echo Baudelaire's salutation to his readers in
Les Fleurs du mal. One need not recall the French poem
for, beyond its literal meaning, it bears not even a remote
kinship with the French. The progress of the contrasting
couplets, set between six-line stanzas, does not move toward any climax; rather, it presents a series of contradictory
views, which gain importance by establishing the observer
and his progenitors from Holland, the country Stevens
claimed in preference to Germany, in their piece of "real-

ity." The poet identifies himself restlessly with the past. Addressing the dead in French, a device similar to that in "Sea Surface Full of Clouds," for another sort of self-discovery, indicates through comparisons with that poem how far he has advanced toward directness, range, structure, and complexity.

This return to his youth in age further underlines the mounting concern about the past but always in terms of what he has already pronounced. In "Adagia" he asks the question: "Which is correct: whether, if I respect my ancestors I am bound to respect myself, or, if I respect myself I am bound to respect my ancestors?" [167b] Exploring such pieties does not divorce itself from the moment; it never repeats an embalmed etiquette. "The work of Picasso is an attempt to get at his subject, an attempt to achieve a reality of the intelligence. But the world of the past was equally the result of such activity. Thus the German pietists of the early 1700's who came to Pennsylvania to live in the caves of the Wissahickon and to dwell in solitude and meditation were proceeding in their way, from the chromatic to the clear." [258–59b] The indicative phrase, "from the chromatic to the clear," sums up Stevens' own maturing, if one remembers that the clearest light includes a diamond's spectrum; or, if one takes *chromatic* as a musical sign—to extend the pun—it can stand for the swelling range of musica ficta. By this route he comes to grips with time, like matter both friend and enemy. If it destroys through change, it can aid—not through mere repetitions, worthless as junk on a pedestal in a public garden—with the assurance that human striving rejuvenates a pattern of partial renewals. By such a formula one draws closer to those vexing concepts, some already quoted, others set forth in titles: "Description without Place," "The Good Man Has No Shape," "Men Made out of Words," "The Search for Sound Free from Motion." To say this much does not mean that by reference to the past one arrives at future triumphs nor that because something has happened before it fixes its characteristics for all time. A dispensation so irrevocable belongs only to the world of the dead. In a way awareness of the past imposes heavier burdens, although it may lighten some of them.

These late poems explore fewer areas, but they map their confines with greater detail. Often, one feels, Stevens took one of his insubstantial concepts and deliberately tracked it to an arcane, although not an ultimate, source, which always lies a bit beyond human knowledge. One example of such an exercise has the forthright title, "Two Versions of the Same Poem." In the first a man ponders the spirit which disturbs the water; one has, of course, encountered such speculations before, and by themselves they contribute little more than a romantic poem. The opposite view brings them in line for another pattern. In the second a spirit, John Zeller, presumably one of Stevens' ancestors, stands bodiless and contemplates the agitated sea as bare movement. The two versions exemplify the same extremes, the brilliant surface and a central being, with the irony that neither presents the last word. Undoubtedly getting at such an image through an ancestor helped Stevens qualify his outlook. He returns to this figure again in "The Bed of Old John Zeller," and, in a way, this one reconciles the two hostile forces in the preceding work. Here the poet reconstructs the turbulent thoughts of a ghost and almost wishes to escape them with the accompanying realization that he cannot. As in the prose passages, the man now alive belongs to the same cycles as his forebears. Such providential creatures do not represent banshees lurking in the night to mock Chocorua or shadows cast across a summer day. He eventually accepts all versions of this world. His Pennsylvania countryside partakes of rightness which few poets in the United States have ever managed. Others, emulating expatriates, deny their birthplaces, or, copying James Joyce, make eternal cities from hometowns, or mourn the loss of the place they rejected and cannot go back to, or truculently celebrate its vulgarities. Stevens graciously makes it yet another part of his poetic universe along with museums and scovy ducks, Oxidia and Olympia: all with potentialities for harmony or ugliness. This return to his home, after emigrating through the imagined cosmos, adds yet another badge of uniqueness for this century.

Less austere than New England generally looks to him, less flamboyant than Florida, southeastern Pennsylvania encourages quietness. "For example, two traditional colors of the Pennsylvania Dutch—blue and black—are very significant in the color symbolism of Stevens' poetry. [As a local couplet puts it: "Black and blue, | Dutch all through."] In a letter to Professor Dick, Stevens commented on this similarity. 'There may be something to your idea that my colors are the colors of my origins. This is not so if what you are really thinking of are the so-called gaudy Dutch colors, for after all, the gaudy Dutch colors were not the true Pennsylvania Dutch colors.'"[8] "From a Schuylkill in mid-earth there came emerging | Flotillas, willed and wanted" to bear the surprises of "A Completely New Set of Objects" [352–53a], whose hidden identity implies a gift surpassing the moment and the physical with its sudden vibrance. An equally persuasive wonder and peace pervade "Thinking of a Relation Between the Images of Metaphors" [356–57a] by showing that "The wood-doves are singing along the Perkiomen. | The bass lie deep, still afraid of Indians." The idyll expands to become worthy of Izaak Walton in an age when the fisherman through his contemplative songs gathers together an entire scene. Youth promises no inevitable escape; the world can remain bleak, as the title "Debris of Life and Mind" [338a] says, "There is so little that is close and warm. | It is as if we were never children." With the later poems this attitude toward the past achieves a deepening mellowness. Although generally the speaker lacks a specified age, in poems where there is one, he now becomes an old man. Wit in regarding children, never conspicuous among his dramatis personae except as a sort of eighteenth-century mannequin, now heightens the familiarity: "In the weed of summer comes this green sprout why. . . . | It is the extreme, the expert, aetat. 2." [462a] Conversely, old men stir a bemused pity, and the aging poet quietly mocks youthful exuberance. "The Old Lutheran Bells at Home"

[461–62a] opens with the solemnity of early church fathers, but its tones change. "Each sexton has his sect. The bells have none." The past generations follow into the edifice, but no dogma rises triumphant from it. "Each truth is a sect though no bells ring for it." The poem ends on a jangle of bells as the ringers fly through the air with them. Backed by such assurances of his past in both his own life and his ancestors', the final undertakings lead neither to a frozen winter nor an embarrassing Indian summer but to autumn and its auroras, still brilliant, still insubstantial, still of a mysterious origin, still hovering above earth.

Of all the titles heralding the familiar, the most suitable examines "An Ordinary Evening in New Haven" [465–89a], a long poem which needs to be only touched on here. Anyone not conversant with his later books might suppose it ironic, or, even if a pun, that no new haven ever proffered such exotic flittings in the twilight. Having traced Stevens, one spots old acquaintances, some pristine, others matured. The ordinary evening presents him the recherché through poetry, and a grasp upon coalescing reality keeps perspectives straight. It starts with a tested dichotomy and has the two fuse to circulate until "we cannot tell apart | The idea and the bearer-being of the idea." The hero arrives to instill a shape, and, predictably, he lacks external stigmata of his importance. An actor again claims the landscape, but New Haven continues as the stage for him. Moonlight returns to its old, lovely guise, provocative and yet not wholly trustworthy. The double lions face each other as the poet confronts himself among "the metaphysical streets of the physical town." The scholar, this time Professor Eucalyptus, continues to study himself, but a new grandeur infuses the evening. Comedy appears as a wistful failure; the concept no longer contains many wry qualities. The difficulty of being modern—and the impossibility of being anything else—changes New Haven continuously. "The imaginative transcripts were like clouds, | Today," as they are once again addressed and point inevitably to self-knowledge, then back to Professor Eucalyptus, still searching learnedly for a god. The sun rises from "Sunday Morning," "The statue of Jove among the boomy clouds." Even the player of a haunted Spanish guitar helps complete this pastiche which assuredly blends New Haven and all imagined figures. Finally, nature reasserts itself in the color of blooming things, and the scholar returns with cryptic notes which make fact, once again, fact, a term whose meanings attracted Stevens constantly.

> *Real and unreal are two in one: New Haven*
> *Before and after one arrives or, say,*
>
> *Bergamo on a postcard, Rome after dark,*
> *Sweden described, Salzburg with shaded eyes*
> *Or Paris in conversation at a café.*
>
> *This endlessly elaborating poem*
> *Displays the theory of poetry,*
> *As the life of poetry.*

Thus New Haven becomes the world or the world becomes New Haven: both partake of each other. Shades and dust may compose its reality, which here takes its ultimate form from the poet during his semi-private, but not quite hermetic, meditations on a fully ordinary evening, whose darkness reveals what light may disguise without falsifying it.

vii

The harmony between the poet and all aspects of his world continues. Indeed, in the preceding part poems from *The Auroras of Autumn* fit so well with the celebration of his native climates that they could be cited without separate designations. Once again, his transitions almost elude notice, and he never shifts his allegiance wholly to Pennsylvania and Connecticut. One of his last poems, the final one which *Opus Posthumous* prints, asserts again "A Mythology Reflects Its Region." [118b] "In Connecticut, we never lived in a time | When mythology was possible—But if we had—" and he expands the thesis of the title. Nevertheless, *The Auroras of Autumn* reveals him still probing the purlieu of his credo, and "The Rock," as its name indicates, seeks basic tenets. *The Auroras of Autumn*, then, reveals darker topics, the winter shadow after summer, the night sky arching in iridescence over rocks. In encompassing the new elements the verse itself grows austere when subjects before viewed only obliquely now loom in their own guises. The sometimes pared vocabulary provides the courage to push further and discover yet more about reality. "The Auroras of Autumn" [411–21a] itself opening the volume draws upon an impoverished earth and variegated sky. The strands of statement and image, never very remote, fuse in a thoroughness unlike any other twentieth-century verse. While similar to metaphysical poetry of the seventeenth century in this respect, otherwise the style differs notably. By exploring the area between hard, separate images and an undefined mythology, its difficulties increase.

The serpent in "Farewell to Florida" and "Owl's Clover," reminiscent of Valéry's emblem based on the traditional icon for this creature, joins the aurora: "His head is air. Beneath his tip at night | Eyes open and fix on us in every sky." This figure belongs to those which Stevens sometimes offers without sufficiently qualifying them; in general it conveys a mood and prepares the way for what follows. Doubt, uncertainty, disturbances, and departure mark the next three parts, and they all take up the motif, "Farewell to an idea. . . ." Whether this leave-taking induces only regret, whether necessary knowledge also accompanies it, the rest of the work must explain. After the serpent, the land presents an empty cabin on a beach and contained in its own stillness to suggest "Credences of Summer." Autumn ages it as the northern auroras sweep down. Inside, the mother and whatever gave the house warmth fade; "Upstairs | The windows will be lighted, not the rooms." The father, allied with the principle of motion, remains sternly brooding. Saying farewell to house, mother, father, and ideas disguises the drifting concepts of both relationships and emotions. In the fifth section the parents preside over their rites, the father particularly as master of ceremonies without much elation. "This then is Chatillon or as you please. | We stand in the tumult of a festival." The celebration becomes hallucinatory, insubstantial as the auroras themselves born from cold and light. The creation of each thing by its own opposite involves the flashing sky in a universal activity, even at the height of summer. In their remoteness the northern lights become an innocence contrasting with the serpent of the opening.

Stevens' poems reflect one another by enlargements and qualifications. In the early "Anecdote of the Prince of Peacocks" [57–58a] the conclusion "As sleep falls | In the innocent air" sounded right for elusive reasons. Such a line by itself defies explanation, but the quality of innocence here emerges. Granted, then, human knowledge of impermanence, how does one react? After such fine points of clarity comes a rumbling question which only German metaphysicians should ask: Friedell's starting his three-volume modern history with "Durch die unendliche Tiefe des Weltraums wandern zahllose Strene, leuchtende Gedanken Gottes, selige Instrumente, auf denen der Schöpfer spielt. Sie alle sind glücklich, denn Gott will die Welt glücklich. Ein einziger ist unter ihnen, der dieses Los nicht teilt: auf ihm entstanden nur Menschen. Wie kam das?" [9]

> An unhappy people in a happy world—
> Read, rabbi, the phases of this difference.
> An unhappy people in an unhappy world—
>
> Here are too many mirrors for misery.
> A happy people in an unhappy world—
> It cannot be.

The universe for Stevens becomes acceptable as an entity which contains, through the innocent air, all necessary bridges, gossamer or marble, in themselves the essentials of changing life. "In hall harridan, not hushful paradise." Confronting the serpent, ambiguous as the auroras, allows this poem to rejoice in defense of necessity. The work partakes of pure poetry to the degree that its statements at first defy paraphrase. Some will probably stay conjectural, such as the exact iconography of the serpent. Nevertheless, one of the wonders of Stevens' poems, he withholds nothing: his own efforts to contain a mystery, consequently, result in unsatisfactory segments. When he has lived through a concept, it emerges with his special style between music and thought. Even parts which never unlock themselves help illuminate other works more fully. In many ways one can comprehend his whole output more easily than some of its components, a condition which his candor makes inevitable.

Although the subject of poetry, its uses and applications, keeps recurring, the final statement for the present purpose and the most delicate is "A Primitive like an Orb." How graciously—to digress briefly—these poems can share a page with drawings which at first glance seem antithetical to them surprises one. The two made by Kurt Seligmann for this poem (included in the pamphlet by the Banyan Press) with their distorted cabalistic figures should weigh on the verse too heavily; instead, while doing little for the poem, they commit no violence against it. At an opposite extreme, within a nonobjective range, Wightman Williams' thin and spidery lines which crowd upon the pages of the Cummington Press edition of "Esthétique du Mal" extend one aspect for that text. This flexibility suggests once again how difficult restricting Stevens to a limited interpretation is. Likewise, it makes hazardous conjectures about how unified any modern artist's general standards are when measured against contemporary vogues in the other arts. The comparison is already advanced and the ensuing pages take for granted a correspondence between Stevens and the so-called "modern" in art, centering in Paris for painting and Vienna for music. "Thirteen Ways of Looking at a Blackbird," for example, in a composition by Boris Blacher as a text becomes one instrument among several, and "Tea at the Palaz of Hoon" gave a name to a ballet danced by Aileen Passloff and Company with lute music. As a matter of fact, it appears that personally he cared for little in painting beyond the style of late nineteenth-century impressionists, with the exception of Klee, and had slight sympathy with atonal composers. Perhaps the discrepancy derives from a fundamental divergence between the temperaments of artists and annotators, creator and historian. Whereas the one builds assuredly in his own field and feels free to enjoy the rest, the other must beg assurances on every side and in the process enforce a totality never existing in any artist's mind. In a way this conjecture contradicts Stevens' views on the concord of outlook within epochs; further observations upon it fit more conveniently in the final chapter.

"A Primitive like an Orb" [440–43a]—to return to the topic—makes its statements about practicing poetry through a series of sustained images, although Stevens in his own work frequently goes beyond them.

> The essential poem at the centre of things,
> The arias that spiritual fiddlings make,
> Have gorged the cast-iron of our lives with good
> And the cast-iron of our works.

This quality exceeds all matter: "It is and it | Is not and, therefore, is." Inside this nonexistence as existence, being creates effects with the responses it rouses from the dedicated. It again partakes of some diamond as the matrix of creations. If "The Man with the Blue Guitar" places the player drawing his effects at random, here the course of inspiration requires notice. This tendency keeps up the penchant in the later poems for treating not so much the thing but the elusive atmosphere which subjects cast about themselves. All these individual aspects, each in itself responding to the central core of the poem and world, come to inform each other and join as the fifth section ends, "It is | As if the central poem became the world." Then, through one of those leaps, which nearly justifies Stevens' sometimes excessive addiction to Roman numerals for breaking poems into their moderately arbitrary subdivisions, the sixth section opens, "And the world the central poem, each one the mate | Of the other." Taken too literally this state resembles a yin-yang of hermetic

tightness. To vary the assertion beyond this point, without
denying it, tests both the theory and its poet.

The essence of the object rests in its almost unknowable
nature, which must hover always at a remote distance,
existing, as it does, through tangential human impulses.
The final summary, without violating the rest, manages
the saving qualification generously. The third to sixth lines
concede poetry a more extensive sway than it claimed in
Harmonium, but the vocabulary, commensurately, must
likewise jangle more roughly.

> *That's it. The lover writes, the believer hears,*
> *The poet mumbles and the painter sees,*
> *Each one, his fated eccentricity,*
> *As a part, but part, but tenacious particle,*
> *Of the skeleton of the ether, the total*
> *Of letters, prophecies, perceptions, clods*
> *Of color, the giant of nothingness, each one*
> *And the giant ever changing, living in change.*

This figure bears a decided kinship with Chocorua and its
giant, but there in spite of the remoteness—at least a
seeming detachment—man and poetry share a closer relationship, one never any distance from the other. Nevertheless, time and place keep no very sharp boundaries and
alter from poem to poem in terms already promulgated;
the extreme of order becomes disorder when pushed too
far into unchangeable rigidity, while the greatest disorder
adds up to a promised order. Close as these poems come to
explaining and expressing, the awareness of a mystery stays
at their heart; even the orb-like primitive does not join the
world. "The Plain Sense of Things" [502–3a] has "No
turban walks across the lessened floors," a contrast with
the boatman's red headdress rising bravely over "The Load
of Sugar-Cane." Lack of gaudiness does not indicate any
basic change because "the absence of the imagination
had | Itself to be imagined."

viii

Try as the language will, it cannot bring all subjects—too obviously present or fleetingly clutched—round
through the autumn air. "Bouquet of Roses in Sunlight"

presents flowers through ornate language only to denounce rhetoric itself. "The Bouquet" betrays a similar fumbling at a facsimile. After the modulated metrics which almost create an impressionistic still life from the vase, bright beyond Matisse, a soldier enters and upsets it. The world rarely intrudes with such violence, but the poems continue to offer surprises, and one dare not take Stevens for granted. At the very moment when he seems to have reached an ultimate limit, either by having whittled down his données as thinly as possible or by having cast them outward toward the zenith, a slight swerve incorporates yet other materials comfortably between minutiae and the cosmos. The exercise for a cavalier assertion about the taming of chance, which would otherwise destroy his outlook, by the end can develop the strength to accept even death, seen at its most tortured in "The Owl in the Sarcophagus." Here the interview with cessation, necessarily a one-sided affair, pushes beyond the ease of "Sunday Morning." The triumvirate of sleep, limbo, and nothing—approximately—end as, once again, projections from men and children. Such autumnal shadings derive from Stevens' desire to exhaust poetic potentialities and do not allude to his advancing age necessarily. For example, the tribute to Santayana, written at this time, could have been composed by no one else with the same gentle firmness. However strong his sympathy with the old philosopher in Rome, one should not read it as Stevens' elegy to himself. The loyalty to abstraction continues unabated, and one may interpret him in neither Crispin nor Santayana. No author can always exile himself from his poems, but Stevens' reticence carries him almost to self-effacement. The total effect of these late poems strengthens through simplified details aspects of the earlier ones. One might compare them with Klee's last canvases, such as *Paukenspieler*, where a slowly evolved technique revels in a strength, indeed brutality, hitherto unavailable. At the same time the scope, medium, dimensions, and attitudes need not expand. The style no longer improvises phantasies to impart a vision but presents directly a transcript through revealed discoveries. In Stevens the newer concepts of the rock and the skeleton expose what all along has subsumed the views and help further round out his world.

If not precisely melancholy, former colorations often survive like faded remnants of a summer day. Although less resplendent lines glitter in *The Auroras of Autumn,* their declining atmosphere, a brilliant foliage tough against heavy clouds, dazzles one anew—yet another instance of how nothing bears a single aspect for Stevens. The mood may have expanded from the preceding volume, but it signals no regret for lost pleasure. In fact, as early as *Harmonium* "Domination of Black" toned down the spectrum to near darkness. There, lack of all commentary suspends the deliberate irresolution; a charm and vagueness ameliorate the discontent. Now, he insistently tries to name aspects of the restlessness. The most ambitious in this vein, "Things of August" [489–97a], must fail; it stretches its lines beyond the limits of the subject, at least those parts which it presents. Granted that the opening wishes to establish a point about weariness, nevertheless, it frequently sounds like a dutiful exercise in which the poet has not sufficiently thought his way through the matter. After a moderately literal descrying of August, the next stanzas group their related images in an enigma; everything lives within an egg. How an interrelationship can function inside an area so encased does not emerge from the next part. Further opposites, this time between Persephone and a widow Dooley, establish no tensions in contrasting, one supposes, a true spring, long vanished, and a false autumn without promise. The rabbi, again studying this world, turns his pages, but his conclusions about it stay locked. Perhaps the nature of this season depends upon a comfortable decline, less open and available to human belief than summer or spring. As the last poems will, this one turns at length to certitudes, although with resignation rather than triumph; "He could understand the things at home." From the denial of fancies, the trying for too much, the theme of autumn itself surmounts the doubts. What emerges is "A new text of the world, | A scribble of fret and fear and fate," with the realization that such stern subjects and not any others will make points correctly. The ennui remains with a weary moon: "She has given too much, but not enough. | She is exhausted and a little old." The license taken with form also hints that Stevens may have found his chosen subject unmanageable, that as new qualifications presented themselves he accounted for them as best he could.

Everywhere "The Rock" conjures a baroque garden trembling before winter with still the energy of former elegance to oppose quiescence. Suitably for such décor and mood, the several poems which make Ulysses their subject, while inevitably more traditional than those which encourage Stevens to his freshest discoveries, elevate the old explorer as a man addicted to comprehending his world through his own faculties. If not a Tennysonian colonizer, he bears slight resemblance to Homer's crafty man. In his image the late park continues, now deep in its shadow, now with nearly intense strength of avenues reaching against space. Sometimes the mood sounds only resigned [504a]:

> I am the archangel of evening and praise
> This one star's blaze.
> Suppose it was a drop of blood . . .
> So much guilt lies buried
> Beneath the innocence
> Of autumn days.

Likewise, the essential gaiety of its title notwithstanding, "Lebensweisheitspielerei" shows that nothing remains but a stark season and people who by themselves have a derelict majesty in a world grown cold. In surviving autumn, "The Green Plant" [506a] contrasts with a direct statement as "The effete vocabulary of summer | No longer says anything," and the visible foliage menaces. Even the titles, for example, "Long and Sluggish Lines," suggest that weariness and sleep dominate. "Final Soliloquy of the Interior Paramour" [524a], if less contrite than T. S. Eliot's guilt-ridden "Ash Wednesday," echoes the song of its bones:

"Forgetting themselves and each other, united | In the quiet of the desert"; "Here, now, we forget each other and ourselves. | We feel the obscurity of an order." Fortunately, all the poems of "The Rock" do not stop here. The concepts to provide what would, in any event, have seemed their final configurations have already appeared. In Stevens' poems, as with the coming of dawn or evening, one cannot quite point and say that here a topic begins, one of the many advantages of his manner of writing.

ix

The poem called "The Rock" [525–28a] delimits its own attributes. Dramatizing a renunciation of past life and works, a casual meeting becomes "An invention, an embrace between one desperate clod | And another in a fantastic consciousness." The inscrutable rock subsumes all, even change. Poetry may hide this metaphysical stone as leaves do an actual one and soften its contours if not its quantities. As before, an absolute substratum repels an entrance, and the glistening surface becomes an actuality. The qualities among and through which people live transcend without destroying the base which eventually assumes properties of a source, although not a first cause. As though Stevens before had sought an actual ladder by which to ascend as far as possible into an ether, here he sets the rock as a necessary particle at the other extreme. It has no evil connotations, nor any pejorative ones. If the earlier one of fictive music seemed too remote and the supreme fiction tolerated only notes toward an approach, here the rock becomes nothing to be embraced or feared but a reality accepted as an undeniable if less interesting, more obvious, component in experience and art. He never excludes anything which pertains to poetry. The volume ends not on this note but with the arrival of another spring and a bird's cry which, insubstantial though it sounds, promises that fresh discoveries may await; the image of Ulysses persists. While clutching insistently after whatever continues in its barest qualities, "The Rock" never denies that poetry, too, perpetuates its own existence.

The concept goes back to the very beginning, surely as far as Crispin who learned that poems and plums, as well as curls and turnips, survive in nature. More clearly it inscribes "A Postcard from the Volcano," where the children found bones of those long dead. In turning inward from the outside, Stevens confronts in himself a similar matter, the skeleton. His program for accepting this menacing part of reality uses a tested process. He faces it as a fact for which he has no particular regard and, nevertheless, brings himself to analyze its components and to make himself its equal. The assured "As You Leave the Room" [116–17b] takes exit in terms not defiant but forceful: "*You speak. You say:* Today's character is not | A skeleton out of its cabinet. Nor am I." The skeleton, more a part of the external world than of man, would question the stuff from which poetry takes shape and regard it as mere ectoplasm. The poet affirms his belief in the validity of his work until, at last, it endures beyond bone: "nothing has been changed except what is | Unreal, as if nothing had been changed at all." Although the skeleton exists internally as the rock does outside man—both as substances on which one may have to fall back—neither symbolizes a final negation or denial. Nor do they, of course, provide a precariously wedged cornerstone in the fully worked out aesthetic. Stevens might have gone on, had he lived beyond 1955, to write more which would have rounded off the older concepts with yet greater finality or have introduced yet new speculations: conjecture is futile. By these last postulates a deeper assurance attends offering not a versified philosophy but an area which proves at once consistent and elastic, a way of writing poetry which erects no signposts but, instead, a fully developed map with most regions well charted through the detailed jottings en route. In this particular, Stevens again proves himself of his time, not falling into a nineteenth-century trap: "His [Meredith's] teaching seems now too strident and too optimistic and too shallow. It obtrudes; and when philosophy is not consumed in a novel, when we can underline this phrase with a pencil, and cut out that exhortation with a pair of scissors and paste the whole into a system, it is safe to say that there is something wrong with the philosophy or with the novel or with both." [10]

Asserting this much should not imply that the late poems, dealing now and then as they must with rocks and skeletons, come nearer to what Stevens really means or what he feared admitting in the earlier verse. If he continued exploring, he never surrendered his old territories but drew from them constantly. The skeleton does not dominate the imagination and its works but takes its garb from them and keeps within the flesh a frame which the eye must have. If "The Rock" grows austere, it heightens certain images and asserts their wisdom quite directly; one must insist again that really nothing has changed at all. "A form of fire approaches the cretonnes of Penelope" might have graced any of the poems, as mentioned in section iv, Chapter 1. It comes from the late "The World as Meditation" [520–21a] with its prefacing motto from Georges Enesco, "Je vis un rêve permanent, qui ne s'arrête ni nuit ni jour." In it Penelope awakens and experiences the sun which may precede her returning husband. The mere act of awaiting Ulysses has enabled her to accept the world almost gracefully. In her deprivation this vigil comprises no negative. Rather, by living fully an existence which, in terms of life itself, can never be complete, one comes to annex the part of the world which one inhabits. The legend has never had so delicately effective an embodiment. For Stevens two principles must always bolster each other, sometimes obvious dichotomies, at others merely objects side by side, and one of them may, indeed, make itself felt through its very absence not as a lack but as that which adds to composing a positive. Thus, the Ulysses of "The Sail of Ulysses" [99–105b], himself a *Symbol of the Seeker*, muses his complementary interior monologue and discerns a truth, "As if abstractions were, themselves | Particulars of a relative sublime." In this way the skeleton, the rock, the pared verse, as well as the entire corpus of his work all become exchanges of fealty with the imagination, which needs all matter. Each title represents an effort to illuminate a bit more clearly an increasingly deep world. The faith in wholeness depends, basically, on the efficacy of metaphor.

x

Modern criticism has painstakingly investigated the structure and effects of metaphor. In this matter, as well as for other tacks taken by recent critics, one's gratitude about their undeniable advances shades off into regret that for Stevens these methods distort as much as they reveal. Taking its cue from metaphysical poetry, much twentieth-century verse moves easily from the dim myth to the striking foreground because it establishes one object as another, then as another, then as another. This manner gives birth to symbols, which gather to themselves a traditional authority as well as a striking modernity, which may, however, stale rapidly. If almost everything partakes of something else, ultimately anything may equal nearly everything else. What looks like reality in the daily world becomes a twilight where nothing long remains stable. Although Stevens talks about metaphor, he tends to leave any exact meanings it has for him up in the air. One critic has complained about the failure to conform to the more popular definitions, as though a prophet had announced the norm for all time. "His conception of metaphor is regrettably unclear, though clearer in the poetry than in the essays. . . . But nowhere in his essays does he suggest that metaphor is anything more than likeness of parallelism. . . . Clearly, if poetry is 'merely' this, the use of metaphor could only accentuate what Stevens' poetry tries to annihilate, the sense of a contrast or great gulf fixed between subject and object, consciousness and existence. And in fact we often find metaphor used pejoratively in the poems as a form of avoiding direct contact with reality." [11] All this sounds peevish, like a schoolmaster's lecturing a bright but headstrong student to pay more attention to the rules and not try to prove new solutions to set problems for which the centuries have already demonstrated a single, correct answer. One can readily sympathize because in terms of approved categories Stevens ignores the precision one wishes, in defiance of the subject and its nature. Like the imagination itself, metaphor has its proper and overweening functions. When, however, the same critic proceeds to lecture Stevens on what he really did, presumably in spite of himself, one feels that authority may venture too far. "The theoretical postulate of Stevens' poetry is a world of total metaphor, where the poet's vision may be indentified with anything it visualizes." [12] It may, but such a surrealistic jumble would not hide the minimum demanded by Stevens as a connoisseur of chaos which conceals order.

Granted that his definitions will not stay in one spot, the whole outlook comes close to centrality; in addition to the lines at the beginning of this chapter, one might also cite, "Metaphor creates a new reality from which the original appears to be unreal." [169b] Properly, metaphor implies two objects which through any kind of resemblance, even attentuated as in the anecdotes, partake of each other. The result of this coupling produces a new thing which transcends its origins. One and one make no metaphoric two, joined as a whole. Rather, the invention invalidates neither of its sources, while the new contrivance looms more vividly than its origins. The danger is that from this novel object one may push too far and produce yet another thing and, thus, lose touch with what originally passed for reality. Hence, Stevens must keep his suspicions of metaphor at all times, persistently as he invokes it. Another definition might help somewhat:

> The only *general* attribute of projected romance that I can see, the only one that fits all its cases, is the fact of the kind of experience with which it deals—experience liberated, so to speak; experience disengaged, disembroiled, disencumbered, exempt from the conditions that we usually know to attach to it and, if we wish to put the matter, drag upon it, and operating in a medium which relieves it, in a particular interest, of the inconvenience of a *related*, a measurable state, a state subject to all our vulgar communities. . . . The balloon of experience is in fact of

course tied to the earth, and under that necessity we swing, thanks to a rope of remarkable length, in the more or less commodious car of the imagination; but it is by the rope we know where we are, and from the moment that cable is cut we are at large and unrelated: we only swing apart from the globe—though remaining as exhilarated, naturally, as we like, especially when all goes well. The art of the romancer is, "for the fun of it," insidiously to cut the cable, to cut it without our detecting him.[13]

In his essays, as remarkable in their way as James', Stevens points out how every resemblance reaches limits, that one cannot go on to make a new world metaphorically but must restrict one's self to creating novel elements out of the only home man has. He may, as, for example, in "Extracts from Addresses to the Academy of Fine Ideas," let himself swing to the moon, but he retains the cable and returns to earth. The balloon never serves for an unlikely interplanetary vehicle. Consequently, through their metaphors the poems keep referring back to actualities, and the resemblances neither create a new cosmos nor allude to a private world constructed from figurative stepping stones. Moreover, he does not present absolute categories; at times his metaphors may consist of simply calling one thing by another name; at others, he may take the most elusive connections, based on nothing more substantial than the air itself, and from it conjure a heightened object, a diamond, perhaps, at the center of existence which connects all parts with a slowly revolving wholeness based on itself. Nothing quite isolated exists in nature and nothing duplicates anything else for him. All must turn back to its origins, or, otherwise, resemblance deals with the gossamers of romanticism shaping a subjective phantasy outside the bounds of any experience. This firm grasp on actualities further explains why his gifts function in so tantalizing a manner: marmoreal though his poems with their metaphors look, they never wholly depart from life to become quite independent creations. Words may become almost things, but they must always return back to the soil from which they grew. Stevens subscribes to no faith in magical doctrines nor in any enchanter-poet as ruler of the world. Nevertheless, with all his fondness for an aloof tolerance of life, he could not always suspend his judgments about experience, which sometimes provided him unpleasant metaphors. Consequently, his resemblances have to refer to some sort of scale, the most important aspects of which arise out of his practices themselves.

> *It was from the point of view of another subtlety that Klee could write: "But he is one chosen that today comes near to the secret places where original law fosters all evolution. And what artist would not establish himself there where the organic center of all movement in time and space—which he calls the mind or heart of creation—determines every function." Conceding that this sounds a bit like sacerdotal jargon . . .*
>
> WALLACE STEVENS [174C]

THE QUESTION OF FAITH AND POETRY comes and goes; one had better say that it never departs but that it infrequently lives as a mild boarder and usually tries to rule the household. Faith assumes varied guises and interpretations, and, when talking about it in connection with poetry, one encounters confused prejudices; if one ignores it, one becomes eclectic or sentimental, or both. The history of literature and its immediate areas enlists its industrious chroniclers, but the flowering and decline of faith attract more partisans. Anyone putting the two accounts together generally produces a tract for the times with most of the written words from the past subject to impressment. Problems will remain as long as one asks the nearly inevitable questions. Since Stevens has cavalierly dismissed the past and its shibboleths so often, the moderately attractive temptation of following his example presents itself. Such a procedure would leave him largely in the accustomed position mistakenly assigned him, that of writing and feeling in a vacuum or private preserve. To connect him arbitrarily with traditions may twist his views toward a biased end. The most likely solution would attempt to erect from certain poems themselves a standard. The ones chosen must be arbitrary. Any might, theoretically, serve as well because all cohere within a definite range and none—not even the prose—presents a complete program by itself. Undeniably some, bolstered by extraneous observations, do point toward a general concern a bit more fully. Presumably, also, one may then read back into other ones for implications not fully voiced. Such an undertaking will merely establish a direction and cannot pretend to cover all matters even sketchily. For a beginning one early work, in particular, enjoys—or suffers from, depending on one's prejudices—a number of comments and documents by Stevens himself.

i

Consider the widely publicized "The Emperor of Ice-Cream" [64a], not yet discussed here:

> *Call the roller of big cigars,*
> *The muscular one, and bid him whip*
> *In kitchen cups concupiscent curds.*
> *Let the wenches dawdle in such dress*
> *As they are used to wear, and let the boys*
> *Bring flowers in last month's newspapers.*
> *Let be be finale of seem.*
> *The only emperor is the emperor of ice-cream.*
>
> *Take from the dresser of deal,*
> *Lacking the three glass knobs, that sheet*
> *On which she embroidered fantails once*
> *And spread it so as to cover her face.*
> *If her horny feet protrude, they come*
> *To show how cold she is, and dumb.*
> *Let the lamp affix its beam.*
> *The only emperor is the emperor of ice-cream.*

Explicators have agitated this by turning it upside-down and inside-out. Almost every word can yield three or four meanings. Stevens himself remained mildly reticent. He once named it his favourite poem for an anthology in which poets made their own selections. (Such a choice did not prevent his nominating another one for the similar gathering already discussed in section vi, Chapter 2.) His reason goes: "I think I should select from my poems as my favorite 'The Emperor of Ice Cream.' This wears a deliberately commonplace costume, and yet seems to me to contain something of the essential gaudiness of poetry; that is the reason why I like it. I do not remember the circumstances under which this poem was written, unless this means the state of mind from which it came. I dislike niggling, and like letting myself go. Poems of this sort are the pleasantest on which to look back, because they seem to remain fresher than others. This represented what was in my mind at the moment, with the least possible manipulation." [1]

Later, to a letter enquiring what he made of some close readers going at the poem hammer and tongs, he spelled out his refusal to explain further.

Things that have their origin in the imagination or in the emotions (poems) very often have meanings that differ in nature from the meanings of things that have their origin in reason. They have imaginative or emotional meanings, not rational meanings, and they communicate these meanings to people who are susceptible to imaginative or emotional meanings. They may communicate nothing at all to people who are open only to rational meanings. In short, things that have their origin in the imagination or in the emotions very often take on a form that is ambiguous or uncertain. It is not possible to attach a single, rational meaning to such things without destroying the imaginative or emotional ambiguity or uncertainty that is inherent in them and that is why poets do not like to explain. That the meanings given by others are sometimes meanings not intended by the poet or that they were never present in his mind does not impair them as meanings. On the inside cover of the album of Mahler's Fifth Symphony recently issued by Columbia there is a note on the meaning of that work. Bruno Walter, however, says that he never heard Mahler intimate that the symphony had any meanings

except the meanings of music. Does this impair the meanings of the commentators as meanings? Certainly this
music had no single meaning which alone was the meaning intended and to which one is bound to penetrate. If
it had, what justification could the composer have had
for concealing it? The score with its markings contains any
meaning that imaginative and sensitive listeners find in it.
It takes very little to experience the variety in everything.
The poet, the musician, both have explicit meanings but
they express them in the forms these take and not in
explanation.[2]

One more document by Stevens may throw some light on
this poem, although, obviously, no single source will restrict it to a single meaning, even as meaning. An undergraduate sketch, "Four Characters," centers one episode
upon a narrator who accompanies a friend, a reporter, to a
house where someone has died. A woman admits them
briefly; they start to leave.

> She pulled the cloth back over the thin, somber fea-
> tures, put the lamp on the table, and went over to the
> stove again.
> "Won't you have some tea?" she asked. "I'm just going
> to make some. Bigsby [the dead husband] hated it."
> We thanked her and started to go.
> "I will light you to the stairs," she said. As she crossed
> the room the lamp lit up the hovel, and we saw a bed that
> had not been visible before. It was made of a tattered
> mattress with straw sticking out at the edges. It was
> perfectly bare, without pillow or sheet.[3]

Let this much in prose stand for what Stevens calls
the plain dress of the poem. Many aspects correspond: the
corpse might be the woman herself a few years later. The
bare bed has given up its sheet which may represent the
embroidery of poetry. The lamp, the finality of death,
the kitchen cups, and poverty appear in both; here is no
tragedy but a routine happening made a bit grotesque and
pathetic. On the surface "The Emperor of Ice-Cream" has
the same, flat qualities, but the reporter has departed and
the poet taken over. The poem obviously does describe an

amiable wake without any demand for mystery by jeweled unicorns or forgetfulness by Irish usque baugh; no hysteria needs assuaging and no hope of resurrection asks bolstering. The dead and the living exist under a single dispensation: an emperor of ice-cream. The improvised festivities disrupt daily chores a bit: the maker of cigars transferred from the dry tobacco to the white curds; the relaxed women who sit for an interval; the passé news from yesterday flowering into its ultimate oblivion. Death lies beyond comprehension, and its essence does not matter. Quite honestly, a corpse, even Badroulbadour, does not present an attractive sight, and her homely dream of beauty becomes a banal vision shaped merely in those fleeting fantails, whether stylized tails, pigeons, fish, or edging. Whatever hardship she suffered, all has gone anonymously. One neither mourns her passing nor rejoices in her salvation. Nevertheless, the vocabulary, the juxtaposition, the imperatives, and ellipses do make it vexing, plain and gaudy at once. Beneath it lurks a twitch that all has gone awry, that one cannot wish death away. Its very reasonableness verges on hilarity or gloom. One might recall the revealing remark attributed to Stendhal, who, upon having finished a plate of ice cream, said, "What a pity it's not a sin."

"The Emperor of Ice-Cream" transcends a report about poverty and death. It implies that nothing can be ascertained about the end of life but, likewise, that one cannot wish away a certain mystery. How, for example, does one interpret the Emperor, whether he himself or his realm (or both) owe their existence to a confection? One might note, too, that the whole poem tells how to conduct a funeral and does not hint whether all works out according to plan. Stevens, it has been suggested, wrote the poem because his daughter liked ice cream, and it does playfully offer the beguiling contradictions which confront Alice in her fanciful travels, if the undercurrents imply more. Indeed, the sheeted corpse could be a girl's. Rolling cigars, a definite step at the time before they were manufactured by machines, requires no strength; indeed, women frequently were employed for it. Making the largest cigars would demand no extra force. The emphasis on muscles twists the logic quaintly. In the kitchen the tempest of energy incongruously whips about cups with their unchildish curds. The staging directs the wenches, not aspiring to the verbal dignity of mourners, to waste time as usual, and such lethargy prevails that flowers should arrive wrapped not in the accustomed green tissue but in the handiest container. (To suggest that death transforms yesterday's news—which proverbially nothing is so dead as—makes a metaphysical point at the expense of decorum.) "Let be be finale of seem" says again that these poems seek to escape from popular sentimentality and that, nevertheless, the reduction of the thing to itself proves equally evasive. In the second stanza a discordant harmony replaces the flat contradictions of the first. The dead creature had indulged her desire for a popular elegance, the old-fashioned wood dresser with its glass knobs—probably not all are missing and some remain—and the wistful embroidery on the coverlet. Whatever quality her presence might have bestowed upon them, their very bleakness testifies to the disruption by death. The use of *horny* focuses on the passing of pretense. Inadequate illusion in disguising the sordid makes the Emperor a sinister power. Then, the lighting of the covered body, the final gaze: of course, things are this way. But, if they are, then everyone shares traits with the uncomprehending snow man for, like that simulacrum, the Emperor of Ice-Cream may be an effigy of the substance which he dominates and which he alone can understand by not knowing. Thus, the discords of life, the discontinuity between being and death, the failure to achieve grace anywhere, and the admission that one cannot quarrel with such contradictions, link this poem suitably with the early anecdotes, which have it both ways. One despairs neatly by wit. In denying death its absolute terror one escapes the guilt of wrongs and, perhaps, falls into the sin of pride. The suppressed feelings came forth in expression only later as an "Esthétique du Mal" [312–26a]: "The death of Satan was a tragedy | For the imagination."

ii

While most twentieth-century poets played fast and loose with their own epoch, Stevens studied it steadily, intent as Nietzsche staring at the lake but less haunted. Sometimes he castigated it obliquely but seldom directly. It took a long time before he could come right out with "Another American vulgarity" [438a], whose context softens considerably its force. This reticence helps explain the multiple qualifications, the stalking of an object from every angle: the penchant for rounding off poems with a flat statement or leaving them quite unresolved, and the preference to champion perfection which springs from a center of disinterest and which can shut itself against the unpleasant or raise a lamp to point up a tawdry wake. The squeamishness indicates a partial blind spot, as though Stevens borrowed the uncle's monocle. Perhaps for these reasons, among others, "Esthétique du Mal" strikes its necessary note, although true to its character, it proposes no final word. From it evolve the bases for suspending verdicts or judging with rectitude.

> He was at Naples writing letters home
> And, between his letters, reading paragraphs
> On the sublime. Vesuvius had groaned
> For a month. It was pleasant to be sitting there,
> While the sultriest fulgurations, flickering,
> Cast corners in the glass. He could describe
> The terror of the sound because the sound
> Was ancient.

Vesuvius and all its potential destructiveness, which impinges by implication upon Pompeii and Herculaneum, exist only in an ironically sketched present. The sky by night disdains the signs: "The fault lies with an over-human god, | Who by sympathy has made himself a man." The tone becomes almost existential in a revolt against the smugness which contrives a supernatural deity, who by bestowing favors makes too much of, and consequently diminishes, the world. Phrases, "A too, too human god,

self-pity's kin | And uncourageous genesis," likewise bring
to mind Nietzsche, although not as a philosopher to whom
one can turn as an avowed disciple. At the same time,
Stevens' theory, here and in general, about the power of
poetry to reach truth through fictions may also stem partly
from him but also, with an entirely different impetus, from
Santayana.

Camouflaging what one experiences as richer or poorer
than it is—to wishfully indulge or escape it—leads to evil.
Accuracy alone can recognize and arrange; precision determines values, although the familiar will always impose
ambiguities on choices.

> *Be near me, come closer, touch my hand, phrases*
> *Compounded of dear relation, spoken twice,*
> *Once by the lips, once by the services*
> *Of central sense, these minutiae mean more*
> *Than clouds, benevolences, distant heads.*
> *These are within what we permit, in-bar*
> *Exquisite in poverty against the suns*
> *Of ex-bar, in-bar retaining attributes*
> *With which we vested, once, the golden forms*
> *And the damasked memory of the golden forms*
> *And ex-bar's flower and fire of the festivals*
> *Of the damasked memory of the golden forms,*
> *Before we were wholly human and knew ourselves.*

Only through an openness to all the risks of misfortune
does pain play itself out in becoming realized, a necessary
process for surmounting it. By personal vanities, by making
too much of events, by seeing particulars rather than the
general, one manufactures a false self. "The sun, in clown-
ish yellow, but not a clown, | Brings the day to perfection
and then fails." The sun exists incompletely, as does almost
everything else, and lives as the victim of time, which
makes its nature possible. From its tracing of personal
disasters, the poem has moved to cosmic ones, which
ultimately depend upon men. The overwhelming catastro-
phe of war, as defined in the poems already mentioned,
comments on itself; soldiers, dead beyond reconciliation,
enjoy a deathless pathos. "How red the rose that is the

soldier's wound" may sound derivative for Stevens, but roses run as a leitmotiv in this part to embody the multiplicity of sorrow and its eventual transformation. Death and inflexible singleness both belong to the frozen kingdom of the emperor of ice-cream. The verse gets to its paradox that admitting evils and not resisting them robs them of their power and may transform them; evading them or battling them arms them with advantages. Lacking a modern Satan, captain of evil, one can neither affirm nor rejoice so that evils may hide everywhere.

> How cold the vacancy
> When the phantoms are gone and the shaken realist
> First sees reality. The mortal no
> Has its emptiness and tragic expirations.
> The tragedy, however, may have begun,
> Again, in the imagination's new beginning,
> In the yes of the realist spoken *because he must*
> Say yes, spoken because under every no
> Lay a passion for yes that had never been broken.

If the sun has its ambiguous kingdom, so, too, does the moon, whose rays shine overwhelmingly. Only by regarding the moon, here, although not everywhere, standing for the widest range of the imagination, can one grasp "Truth's favors sonorously exhibited" with nothing vital excluded. Just as awareness of the perishable earth stirred deeper probings for assurances in "Sunday Morning," here truth turns to other evasions. A nearly mythic mother appears, but she provides, ultimately, another subterfuge; even when Stevens invokes myths, as with Crispin, he rejects them as falsifications: "Natives of poverty, children of malheur, | The gaiety of language is our seigneur." From catastrophes, always present, one can seek another escape into the third sphere which denies knowledge of self and others. If one composes this remote world, it remains stubbornly beyond imagining, too distant for habitation, as one would expect it to be. The point again appears that only by confronting evil and not resisting it can one deprive it of its force, if not its essence and roots, sometimes usable for poetry. In a passage of uncommon grace the poem reviews multiplicity which presents good by reducing evil to its inane role: "Evil in evil is | Comparative." Back in Geneva the reasonable lake once again introduces the proper world which might harbor the refugee Konstantinov.

> *He would not be aware of the lake.*
> *He would be the lunatic of one idea*
> *In a world of ideas, who would have all the people*
> *Live, work, suffer and die in that idea*
> *In a world of ideas. He would not be aware of the clouds,*
> *Lighting the martyrs of logic with white fire.*
> *His extreme of logic would be illogical.*

This part concludes with the passage already quoted in section iv, Chapter 1 as an affirmation of life itself. Evil, therefore, exists as an evasion of living, and the other poems show abundantly of what the good consists. For Stevens pain and fear become maladies only when denied or optimistically called blessings, both rationalizations and likewise deceptive. Each day with, obviously, its evils must be sufficient in itself, and one judges it as seldom as possible.

iii

The matter which one sees depends upon how one looks at it, and this exercise concerns the very center of poetry. Although Stevens has commented on this topic repeatedly, both those whom he has influenced and his critics have found his statements in verse and prose puzzling. The very singleness of his pursuit means that the essays nearly depend on the poetry for illustrations; they offer no diagrams. For this commentary it seemed most suitable to treat the two as a unit [vii c]:

> One function of the poet at any time is to discover by his own thought and feeling what seems to him to be poetry at that time. Ordinarily he will disclose what he finds in his own poetry by way of the poetry itself. He exercises this function most often without being conscious of it, so that the disclosures in his poetry, while they define what seems to him to be poetry, are disclosures of poetry,

> not disclosures of the definitions of poetry. . . . In short,
> they [the collected essays] are intended to be contribu-
> tions to the theory of poetry and it is this and this alone
> that binds them together.

This passage from the introduction to *The Necessary Angel* reveals how the verse and prose, each in an appropriate style, share paring away extraneous matter toward exactitude, an enlargement of concepts by defining them in their own terms, the only ones available. Seldom has so elegant a style cared so little for the elegant variation in its own right. The method belongs essentially to its subject. It seeks always to get at a central meaning about poetry without impoverishing, for Stevens, its innate panache. On the other hand, because the manifestations of this vital nucleus proliferate throughout poetry, the subjects can range almost at random and still keep firmly to the point of origin. This double movement explains, also, in part why so many of Stevens' poems echo each other and why so few fail to say something slightly different or present the familiar in a novel fashion.

The essays set forth the same views in many instances, and the ease with which the prose blends into the origins of the poetry the quoted passages should have amply demonstrated. Going through the poems in order of their original publication, then following them up with the prose pieces, which have their moderately casual air because Stevens delivered the majority first as speeches and preserves their occasional character, instructs one best about his beliefs and methods. While less overwhelming than James' prefaces, they touch the same, elusive area, where the artist and theorist join and provide both example and explanation with an authority which neither a critic nor a philosopher matches by himself. Both James and Stevens have the virtue of showing an established and masterful practice with its rationale. This very fusion of the two qualities may, however, sound a bit too pat, as though a prophet spoke an inevitable and final word. Such fullness can discourage study. The very point is that, of all his contemporaries, Stevens still troubles critics most, still receives tentative, if deeply respectful encomia, as reviews of the *Collected Poems,* even those by practicing craftsmen, testify. For example, the "Adagia" at first glance present dicta with an air of greater superiority than self-conscious epigrams have a right to, and consequently some flounder as mere clichés or strive vainly for the mot juste. Upon more careful study, in the light of the poems, they attain the precision of idioms. Their sentences say things well in Stevens' native language, although to a foreigner they strike the ear as irritatingly clipped or cumbersome. No self-sufficient gloss for the poetry lies buried in them, and they demand the same alert reading which it does.

Two essays particularly culminate in substantial creation, although all have significant passages. The circumstances under which he read "Three Academic Pieces," as a lecture at Harvard, in 1947, may have dictated its style. Although in no way a dramatic monologue, it offers a prim Professor Stevens, more allusive and distant than usual, given to niceties: "The accuracy of accurate letters is an accuracy with respect to the structure of reality." [71c] Looking tolerantly askance at nonacademic matters and proudly humble before his topic, he treats resemblances in reality. Passages pilfered from it have been strewn through these chapters. At the end of the prose, without explanation or transition, two poems follow, which fully demonstrate the thesis. "Someone Puts a Pineapple Together" focuses steadily on the fruit, which partakes of all its surroundings. By itself it would pass as an acceptable poem; in context it elaborates more clearly than extra appended prose could on his implications. The second "Of Ideal Time and Choice" [88–89c], treats the insubstantial qualities of time and space.

> Since thirty mornings are required to make
> A day of which we say, this is the day
> That we desired, a day of blank, blue wheels,
>
> Involving the four corners of the sky,
> Lapised and lacqued and freely emeraldine
> In the space it fills. . . .

The poems illustrate two of the extremes between which Stevens constantly moves: the very specific and the quite rarefied. The voyage from the one to the other, without stopovers into more practical affairs, can become poetry. Of course, the two likewise exist almost side by side, when counted as two of the four areas, advanced in the first chapter, in which poets work. Although "Three Academic Pieces" coheres tightly, it cannot argue from premises nor proceed from induction; like the rest, it circulates to sketch boundaries around poetry. The same method operates in a second, more ambitious, essay.

"The Noble Rider and the Sound of Words" draws upon a similar organization, or freedom from it. It opens with a survey of equestrian figures: in Plato, by Verrocchio, in Cervantes, by Clark Mills, and *Wooden Horses* by an unidentified contemporary painter who must have found refuge for a while in a WPA project. Each horseman represents an interchange between the imagination and reality, but they remain sealed in the past, largely. Drawing closer to the present, Stevens sketches developments in poetic language through the nineteenth century and into the present and finds dissatisfaction with all the modern arts. "It may be that Braque and Picasso love and feel painting and that Schönberg loves and feels music, although it seems that what they love and feel is something else." [16c] He turns to the modern pressures of reality as a factor in the decline but always with an owlish wit. "We are intimate with people we have never seen and, unhappily, they are intimate with us. Democritus plucked his eyes out because he could not look at a woman without thinking of her as a woman. If he had read a few of our novels, he would have torn himself to pieces." [18c] Such minor irritations might be borne, but the overhanging catastrophes throughout the globe, and the concomitant deterioration in language and sensibility, work against the arts. Conceding all this, Stevens proceeds to present his poet, the emerging noble rider, with past artifacts at his back, going bravely through modern realities, whatever their terrors and ravages. More positively, the poet must renounce social and moral allegiances. "His role, in short, is to help people to live their lives. Time and time again it has been said that he may not address himself to an élite. I think he may. There is not a poet whom we prize living today that does not address himself to an élite." [29c] Through presenting reality in a new guise, that of his own time and temperament, and then offering it in accurate words—quite apart from any social or moral obligations—the poet transcends contemporary chic and achieves, again, nobility.

Deprived of its body, the outlined essay sounds pretty, if unconvincing. It needs the echoing examples, the modulations from irony to statement, the short sentences whose repetitions strengthen concepts, and the tantalizing ellipses. All such devices belong to definition not argument, to the philosopher not the propagandist, to understanding not proof, and to insight not logic. In composing his prose, it would seem, Stevens worked in the same manner he did when setting down a poem. He defined his general intention throughout and then began shaping it with phrases and examples. Although not whimsical enough to be coupled with the nearly extinct familiar essay, his work shares traits with this genre. For this reason isolated passages enlarge upon the poems well, and extracting parts without context does them slight violence. At the same time, no finely argued theory can be coaxed from *The Necessary Angel* and the pieces in *Opus Posthumous*, as his inconsistencies in using *metaphor* show. His one outright foray into a systematic scheme, "A Collect of Philosophy," was turned down by a journal of philosophy, and one must sympathize with the editor who rejected it. Having exhausted all visible approaches, then, and resigned to handicaps, one must turn to counter judgments against Stevens. Recent criticism has loved schematizations for their own sake. Methodologies provide impregnable defenses against assaults by unorthodox works. Fortunately, such bulwarks have, likewise, aggressively banished much nonsense which once passed for analysis. At the same time, their unheeding rigors may have clumsily destroyed, or failed to appreciate, valid subtleties, which became, in a fashionable term, heresies. In surveying unfavorable comments one had best try to negotiate by noting failures to take account of all Stevens' assumptions. At that, the topics, so inextricably does he intertwine them, will not march out in completely separate files.

iv

Taking Stevens more or less at his own evaluation, John Crowe Ransom in *The World's Body* observes, "Stevens, however, is objective from beginning to end; he completes all his meanings, knowing these will have little or no moral importance. . . . [as one kind of modern poet], he will not consider a subject which lends itself to moralization; that is, a subject of practical interest. It is his chief problem to find then a subject which has any interest at all." [4] Judged on the basis of *Harmonium* alone, Stevens might deserve this verdict. At that, however, one may debate where "meaning" and "moral importance" (and what, poetically, bestows "importance"—high seriousness?) part company in any poem. John Crowe Ransom, one assumes, does not attach quite the same significance to the term as Stevens does in "The Noble Rider and the Sound or Words" and in "The Figure of the Youth as Virile Poet," where he notes, "The morality of the poet's radiant and productive atmosphere is the morality of the right sensation." [58c] Of course, *The World's Body* preceded his more pretentious book, *The New Criticism*, by a number of years. Being wise not too long after the fact, one can see that "Sea Surface Full of Clouds," the poem selected to illustrate the point in *The World's Body*, represents a peak for one kind of poetry and, within its limits, says quite a bit more than Stevens is usually given credit for. To bring subject and treatment to qualify each other poetically, a technique about which John Crowe Ransom himself later makes penetrating observations, one must steer between the shallows of sententiousness and commonplaces, drama and sentimentality. Whether from this manner one learns about the world or about one's response to abstraction has no easy answer, but Stevens devotes his whole output to formulating just this topic. His desire from the outset is to show how the trivial and grand interact neither in terms of a buried trauma nor through trite externals but by a fusion of the two afresh. Aware that judgments by aesthetics or morality, two entities never separate in his view, should not become mechanical, Stevens has the courage to explore the implications of his refusals and beliefs. Suspended judgments do not mean fear of discriminating itself but, inevitably, respect for it. A review of his own piece on John Crowe Ransom, already discussed, in some ways provides the best answer because it proves how poetry can evolve from a place itself without extraneous matters.

Permitting morality to intrude at this point obscures the problem of "interest." Throughout his poems Stevens often insists upon pleasure as an almost absolute criterion, nearly interpreting aut prodesse aut delectare as either/or with no third alternative. Such candor embarrasses critics who wish to anchor their judgments on a less transitory and shifting base than enjoyment, a question which haunted Arnold and which, despite his diminished reputation in the twentieth century, theorists still try to exorcise. Nevertheless, pleasure can have its positive aspects, not in the sense of irresponsibility but merely because, from all the things which go to make poetry, many obviously do please. The subject of this enjoyment does not derive from memory, as in sentimental verse, nor from future promises, as in hymns. Rather, it seeks its own transcendental values which need not rove beyond the bounds of the lines themselves. As Stevens illustrates it: "Yet Narcissus did not expect, when he looked in the stream, to find in his hair a serpent coiled to strike, nor, when he looked in his own eyes there, to be met by a look of hate, nor, in general, to discover himself at the center of an inexplicable ugliness from which he would be bound to avert himself. . . . Narcissism, then, involves something beyond the prime sense of the word. It involves, also, this principle, that as we seek out our resemblances we expect to find pleasure in doing so; that is to say, in what we find." [79–80c] The trouble with Narcissus as a figurehead for such activity is that, like Nietzsche and Lenin beside their respective bodies of water, he becomes the person chained by one idea, as disastrous in pleasure as with any other activity. For Stevens poetry neither starts nor ends with introspection (nor projecting that mood upon the world), and he praises euphuism as an effort to arrive at the proper kind of pleasures in style: resemblance, musicality, balance, and completeness. His poetry need have no further requirements. Too often criticism feels an obligation either to substantiate theology or take its place, and rejoicing in the world has distinguished few of the polemics designed to defend literature before an ecclesiastical council.

One must concede that a credo proposing only enjoyment rarely has graced arts which long endure, and, further, that the younger poets who imitate Stevens have not managed his sane balance. They forget that poetry must have its commonplaces and elegance. Such examples do not vitiate his own practices, which stand like beacons for both directions and warning. He himself knew where he wished to go. "To give a sense of the freshness or vividness of life is a valid purpose for poetry. A didactic purpose justifies itself in the mind of the teacher; a philosophical purpose justifies itself in the mind of the philosopher. It is not that one purpose is as justifiable as another but that some purposes are pure, others impure. Seek those purposes that are purely the purposes of the pure poet." [157b] Poetry has its limits and within them it can, it must, give pleasure. It may also supply grist for the mills of teachers, philosophers, and the gods, but the secondary functions do not deter the poet in making poetry. By championing this claim, Stevens evades nothing. To deny it he would, by his lights, have impoverished his work and its goals. If the usual subjects vanish, if no moralizing mars his lines, he seeks to delimit more honestly poetry itself, always the subject of the poem and, thus, interesting to anyone, presumably, who cares about it. One dare hardly suggest that citing morality as a defense argues an insecurity in its proponents about their own conduct and taste. Certainly varied epochs, and most aristocratic ones, took their literature for enjoyment without compulsively enquiring after edification. Stevens' defense of pleasure has, however, been termed an evasion by a variety of critics, and not just those of a Marxist persuasion, either.

v

A modification of John Crowe Ransom's view occurs in Kenneth Burke, who in *A Grammar of Motives* had later poems to work with and refers specifically to the essay "The Noble Rider and the Sound of Words." His conclusions present a modification commensurate with changed tastes in the war years separating his book from *The World's Body*. Here poetry both occupies a less unquestioned position and champions a more urgent cause.

On the Symbolic level, philosophy and reason here seem equated with the vocational (with office hours), poetry and imagination seem equated with the vacational (after hours). Accordingly, when Mr. Stevens tries to illustrate what he means by poetic imagination, he begins: "If we close our eyes and think of a place where it would be pleasant to spend a holiday . . ." [Although expressing mixed feelings for Stevens, including a measure of admiration, Kenneth Burke advances his essay:] But Shelley, pantheistically merging divinity and poetry into one, similarly brings the poetry and the knowledge together. The next step is to drop from pantheism the *theos*, whereupon imagination equalling knowledge, one is left with the *pan*: Mr. Stevens' "*mundo* of the imagination." [5]

On the contrary, if one drops *theos*, everything else in the world necessary for the imagination to start seeing resemblances remains. The concept is scarcely novel, for Baudelaire knew in addressing his Muse,[6]

Je voudrais qu'exhalant l'odeur de la santé
Ton sein de pensers forts fût toujours fréquenté,
Et que ton sang chrétien coulât à flots rhythmiques

Comme les sons nombreux des syllabes antiques,
Où règnent tour à tour le père des chansons,
Phoebus, et le grand Pan, le seigneur des moissons.

Possibly introducing this quotation stretches an old pun too far, but a good share, if not all, does remain without a public code, more, for example, than another commentator admits: "Thus we find in Stevens the heart of a romantic pantheist and an intellect inclined toward the caution of a modern positivist. Like Emerson he is a Plotinus-Montaigne, at once inspired and skeptical and as a result capable of a subtle and ironical self-criticism." [7]

Stevens' general attitude toward established religion, as apart from private belief, has caused various explanations on the part of his critics. He refers to the topic frequently, but one might wish for a fuller identification. At times he verges on the views that poetry can become a new religion, but he never plunges over the brink into grandiose delusions. As for his attitude toward older religions, there can be little doubt. From the first poems—and increasingly in his career—he saw the gods as man's fabrication. Mortals assigned them their prerogatives and invented, or surely gave voice to, their mysteries and myths. Such a development of human knowledge about the gods was not fortuitous, and they transcend any single worshipper because, otherwise, they would want authority. Yet, if they arose from man, who expressed his soil in aspiring toward heaven, they also died after a period because time passes and no past endures without change. To this degree, then, poetry can bestow no immortality upon a deity, although through it the Olympians can last for a bit longer than in any other guise. Stevens subscribes to no absolutes except, in a qualified way, poetry. Public morality has no place in it. How anyone conducts his affairs simply does not concern a poet. Once again, those who insist that anybody not with them opposes them make Stevens nearly a high priest of secular irresponsibility. Poetically he acknowledges only his craft, which he does not try to draw into daily life where it may or may not function. The errors of the decadents, storing up exquisite sensations, do not touch him. Because his poems refer to themselves, he favors abstractions. The general qualities treated establish no golden commandments for conduct or riot. They offer a world available to anyone. In some ways the manner does resemble taking a holiday, but the office and the vacation depend upon each other, as do the farm and the museum, as do all polarities for Stevens. In this rigor he may deny an academic humanism, but, from another point, he simply asks for a more fully realized twentieth-century humanity. From both positions his credo respects every individual as an end, not a means to profit, power, fame, or publicity. As poet he legislates for no one; instead, he pronounces an insight initially obtainable only through his chosen medium and, afterwards, partially open to readers. Once a work leaves its creator, meanings, as he noted, must shift for themselves. In such terms poetry does not become a relaxed weekend for him but one real aspect of life, present each hour along with other actualities. Although lacking the solemnity of a cathedral and its organ it also mocks the sternness in a gallery which one trots through dutifully after attending a Sunday sermon. Finally, if Stevens ignores god and his temple, he does not reduce him to strolling about the marketplace and bartering for souls.

Saying this much may saddle Stevens with the frequently noticed flaw in protestant art and business: that both pursuits go their ways cut off from any theological roots and, as a result, end up quite immoral or, at best, accidently moral, an adjunct of Kenneth Burke's observation that a poetic such as his verges on pantheism or worse. Enough examples exist to provide partisans of the twelfth century with wearying lists of contrasts between then and now. To argue that the rule has no exceptions makes art as repetitious as a mechanized nature or universe, a condition it has not yet exemplified to everyone's satsifaction. One may admit that the force (and depraved splendor) in *Les Fleurs du mal* sometimes rests on Baudelaire's consciousness of a loss of faith; it does not follow that Stevens' freedom from this anxiety makes him an innocent voyager through imaginary kingdoms whence he returns with his sheaf of souvenirs labeled "Les Fleurs de la malle." Because for him poetry can, and demonstrably does, impose its own rules, the practice of art becomes his discipline toward morality. It leads to a different kind of art and morality, both rich enough in achievements so that they do not turn out to be fool's gold. The point has no absolute proof either through evidence or intellectually; those who believe from whatever motives that an inviolable standard controls poetry have their built-in arguments and marshall them. It does not matter whether the dogma derives from earth or heaven; it seeks to destroy what it cannot contain, a condition which Stevens showed in "Life on a Battleship." That poetry does not suit such martial spirits has not yet deterred anyone from putting it to this use. Not all onslaughts from this position need revel in crudities; some wax very subtle indeed. In general, the higher the thought, the more apologetic the attack.

vi

Allen Tate takes time out during an essay to remark in a packed aside:

> The obscurity of Poe's poetic diction is rather vagueness than the obscurity of complexity; it reflects his uncertain grasp of the relation of language to feeling, and of feeling to nature. But it is never that idolatrous dissolution of language from the grammar of a possible world, which results from the belief that language itself can be reality, or by incantation can create a reality: a superstition that comes down in French from Lautréamont, Rimbaud, and Mallarmé to the Surrealists, and in English to Hart Crane, Wallace Stevens, and Dylan Thomas. (I do not wish it to be understood that I am in any sense "rejecting" these poets, least of all under the rubric "superstition." When men find themselves cut off from reality they will frequently resort to magic rites to recover it—a critical moment of history that has its own relation to reality, from which poetry of great power may emerge.) [8]

The cautious charge accuses Stevens, and strangely assorted fellows, of caring excessively about "pure" poetry and of making a mystical, religious doctrine from his aesthetic. At the same time it reverses John Crowe Ransom's verdict about Stevens' essential triviality to say nothing of Yvor Winters' testily placing a wreath on the altar of nominalistic hedonism, where he claims that Stevens worships. It also elevates Stevens' poetic activities several notches above a pastime. Granted the eminence from which Allen Tate beholds poetry, his strictures carry an orthodox authority. Also, since he, along with John Crowe Ransom, Kenneth Burke, and Yvor Winters, may roughly be said to head the full phalanx of what loosely passed for the new criticism, whose opinions still dominate interpretations, their judgments help explain why Stevens remains celebrated and comparatively obscure. They tend to resemble men of one idea in Stevens' world of ideas or anti-ideas. Stevens also manages to avoid the dead-end to which another critic sentences him on the same charges.

> Beginning where he began, development was impossible except as abstraction, progressive refinement, development to a stripped simplicity; it is as though what he developed was primarily the sense of what he was about, the simplifying consciousness of his poetry as an assault upon conventions of meaning, conventions of language, upon those people who, as Valéry once wrote, are so little aware of the pains and pleasures of vision that they have invented *beautiful views*.
>
> It is the tragedy of poetry so conceived that, in a certain sense, it produces beautiful views despite itself; and a greater tragedy that all success is briefly sustained upon failure.[9]

If a loss of belief has tormented the major artists and critics during this century, the one greater obsession has been forging a new creed or revitalizing one rooted in a tradition, a term which always bears an ironic tinge in the United States. This crisis has endured so many tiresome investigations that a catalogue of them here would amount to a boring impertinence. At times it nearly seems that the critics have set out to construct a summa based on that paradise lost by the generation of the 'twenties. The physical world itself offers Stevens both signs and rewards, not because of its goodness, evil, beautiful views, or mysteries but merely because it has to be "enough," a condition about which one neither despairs nor rejoices. He does not erect a religion from art because he wishes to formulate no absolutes whatsoever for dominating others. In this fashion he can share, for quite different reasons, the exiles' contempt of the bourgeois while remaining happily highbrow at home and keeping his art, incidentally, somewhat purer. The matter in this light has simply little to do with a single dogma at all. Although he cannot shake off entirely the inherited attitudes toward death, grace, salvation, and eternity, he manages to oppose the necessary angel of earth to them almost successfully. The contest involves no mighty opposites but says that the pleasures of living contribute all one dare expect and may anticipate no heavenly rewards. If such a predilection removes penalties often deemed essential, it likewise diminishes profits. The world does have limits, granted one knows nothing about what lies beyond them, and its chief enjoyments reside in the quite literally immaterial uses which each man makes of it himself as practicing poet. To the orthodox such a program must sound unconvincing, probably sentimental, perhaps superstitious, certainly barbarous. For Stevens it simply did not look that way, although nothing would dispose him to debate it.

He stops short before every absolute and first cause. No desire bedevils him to penetrate the heart of the universe and, like Faust, to master all. At the outset of this chapter, in quoting Klee, Stevens found the opinion tempting, indeed, but a bit haughty. The imagination notes resemblances among all that confronts it and extracts from worlds abstract patterns whose accomplishing fulfills their only end. The method, admittedly, does not compulsively need the cautious intellect, but it does not jettison it, either. An enduring rivalry exists between the two. The intellect, given to facts, can never quite catch up with the imagination as manifested in poetry. Nevertheless, the imagination, struggle as it will for complete independence, returns ultimately for support to the rational, the force which constructs power dams and dogmas.

What, then, is it to live in the mind with the imagination, yet not too near to the fountains of its rhetoric, so that one does not have a consciousness only of grandeurs, of incessant departures from the idiom and of inherent attitudes? Only the reason stands between it and the reality for which the two are engaged in a struggle. . . . Is there in fact any struggle at all and is the idea of one merely a bit of academic junk? Do not the two carry on together in the mind like two brothers or two sisters or even like young Darby and Joan? Darby says, "It is often true that what is most rational appears to be most imaginative, as in the case of Picasso." Joan replies, "It is often true, also, that what is most imaginative appears to be most rational, as in the case of Joyce. Life is hard and dear and it is the hardness that makes it dear." [141c]

Stevens readily concedes that the contest ranges from Darby and Joan to violence, but he never denies the symbiotic dependence. The irrational, in his terms, never ventures demoniacally to demand servitude from the intellect, as in much romanticism.

Under this dispensation, too, other inferences about his position and its ramifications lose their force. If by ignoring dogmas Stevens closes his ears to seraphic voices, he, likewise, frees them from heeding more worldly temptations. The fictive hero may become the real but never in public terms of office and authority. Propagandists of both the conservative and radical persuasions have praised or castigated his supposed political views. For whomever he voted—whether in fact he did—a case can be made out from either point. The disbelief in a firmly fixed order would place him among the somewhat liberal, along with his poetry, often termed avant-garde. On the other hand, horror of arriving at a single idea and fixing on it, the culminating point in "Esthétique du Mal," and an awareness that persistent qualities prevail would tend away from rebels toward conservatism. The crux refers back to the imagination and its limits. If the imagination has its bounds, so does the rational planning of politicians; both, of course, hold a place in man's affairs and in their encroachments on his time. Projecting a future order based on the present involves politics but not poetry. To a degree the catastrophes in the world may emanate from governmental bungling, but a remedy for them will not spring out of poetry, which utilizes such materials for its own purposes. In every way, then, Stevens champions freedom, his own and others', to such an extent that, beyond the bounds of poetry, he legislates for no one either in his own guise or behind a shield of superior authority. Yet, even well disposed commentators have done him a disservice in translating the extent to which he allots power to the imagination and reason.

vii

In praising the imagination he does not assign it the idolatrous function of working upon intractable matter, a pursuit open to reason. No Gnostic heresy in terms of aesthetics embarrasses him. The thoroughgoing romantic poet believes not only that he can summon spirits from some vasty deep but that they will come in their sieves from as far as Aleppo . . . The allusions could fill volumes. All such views ultimately depend on some arcane construct, the poets' rather than philosophers' stone, which exists somewhere and which the poet-priest can control. Stevens deliberately eschews such communications with the supernatural. "I am not competent to discuss reality as a philosopher. All of us understand what is meant by the transposition of an objective reality to a subjective reality. The transaction between reality and the sensibility of the poet is precisely that. . . . Poets continue to be born not made and cannot, I am afraid, be predetermined. While, on the one hand, if they could be predetermined, they might long since have become extinct, they might, on the other hand, have changed life from what it is today into one of those transformations in which they delight, and they might have seen to it that they greatly multiplied themselves there." [217–18b] Nevertheless, the view of Stevens as some spinner of charms, which alter, instead of taming, the actual, persists even among those not likely to fall victim. "Set against the imagination as shaping spirit is the desire of Stevens, expressed with equal vividness, to face things as they are. It may be that these two contradictory views are merely another instance of those opposites which fuse into a third and perfect singular—but on the other hand their incompatibility may constitute a crucial lack of clarity in his aesthetic, though perhaps the clash might better be described as a sign of countries of the mind yet to be explored." [10] Much of the thesis in which this conjecture occurs expands from the view that Stevens' poetry indulges in a sort of metamorphosis.

The concept has a certain importance in his poetry, and the word itself does appear a number of times. For literature, however, as distinguished from religion, the practice looks rather crude unless, of course, it pretends to transform the whole world in which case it becomes, except to the deluded practitioner, only puerile. Suitably the author who collected the ancient legends of metamorphoses and retold them for rationalists was a Roman citizen. The nature of simultaneously rearranging matter rests on duality; the spirit can retain its identity in new coverings: the laurel was once a fleeing girl, and the jonquil once lay by a pool as a youth. Although in other trappings to the eye, the object metamorphosed retains inside its altered shape a hidden soul or essence. Stevens begs from credulity no such easy disguises for his poetry. His need for wholeness scorns dividing the world between matter and magic. Resemblances may beget a third, or more, qualities between two objects, but the initial ones must retain their attributes. No new country of the mind will open to this shaping spirit; indeed, if such a land existed, it would be a nightmare of distortion. An outlook such as this further helps explain his suspicion of metaphor. Consequently, freely as subjects impinge upon one another, they retain their identity. If words almost equal things, objects exceed building blocks to be joined or split at will. One poem called "Metamorphosis" [265–66a] finds autumn naturally through summer as sounds and presentiments.

> *Yillow, yillow, yillow,*
> *Old worm, my pretty quirk,*
> *How the wind spells out*
> *Sep - tem - ber. . . .*

Summer is in bones.
Cock-robin's at Caracas.
Make o, make o, make o
Oto - otu - bre

. . . and so on to the end of autumn. Man, however, can do nothing to change the seasons, which revolve because they must, in the same way clouds cross the sky and birds return. For Stevens metamorphosis means "as if" and does not produce a scientific demonstration on the regrouping of atoms, molecules, and finer particles.

Poetry, then, mediates between its own transcendency and this world and by its very nature shows how it infuses, without altering, the physical. Stevens borders on admitting deeper interconnections, but generally draws back. "The truth seems to be that we live in concepts of the imagination before the reason has established them. If this is true, then reason is simply the methodizer of the imagination. It may be that the imagination is a miracle of logic and that its exquisite divinations are calculations beyond analysis, as the conclusions of the reason are calculations wholly within analysis." [154c] One comes back to the qualities for poetry as a supreme fiction. Being human, it depends on its singular creator and solitary reader or listener. Consequently, it does not have the universal inalterability of the multiplication table, but its abstractness redeems it from effete frivolity. As suggested above, abstract does not imply conceptual but rather idealized, the sort of mode decking the heroes and heroines in Greek drama. Unlike the tragic protagonists, the characters in Stevens' verse do not tower beyond this world and do not dispel their essential natures. Stevens' hero, if more than human, can inhabit a rational world. Part of the concept may derive from Nietzsche, but it indicatively shares traits still prevalent in the French theater: one thinks of Gide's plays and his analysis of fiction in *Les Faux-monnayeurs*. Giraudoux exhibits another possibility, although dramatically he pushes further into actual metamorphoses than Stevens will; his examination of the French hero in a time of war does match Stevens' poems on the same topic.

Les lieux en France où l'on peut enterrer un guerrier illustre, où puet naître un homme illustre, sont infiniment moins rares que ceux où l'on peut enterrer un soldat inconnu, où peut naître un héros anonyme. Nous n' avons pas à compter sur nos collines, nos forêts, nos rivières, nos roches pour nous fournier, au moment critique, l'aide de leurs habitants imaginaires, car chez nous collines, forêts, rivières, composent un paysage qui, loin d'être créateur, semble plutôt créé et dessiné par nos héros eux-mêmes. C'est sans doute ce que l'on a voulu exprimer en disant que la Français n'a pas le génie épique: c'est que son épopée ne comporte pas la légende, c'est que son héros n'est pas d'une race qui surclasse ou déclasse l'humanité par son corps illogique et son âme impulsive, mais un être que la fiction même ne dote que d'une taille moyenne, d'une force moyenne, dont la raison et la vérité sont strictement humaines. Comme la danse, art sans légende, la vérité française ne demande que le mouvement.[11]

Poetry causes nothing to transpire outside itself, and its own nature, even idealized, cannot give birth to actualities. It may utilize maskings, which never basically alter the thing or person covered. On every level, then, Stevens rejects miracles, obfuscation, magic, and metamorphosis except in the world of words, which may now be delimited a bit more fully.

viii

The assumption at the outset of this survey ran that what once passed for modern, experimental poetry now looks, sounds, and, therefore, is perfectly familiar. One reason for improved comprehension of such works stems from the industrious work of so many theorists linking it with the past. Beneficial as the process may have proved, particularly for those holding provincial prize days under the aegis of a great tradition, it forgets that the modern monuments represented, at least among those participating originally, a break with the past and that, thanks largely to their accomplishment, one now apprehends history partly in terms of what they have done. To work the other way and project the past into and through these works frequently distorts them. They do belong to the whole development of poetry, but they also retain individuality. Indeed, the problem, as has been noted repeatedly, of how Stevens takes a special attitude toward the past in terms of the one knowable present, has a bearing on his poetic practices and attitudes.

There are certain connoisseurs who can tell you merely from the appearance, taste, and behavior of a wine the site of its vineyard and the year of its origin. There are antiquarians who with almost uncanny accuracy will name the time and place of origin and the maker of an *objet d'art* or piece of furniture on merely looking at it. And there are even astrologers who can tell you, without any previous knowledge of your nativity, what the position of the sun and moon was and what zodiacal sign rose above the horizon in the moment of your birth. In the face of such facts, it must be admitted that moments can leave long-lasting traces. . . . The causal point of view tells us a dramatic story about how D came into existence: it took its origin from C, which existed before D, and C in its turn had a father B, etc. The synchronistic view on the other hand tries to produce an equally meaningful picture of coincidence. How does it happen that A', B', C', D', etc., appear in the same moment and in the same place? It happens in the first place because the physical events A' and B' are of the same quality as the psychic events C' and D', and further because all are the exponents of one and the same momentary situation. The situation is assumed to represent a legible or understandable picture.[12]

Stevens puts it in much the same way, although one would hesitate to call him a synchronistic connoisseur [68b]:

> The solid was an age, a period
> With appropriate, largely English, furniture,
> Barbers with charts of the only possible modes,
> Cities that would not wash away in the mist,
> Each man in his asylum maundering,
> Policed by the hope of Christmas. Summer night,
> Night gold, and winter night, night silver, these

Were the fluid, the cat-eyed atmosphere, in which
The man and the man below were reconciled,
The east wind in the west, order destroyed,
The cycle of the solid having turned.

The first quotation comes from Jung's introduction to the collection of Chinese oracles, *I Ching or the Book of Changes*, and the second a passage, by no means exceptional, from "Owl's Clover." Without advancing any conjunction so improbable as a borrowing, one might profitably consider Stevens' view as more nearly akin to the synchronistic than the causal. The analogy stands, of course, less than perfect, but it should dispel one major misapprehension. Such an outlook excuses him from answering the pointless charges brought against him. The disappearance of dramatis personae, chaos merging into order, the refusal to exclude seemingly accidental touches, and the tolerance—all tend toward this direction. Furthermore, taken in this guise, his role of connoisseur assumes, at last, its proper dimensions. His poems consider the relevant aspects within a situation by synchronistic resemblances almost apart from causes, always beyond the demonstrable except for science, which must by its nature believe in absolute causality. At the same time, rejecting science for poetry does not, in this way, become antirational. The resulting easy interchange between the physical and psychic discerns congruity in whatever exists together; imbalance, the erection of an eternal cause, creates evil falsely whether as an African Ananke, Marx laying bare the cogs of history, the rejected imagination, or an inviolable Good. In light of the way by which *I Ching* orders matter, Stevens' reluctance to construct a set of private symbols becomes necessary. A symbol tends to radiate qualities until it approaches the rigidity of myth or allegory.

Although often compared with Mallarmé's concept l'Azur, his associations with sky and air project none of the richly inflexible French connotations. He does not, however, shrink into a pedantic literalist, either. Rather, as the basic eight aspects of the oracles in *I Ching*—heaven, earth, thunder, water, mountain, wind (wood), fire, and lake—keep shifting through perpetual unions, so Stevens' recurrent images impart comparable nuances. Water in the Chinese often warns of danger, but it does not always assume an unfavorable aspect. For example, in the sixty-third oracle it betokens a time between Peace and Standstill when it hovers over fire. "If the water boils over, the fire is extinguished and its energy is lost. If the heat is too great, the water evaporates into the air. These elements here brought into relation and thus generating energy are by nature hostile to each other. . . . In life too there are junctures when all forces are in balance and work in harmony, so that everything seems to be in the best of order. In such times only the sage recognizes the moments that bode danger." For another oracle, fire burns over water, and the situation changes. "When fire, which by nature flames upward, is above, and water, which flows downward, is below, their effects take opposite directions and remain unrelated. If we wish to achieve an effect, we must first investigate the nature of the forces in question and ascertain their proper place." [13] Stevens, of course, does not predict any future from the patterns discerned in his poetry nor does he draw model conduct from them; they remain intensely genial revelations about the moment. Nevertheless, he veers closer to the synchronistic than to any "scientific" causality, and he keeps his counters quite uncommitted.

Furthermore, *I Ching* revels in resemblance nearly as avidly as does Stevens. Not only do the eight basic objects alter themselves and each other constantly but they also present added designs with their shiftings, not as superimpositions but in more discoveries. They can, thus, stand for patterns in family relationships and chart the educating of the emotions. The uses to which this book has been put vary, but it need not serve only to warn about the future. In Jung's reading the oracles uncover possibilities for the present scene to the mind, which, because of its steady preoccupations, might otherwise overlook them and itself. Stevens, naturally, codifies no set program, and his re-

peated scorning of mystical numbers would invalidate any
prefabricated system. His poems do share traits with the
Chinese images to the degree that they arouse the imagination to perceive the moment fully in terms of each individual. Nothing in a situation need be superfluous; if one
forgets the history of each object and consents to understand it as contributing a significant construct with different aspects for each beholder, one has grasped something
like potentiality. All such procedures, in light of Western
thought, could be deemed, at best, irrational, and so Stevens insists that poetry defies the intellect, almost successfully. His method, in contrast, simply may appeal to another sort of appreciation and knowledge. From this position, one can advance a counter proposal to Stevens' more
ambitious critics who have turned out four books devoted
to codifying his works under disparate rubrics.[14] Without
aspiring to the last word, the following segment may
illustrate why his view of art and the universe includes
much which they omit and ignores certain of their stoutly
championed creeds.

First, however, a note about another book, which makes
him a nearly tragic victim of American culture, may free
him from another verdict. If not without its insights, this
study considerably reduces his awareness of his own attain-
ments. "The greater paradox is this: that Stevens' quest
for an ultimate humanism (for that surely is what it is)
leads him toward a curious dehumanization. It urges (or
forces) him in the end to purify his poems until they are
hardly the poems of a man who lives, loves, hates, creates,
dies. Rather, they are the poems of a man who does
nothing but make poems; who 'abstracts' living, loving,
hating, creating, dying from his poems, in the hope that
what will be left will be not so much poetry but the
possibility of poetry." [15] Taken in a different sense from
the one which the context implies, the phrase "the possibility of poetry" provides a revealing clue. Whereas the
romantic poet—particularly an American one—requires a
humanistic base decked out in fervently vague Christian
attitudes from which to project his facsimile of living,

loving, creating, and dying, Stevens freely accepts quieter truisms: that all changes but remains, that opposites arise from each other, that intensity does not beget insight, and that poetry stays everywhere—most paradoxically—a perpetual possibility. When it reveals itself nakedly, when its persona masks a puppet sighing, "I, I, I," when it presupposes absolute programs or truths, and when it rivals religions, then, indeed, the poet has betrayed his task and become a tiresome prophet, whatever honors such charlatanism earns him. As "Prologues to What Is Possible" [515–17a], a late poem in which self-discovery still prevails, concludes:

The way some first thing coming into Northern trees
Adds to them the whole vocabulary of the South,
The way the earliest single light in the evening sky, in spring,
Creates a fresh universe out of nothingness by adding itself,
The way a look or a touch reveals its unexpected magnitudes.

To learn *how* such enlargements occur would exhaust poetry and possibility and delight only a behaviorist. Stevens' very freedom from all causes and isms—one might think—would better qualify him as a typical American, if not of New England or the southern colonies, then at least his native Pennsylvania and its tolerance derived from Penn. So far, only one essay has drawn upon this quality with any perception.[16]

Whatever the sources, taken in his way the contradiction that one of the most keenly intellectual among modern poets deals with transient insights sounds less paradoxical. The style seeks to readjust a force that too long, even in poetry, has favored syllogism and absolute symbols unlocked by a key. His words certainly imply more than a single definition, and the prominent irony, wit, vocabulary, and disbelief keep the reader from drawing pat conclusions. The position shows how misapplied the long studies and the briefer comments by John Crowe Ransom, Kenneth Burke, Yvor Winters, and Allen Tate are, however meaningful what they write may be for the philosophies which they happen to propound. Qualities they discover in his poems do not try to exist there, and, if they were to, they would not have any relevance for it. All the fuss about Stevens' making overly abstract observations, or his failures to present them cogently, demands what he seldom seeks. His substitute carries quite enough rewards in its own right. Having argued for his method, one must agree that his demonstrations do not aim to persuade. In *I Ching* the ruling assumption affirms that no condition will endure, that the six lines which compose the oracular trigrams shift with the very process of their coming together but that momentarily something can be known: order and disorder transform into each other ceaselessly. If Stevens' world lacks a first cause, neither has it an end; the final, sixty-fourth, oracle also posits other changes. Unlike the motto which T. S. Eliot reiterates so poignantly, in my end is my beginning, Stevens forever sets his world to rolling to disclose still more permutations. If the argument persists that the modern poet in the United States should not behave so irresponsibly, one can only point to what the work itself has accomplished.

ix

If discovering too many parallels for his craft with origins in the ancient Chinese borders on the fantastic, a contemporary artist may reveal closer affinities. A name frequently linked with Stevens' by commentators is Paul Klee. Drawing analogies between the arts still proves hazardous; the measure, at best, remains subjective; it quickly reaches limits beyond which speculation sounds like nonsense or improvisation. The topic fascinated Stevens, but his essay "The Relations between Poetry and Painting" establishes only tangential bonds. Nevertheless, for incidental insights a comparison might have a value, and one critic already has cited revealing traits.

Klee inhabits, really, the closed, cautious world of the modern aesthete, which admits experience only piecemeal. No grand style here, no panoramas, but many small and precious objects. Let him be put next to Marianne Moore and Wallace Stevens, and we in America shall have a more correct idea of the place of his art and a truer estimation of its intense but circumscribed power. . . . The place where Klee was born, Berne in Switzerland, lay at an intersection of French and German culture. . . . But the provincial atmosphere protected something valuable for Klee: the autochthonous, that which is native to the centuries-old South German cultural enclave and was in part the source of his originality. . . . product of the German bourgeois art style that arose out of a crossing of peasant and Gothic urban art in the late Middle Ages, more intimate and explicitly lyrical than the painting of the Rhenish cathedral masters. . . . Klee is like somebody out of an E. T. A. Hoffman [sic] story about the small-town Germany of the 18th century; comfortable, musical, modest, and fantastic—all these in his work if not his person.[17]

Stevens' art (even life) follows a parallel path. His childhood surroundings among the Pennsylvania-Germans with roots predominantly from the same heritage as Klee's would have presented him comparable initial values, even, perhaps, an ease before abstract folk art. Beguilingly enough, William Carlos Williams also alludes to a related quality: "To me there was something in the dogged toughness of his thought that gave it a Germanic quality. He always reminded me of Goethe, in his youth, when *citronen blümchen* filled his dreams, before the devastations of the moral sense had overcome him." [18] Harvard, during what has been termed its Golden Age, nevertheless, as Santayana and T. S. Eliot both knew, depended on a hub beyond London and Paris. Stevens' fascination with French culture and a semi-tropical climate duplicates Klee's, but both men remained respectably living in cities not notably bohemian. While the Bauhuas, where Klee for a time resided, dedicated itself to art, it encouraged sobriety. This background may suggest why Stevens differs as much from T. S. Eliot as Klee does from Picasso, honestly as the stay-at-homes admired the expatriates' works. Anxiety about dislocation, metropolitan neuroses, scepticism, and a collapsing culture dictated their output less compulsively because they asked fewer overwhelming questions and so had to declaim no reverberating answers. They accepted the external and inner worlds with assurance. They could draw on German metaphysics and avoid its ponderousness; they could incorporate French wit without deifying chic. In a word, they mastered eclecticism not from despair but joyfully and proceeded to create a truly integrated style. The method shares affinities with other twentieth-century artists, although it forms a strand not yet delineated. Merely for a convenient label, without insisting on a precise usage, one might call it a disestablished protestantism: salvation in art, or religion, requires solely an individual faith, which remains content by being itself; it seeks no converts.

Such an attitude has not distinguished much recent culture, if one trusts the historians of art and ideas: the uncommitted standards will not suit their most common categories. The historians, and most critics, have preferred artists who took pride in a status as physical and intellectual exiles: those commentators who celebrated the home scene could attack them because they failed to turn out products praising recent advances; critics championing the expatriates could both interpret difficult works ingeniously and, with the left hand, slap down a world which refused to heed its prophets of doom. The game has grown so popular and the rules so lax that any industrious college undergraduate can mimic the clichés convincingly. Undoubtedly many twentieth-century minds, for whatever cause, have felt disinherited. One should at the same time allow for the possibility that other conditions somewhere prevail. A society may exist which has remained comfortably settled for several centuries. It has prospered in its regional way, and the natives enjoy their possessions without mourning lost grandeurs or awaiting a richer future, without desiring greater wealth to purchase symbols of their prestige. The weather is favorable, and whatever gods the founders of the community had established on altars have, during the nineteenth century, quietly withdrawn as both givers and judges, although no one misses them particularly. In such an atmosphere to one view the sensibilities may have nothing on which to exercise; they just may enjoy an ideal freedom to develop their inner visions through a nearly pure style. Klee's whole progression, if never limited to phases and periods, presents his area with increasing profundity, and so does Stevens'. Others come to mind: Charles Demuth, with a background similar to Stevens', transposed Egypt as native silos; Logan Pearsall Smith, never a professional exile, experimented with prose; still others might include (besides Marianne Moore) Roger Fry and Dorothy Richardson—all similarly in an avant-garde if rarely signing manifestoes and joining movements. Biographical conjectures explain little about this group, who differ among themselves, and its art, which does project the trait of impersonality coupled with a special idiom. All of them, too, may partake of the times; a decidedly different temperament, Max Ernst, reports a similar discovery.

> One rainy day in 1919 in a town on the Rhine, my excited gaze is provoked by the pages of a printed catalogue. The advertisements illustrate objects relating to anthropological, microscopical, psychological, mineralogical and paleontological research. Here I discover the elements of a figuration so remote that its very absurdity provokes in me a sudden intensification of my faculties of sight—a hallucinatory succession of contradictory images, double, triple, multiple, superimposed upon each other with the persistence and rapidity characteristic of amorous memories and visions of somnolescence. These images, in turn, provoke new planes of understanding. They encounter an unknown —new and non-conformist. By simply painting or drawing, it suffices to add to the illustrations a color, a line, a landscape foreign to the objects represented—a desert, a sky, a geological section, a floor, a single straight horizontal expressing the horizon, and so forth. These changes, no more than docile reproductions of what is visible within me, record a faithful and fixed image of my hallucination.[19]

Having said this much, perhaps, sets enough limits around Stevens. Tentatively one might try to establish a sort of system within his work.

x

    To have protested a bit excessively about Stevens' lacking an inflexible philosophic method and then to introduce one so far along must appear quite inconsistent, if not self-contradictory. He knew what he was doing, and its very nature forbids scales of equivalents. As others have noticed, "The late manner does resemble that of philosophical statement; we can almost expect logical forms; we look for a consistent organization of thought; it seems that a paraphrase is almost possible, that we can state a certain meaning for a certain poem, an effort that misses most of its purpose, like telling dreams or describing music. Stevens, in spite of appearance, is never a philosophical poet expect (like other poets) in his interest in the theory of reality." [20] He himself expressed his attitude in saying, "An evening's thought is like a day of clear weather" [159b], a statement which, the longer one looks at it, the more fraught and less explainable it becomes. As a result, the observations below do not aspire to embrace all of his poems, much less propose diagrams to simplify them. In terms of the preceding pages, his fully evolved outlook does have a coherence. Its validity hardly matters outside his poetic universe; within it, it seems to have supplied him a system of faculties. He rarely indulges in the philosophic method: generalization, logic, fullness, and universality. Rather, he resembles the essayist who sketches his opinions graciously as personal preferences. This manner excuses him from rectifying inconsistencies, which worry him little, and tolerates manipulating subtly his preferred, granted rather simple and old-fashioned, opposites from the anecdotes to the late poems. For him, then, man's nonphysical faculties constitute one side and the physical world, including man's body, the other. Such a scheme does not terminate in a vicious dualism. One might arrange these two areas on a scale which implies degrees of evolution but not necessarily values. (The terms are not always Stevens'.)

[Logic]

Thinking	Order
Imaginative	Things
Practical	Quotidian
Subhuman	Rock

[Skeleton]

Communication between these areas varies, and some-times, it seems, messages get through to the wrong level. Also, he arrived at such a division gradually; although the full diagram should apply to "The Rock," only a segment describes *Harmonium*. Ideally, it works in the following way.

The column on the right causes slight difficulty. The rock consists of matter, nearly undifferentiated, intractable, almost unformed, a needed base, a blank substance which subsumes the rest. It may correspond with similar materials in the philosophies of Plato and Plotinus, although Stevens imposes no moral judgments upon it. The quotidian con-sists of items handled daily for commerce or secondary pleasures or just to keep one alive. It covers red cherry pie in a restaurant, birds and animals, an insurance policy, or an exploding bomb. The quotidian substances have no intrinsic value, although excessive prices may be put upon fashionable ones because they can symbolize nearly any-thing. In the social world they are prized for what they will accomplish, and this condition extends to people when treated as anything other than ends. Many of these very items can escape from use and exist by themselves or in a proper company of their species. They may then become things and exhibit truly poetic characteristics. Things range from a blackbird across (not up or down) to the fictive hero, from a dead soldier to an idea. Order belongs to the laws, not quite empirical, upon which the continua-tion of the rest depends: the construct behind the theory of the atom from Heraclitus to Hiroshima. None of this partakes of anything divine nor, particularly, human. The principle is not man's contrivance and exists independent of him, whether he has discovered it or not, whether he has employed it or not. Corruption of uses may disrupt any area, the quotidian being especially susceptible, but such violations cannot destroy any true essence. Stevens' consciousness of man's skill in perverting ends accounts for the dual aspect throughout all his values, particularly for the exalted ones, until he has worked out their full implications. Freedom from a dedicated belief means that nothing dare be taken on faith. "Truth"—whatever it is—belongs to no single category nor, it would seem, the sum total. These four areas impress themselves upon men differently, and here the trouble in most theory and all practice begins. The imperfect communication represents no original sin nor fall of man. The Garden of Eden, had there been any, would have had to endure the same kinds, if probably not degrees, of confusions which afflict the present.

One may as well start with the practical, to move to the column on the left, because it has not yet had much recognition in these pages. Stevens holds nothing against it, really, as long as it keeps its place, not a very elevated but regrettably an important one. The practical handles the quotidian. It tends orchards, bakes, sells, and, with most people, eats red cherry pie. It cannot formulate very much and need not have gone beyond the eighth grade in school, although it may have persisted to an LL.B. or Ph.D., and that pomposity causes part of the trouble. It fails to recognize that things in themselves—properly *by* themselves—exist and that from them the imagination can contrive valid artifacts. Apparently every man should have all four faculties, although no one has them developed in the same proportions. From an exaggerated sense of its powers, the practical supplies public statues of generals, as well as most generals, to say nothing of advertising campaigns, amplified music, organized sports, and all charlatans. Although suffering from delusions of adequacy, it possesses a pride and thus probably scorns the rock or, perhaps, finds that, having no practical value, the rock lacks existence. The subhuman it dismisses as childish or uncivilized. Its attitude toward the imaginative and things ranges from ignorance to hate, and it mismanages order, which it can barely comprehend except when applied by science as inventions. The scorn for intellect, thinking, reflects its engrained prejudices. Most traits of personality, and the more prevalent emotions, arise from this area, and consequently, in Stevens' terms, poetry can do little with character and daily desires. Indeed, poetry makes little of practical manifestations except for satire. Otherwise, it simply recoils in disinterested boredom. However one judges Stevens' attitude toward the practical, it does not rest merely on fastidiousness but shows a genuine concern for the welfare of the imaginative.

The imaginative has so many guises that no one can exhaust them; all the poems themselves cannot do that. Apparently it alone encompasses by intuition the other three areas on the left as well as, of course, all those on the right. Often it appears that the subhuman, the practical, and thinking abandon their proper functions and charter a triumvirate to overthrow the imaginative, but they have no greater chance of prevailing than do Caliban, sailors, and noblemen against Prospero. From the imaginative come all the arts and, for this discussion, particularly, poetry. Basically poetry is the imaginative treating things, and Stevens' fondness for Imagism may derive from such an outlook. The imaginative sees and enhances things nearly in defiance of their quotidian aspects, and as a result Stevens' poetry borders on surrealism, a result comparable with Max Ernst's appropriating catalogues. Likewise, his poetry must prize words because principally through vocabulary can one separate things from their quotidian bondage. For such a reason, too, poetry is "abstract"; it treats not specific daily configurations but discrete entities freed of impure functions and adjuncts. It seeks to get at an essential nature devested of its stale garb and clothed in a new magnificence. The imaginative aspires to encompass order which always eludes it because no individual objects can survive there and because it offers static paradigms while poetry requires the constant change of interplay among things. (Music, it would seem, may almost annex order, and Stevens always stresses this component of verse.) As for the rock, it challenges the imaginative; neither one can wrest all advantages from the other and banish it. Poetry, and all the arts, do not directly communicate things (nor order, nor the quotidian, nor the rock) but attributes which reveal themselves in no other fashion: a poem, or a piece of music, has no single meaning. On the other hand, the imaginative must have things and order, at least, to work with, and if it seeks independence, if it makes its muse fictive music, it betrays itself by aspiring beyond its station. Stevens always insists that the imaginative depends upon reality and that it does reach limits. Finally, the imaginative may observe the interchange between thinking, the practical, and subhuman with the outside, although such a commerce, to him, lacks poetry and belongs, perhaps, to drama and novels.

Thinking, likewise, has limits; because it deals in conceptual matters, it can make little of the rock. Ideally it would arrange values for the quotidian, like a superior parent with a child. It reassures when it becomes scientific but may veer toward sentimentality when it promises goods beyond its powers. In treating things, thinking grows philosophic or theological. The damage it may do things, in light of the imaginative, arises from its addiction to first causes and a hankering for a neat teleology. In this drive it may impose a system where none exists for a violent order and prevent the imaginative from functioning freely. Between thinking and order there can be no direct communication. Could there be, man would walk in unbearable clarity; his habits grace, his gestures art, his sounds music, his deeds charity. Through logic thinking may attempt such a direct assault on order, but it must fail as a satanic enterprise. Thinking must approach order through the imaginative, and in this view Stevens can see logic as illogical, the longest way round as the shortest way home, disorder as order, and an evening's thought as a day of clear weather. If thinking and the imaginative ever could join forces, they might abridge logic, but, so far, they agree like Darby and Joan, at best. When it regards literature, thinking clumsily insists upon moral allegory. As with all the other instances of rivalry between faculties, which should bolster each other, Stevens accepts the condition and does not rail against it. Together they might compose that central diamond, but it cannot become a habitation. The imaginative, thus, cannot work miracles, cannot redeem the supposed evils contrived by other faculties, cannot practice metamorphosis, but it provides the sole refuge from many ills.

The subhuman comes and goes in these poems, and one can make only limited guesses about it. Its force would seem largely negative. Like thinking, it can never encompass order. Intimations about order lead to superstitions, to the worship of false deities: Ananke in Africa or the imago of modern Europe. It may preach an impossible order based on fundamentalist phantasies about an unknowable heaven or hell; it cannot understand the rock, either. Linked to the material world by a skeleton, it would deny any human life if joined with the bones. Because they help compose man, something human may cling to them, so far can the imaginative extend. When the subhuman observes the quotidian, it unleashes the vulgarities of primitive desire corrupted by industrialization, but its lack of restraints may have a pathos which the more genteel practical lacks. If it joins with the imaginative to grasp things, the results provide an antidote to prevailing complacency through valid poems, such as "Domination of Black" or "Like Decorations in a Nigger Cemetery." Such bizarre pieces may express an essential violence understandable in no other way. The subhuman does not match the Freudian concept of the Id, although they share some affinities, nor does it quite perpetuate Jung's postulate of a racial memory. It has little more than any other faculty to do with the emotions. For Stevens, emotions may reside anywhere as an accompaniment of communications between faculties, although pleasure, particularly, belongs to the noting of resemblances and from this pursuit composes poems. Perhaps, however, these conjectures have pushed too far into a topic which engaged Stevens only intermittently. One example shows how these elements cohere in a poem with the engaging title, "The Desire to Make Love in a Pagoda" [91–92b]:

> Among the second selves, sailor, observe
> The rioter that appears when things are changed,
>
> Asserting itself in an element that is free,
> In the alien freedom that such selves degustate:
>
> In the first inch of night, the stellar summering
> At three-quarters gone, the morning's prescience,
>
> As if, alone on a mountain, it saw far-off
> An innocence approaching toward its peak.

On a first reading the poem offers certain difficulties, which soon disappear without requiring external references. To draw upon the categories just defined, the imaginative catches up the practical, likened to the voyager among the quotidian. In comparison with the actual freedom of things, a sailor's rowdy life grows tame. For example, at the approach of a summer evening a star (containing day as well as night) suggests an order belonging to another faculty. For such a view the world may offer a charm not found in foreign ports, especially through the juxtaposition of *innocence* against *love* of the title. With further implications, one may remember other poems: the pacing soldier of "Examination of the Hero in a Time of War," the enslaved sailors of "Life on a Battleship," the innocent star of "Martial Cadenza," and the quiet evening of "Homunculus et la Belle Étoile." The figure against the mountain might step from "Chocorua to Its Neighbor," and the general atmosphere suggests "The Poem That Took the Place of a Mountain." One may find the title still too whimsical. It seems to imply that the wish for happiness in a quite foreign place may be realized more easily through the imaginative than among the quotidian. For most people in the United States a pagoda does not occur as part of the daily scene outside oriental settlements. It may, however, have a more literal denotation. Once again,

Stevens can take a quotidian object, one almost uniquely hackneyed, and make it into a subject suitable for his poem without commentary on its common use.

On a hill above Reading, Pennsylvania, where Stevens was born, stands a pagoda, clear against the sky from the low city. It has no discernible function. Presumably constructed around the turn of this century for a projected hotel otherwise not completed, it rises quite incredible and real. Possibly some association with this incongruous building entered Stevens' mind in putting together the poem. Such a geographical footnote does not further the meaning, and it illustrates the quotidian intruding upon things, as literary documentation has a way of doing. At the same time, that the citizens of Reading have it there at all tells something about them, since they reflect their region; in its stilted manner it may indicate an aspiration toward the imaginative, however crudely expressed. The pagoda can serve only as a quotidian object in the hands of the practical when a local firm calls itself the Pagoda Candy Company and takes for its motto, "The height of quality in the Pennsylvania-Dutch country." The line is more confusing, and less musical, than anything Stevens ever wrote; without the key to the allusion, it is nonsense. Is a pagoda candy company more accountable than an emperor of ice-cream? Why does a pagoda, particularly in the United States, designate height? What do both concepts have to do with the quality of candy? How does a pagoda get among the Pennsylvania-Germans at all? Stevens never takes such liberties in altering the nature of "reality."

The play "Three Travelers Watch a Sunrise" draws these associations more closely together. It places three Chinese wanderers on "a hilltop in eastern Pennsylvania. . . . It is about four o'clock of a morning in August." [127b] Accompanying them are two mute Negro servants. The three observe their ceremonies until a girl interrupts them with the story of the murder of the man who loved her. The discovery of the corpse does not detain the travelers very long. In synopsis the plot sounds thoroughly fanciful, yet it merely elaborates on the most fundamental assumptions throughout these poems. The servants exemplify the subhuman, inarticulate and yet of some use. The violence, with similarities to his earliest story published in the *Harvard Advocate*, "Her First Escapade," stands for all the uncertainties of the quotidian and the troubles it causes the practical. The three travelers with only lightly sketched personalities become the imaginative. The play concludes with a poetic soliloquy about things [142–43b]:

THIRD CHINESE

> Of the color of blood . . .
> Seclusion of porcelain . . .
> Seclusion of sunrise . . .
>> [*He picks up the water bottle.*]
>
> The candle of the sun
> Will shine soon
> On this hermit earth.
>> [*indicating the bottle*]
>
> It will shine soon
> Upon the trees,
> And find a new thing
>> [*indicating the body*]
>
> Painted on this porcelain
>> [*indicating the trees*]
>
> But not on this
>> [*indicating the bottle*]
>> [*He places the bottle on the ground. A narrow cloud over the valley becomes red. He turns toward it, then walks to the right. He finds the book of the Second Chinese lying on the ground, picks it up and turns over the leaves.*]
>
> Red is not only
> The color of blood,
> Or
>> [*indicating the body*]

Of a man's eyes,
Or
                    [*pointedly*]

Of a girl's.
And as the red of the sun
Is one thing to me
And one thing to another,
So it is the green of one tree
                    [*indicating*]

And the green of another,
Without which it would all be black.
Sunrise is multiplied,
Like the earth on which it shines,
By the eyes that open on it,
Even dead eyes,
As red is multiplied by the leaves of the trees.

Around fifteen years before this the blind girl outside the hospital had asked in similar terms about the flowers she held: " 'Red roses, I wonder, red with the Spring, | Red with a reddish light?' " [21] And, nearly twenty years after the play a description without place reaches this culmination [345–46a]

It matters, because everything we say
Of the past is description without place, a cast

Of the imagination made in sound;
And because what we say of the future must portend,

Be alive with its own seemings, seeming to be
Like rubies reddened by rubies reddening.

And nearly ten years after this, one of his last poems contains [529a]:

It is like a new account of everything old,
Matisse at Vence and a great deal more than that,
A new-colored sun, say, that will soon change forms
And spread hallucinations on every leaf.

Far from being a withdrawn connoisseur, Stevens stands in his landscape through all weathers to record its constancy within changes. In his world the ordinary light and what it connects give his imagination all he needs except, of course, the necessary darkness. Ultimately he appears one of the least specialized and most consistent poets. The multiple pleasures which spring from these abstracted things and shifting resemblances order his whole poetic: native and cosmopolitan, vigorous and aloof, uncompromising and witty, primordial and elegant, idiomatic and stylized.

1—Images

1. Wallace Stevens, *Opus Posthumous*, ed., Samuel French Morse (New York, 1957), p. 166. Subsequent citations in the text are to the following:

   a. *Collected Poems* (New York: A. A. Knopf, 1954)

   b. *Opus Posthumous* (New York: A. A. Knopf, 1957)

   c. *The Necessary Angel* (New York: A. A. Knopf, 1951)

   d. *Mattino Domenicale*, tr. Renato Poggioli (Milan, 1954)

To keep many pages from resembling a crenelation, when a poem is discussed a single reference, following its title, appears. Longer poems are broken into subdivisions. The short prose pieces are likewise, if analyzed as a unit, cited only once.

2. *Oeuvres*, (Paris, 1957), I, 482.

3. *Historical Review of Berks County*, XXIV (Fall, 1959); the Wallace Stevens number.

4. William Carlos Williams, *Selected Essays* (New York, 1954), p. 12.

5. Wallace Stevens, reply to "The Situation in American Writing: Seven Questions," *The Partisan Reader*, eds., William Phillips and Philip Rahv (New York, 1946), p. 619.

6. Amy Lowell, *Complete Poetical Works* (Boston, 1955), p. 433.

7. Wallace Stevens, "Part of His Education," *Harvard Advocate*, LXVII (April 24, 1899), 36–37.

8. R. P. Blackmur, "The Great Grasp of Unreason," *Hudson Review*, IX (Winter, 1956/57), 503.

9. Laura Riding and Robert Graves, A *Survey of Modernist Poetry* (London, 1927), pp. 216–17.

10. Stanley K. Coffman, Jr., *Imagism* (Norman, Oklahoma, 1951).

11. *The Partisan Reader*, pp. 619–20.

12. Harry Crosby, *Transit of Venus*, intro., T. S. Eliot (Paris, 1931), p. 45.

13. T. S. Eliot, *On Poetry and Poets* (New York, 1957), pp. 121–22.

14. Jean Cocteau, *Jean Marais* (Paris, 1951), p. 89.

15. John Pauker, "A Discussion of Sea Surface Full of Clouds," *Furioso*, V (Fall, 1951), 39.

16. *The Partisan Reader*, pp. 596–97, 620.

17. Harry Levin, "Statement," *Harvard Advocate*, CXXVII (December, 1940), 30.

18. Wallace Stevens, "Outside the Hospital," *Harvard Advocate*, LXIX (March 29, 1900), 18.

19. Marianne Moore, *Collected Poems* (New York, 1951), pp. 131–32.

20. Randall Jarrell, *Poetry and the Age* (New York, 1953), p. 136.

21. T. S. Eliot, *Complete Poems and Plays* (New York, 1952), p. 145.

22. Stéphane Mallarmé, *Oeuvres Complètes* (Paris, 1945), p. 433.

23. Max Beerbohm, *Around Theatres* (London, 1953), p. 316.

24. Samuel French Morse, "Wallace Stevens: Some Ideas about the Thing Itself," *Boston University Studies in English*, II (Spring, 1956), 57.

25. A. Alvarez, *The Shaping Spirit* (London, 1958), p. 132.

26. Letter quoted in Wallace Stevens, *Poems*, ed. and intro. Samuel French Morse (New York, 1959), p. vii.

27. Henry James, *Novels and Tales* (New York, 1907–9), XII, 138–39.

28. T. S. Eliot, *Complete Poems and Plays*, p. 40.

29. John Donne, *Poems*, ed., Herbert J. Grierson (London, 1951), I, 62.

30. T. S. Eliot, *Complete Poems and Plays*, p. 5.

2—On the Harmonium

1. *The Film of Murder in the Cathedral* (London, 1952), p. 7.

2. Letter to Renato Poggioli, in the Houghton Library, Harvard University.

3. Richard Ellmann, "Wallace Stevens' Ice-Cream," *Kenyon Review*, XIX (Winter, 1957), 103.

4. Edmund Wilson, *The Shores of Light* (New York, 1952), p. 50.

5. Charles Baudelaire, *Oeuvres* (Paris, 1954), p. 283.

6. Wallace Stevens, "Quatrain," *Harvard Advocate*, LXVII (November 13, 1899), 63.

7. Steve Feldman, "Reality and the Imagination," *University of Kansas City Review*, XXI (Autumn, 1954), 43.

8. Letter in *This Is My Best*, ed., Whit Burnett (New York, 1942), p. 652.

9. Allen Tate, *Poems, 1922–1947* (New York, 1948), p. 98.

10. *Grove's Dictionary of Music and Musicians*, 5th ed., ed., Eric Blom (New York, 1954), V, 1014.

11. Paul Valéry, *Oeuvres*, I, 148–51.

12. W. B. Yeats, *A Vision* (London, 1937), pp. 219–20.

13. J. V. Cunningham, "Tradition and Modernity: Wallace Stevens," in *The Achievement of Wallace Stevens*, eds., Ashley Brown and Robert S. Haller (Philadelphia, 1962), pp. 137–38.

14. Andrew Marvell, *Poems and Letters*, ed., H. M. Margoliouth (Oxford, 1927), I, 49.

15. William Carlos Williams, *Selected Essays*, pp. 12–13.

3—On a Blue Guitar

1. *Vision and Design* (New York, 1947), p. 47.

2. Donald Sutherland, "An Observation on Wallace

Stevens in Connection with Supreme Fictions," *Trinity Review*, VIII (May, 1954), 41.

3. Charles Baudelaire, *Oeuvres*, p. 187.

4. Marianne Moore, *Predilections* (New York, 1955), p. 35.

5. Friedrich Nietzsche, *Werke* (Munich, 1960), II, 906–7.

6. Edith Sitwell, *Collected Poems* (London, 1930), pp. 256–57.

7. George McFadden, "Probings for an Integration: Color Symbolism in Wallace Stevens," *Modern Philology*, LVIII (February, 1961), 186–93.

8. Hi Simons, "The Humanism of Wallace Stevens," *Poetry*, LXI (November, 1942), 450.

9. *The I Ching or Book of Changes*, intro. C. G. Jung, tr. into German Richard Wilhelm, tr. into English Cary F. Baynes (New York, 1950), I, 57.

10. Virginia Woolf, *To the Lighthouse* (New York, 1927), pp. 99–100.

11. E. M. Forster, *Virginia Woolf* (Cambridge, 1942), p. 28.

12. Northrop Frye, *Anatomy of Criticism* (Princeton, 1957), p. 367.

13. John Peale Bishop, *Collected Essays*, ed., Edmund Wilson (New York, 1948), p. 371.

14. Georges Braque, "Reflexions," *Verve*, II (September–November, 1940), 56.

4—*On Old Lutheran Bells*

1. Aristotle, *Poetics*, ed., W. Hamilton Fyfe (London, 1953), pp. 88–90.

2. Yvor Winters, *The Anatomy of Nonsense* (Norfolk, Connecticut, 1943), p. 103.

3. Wallace Stevens, *Parts of a World* (New York, 1942), p. 183.

4. Edmund Spenser, *Complete Poetical Works*, ed., R. E. Neil Dodge (Boston, 1908), p. 136.

5. W. B. Yeats, *A Vision*, p. 180.

6. Yvor Winters, *Collected Poems* (Denver, 1952), p. 16.

7. Paul Valéry, *Oeuvres*, I, 298.

8. Michael Lafferty, "Wallace Stevens: a Man of Two Worlds," *Historical Review of Berks County*, XXIV, 111–12.

9. Egon Friedell, *Kulturgeschichte der Neuzeit* (Munich, 1930), I, 3.

10. Virginia Woolf, *The Second Common Reader* (New York, 1932), p. 253.

11. Northrop Frye, "The Realistic Oriole: a Study of Wallace Stevens," *Hudson Review*, X (Autumn, 1957), 363.

12. *Ibid.*, p. 367.

13. Henry James, *Novels and Tales*, II, xvii–xviii.

5—And Judgments

1. Wallace Stevens, Letter in *Fifty Poets*, ed., William Rose Benét (New York, 1933), p. 46.

2. Wallace Stevens, "The Emperor of Ice-Cream," *Explicator*, VII (November, 1948), unpaginated.

3. Wallace Stevens, "Four Characters," *Harvard Advocate*, LXIX (June 16, 1900), 120.

4. John Crowe Ransom, *The World's Body* (New York, 1938), pp. 60–61.

5. Kenneth Burke, *A Grammar of Motives* (New York, 1945), pp. 224–26.

6. Charles Baudelaire, *Oeuvres*, p. 90.

7. Newton P. Stallknecht, "Absence in Reality," *Kenyon Review*, XXI (Autumn, 1959), 546–47.

8. Allen Tate, *The Forlorn Demon* (Chicago, 1953), p. 61.

9. Howard Nemerov, "The Poetry of Wallace Stevens," *Sewanee Review*, LXV (Winter, 1957), 12–13.

10. Sister M. Bernetta Quinn, *The Metamorphic Tradition in Modern Poetry* (New Brunswick, N. J., 1955), p. 83.

11. Jean Giraudoux, *Oeuvres littéraires diverses* (Paris, 1958), pp. 611–12.

12. *I Ching*, I, iii–v.

13. *Ibid.*, pp. 261, 266.

14. William Van O'Connor, *The Shaping Spirit* (Chicago, 1950); Robert Pack, *Wallace Stevens* (New Brunswick, N. J., 1958); Frank Kermode, *Wallace Stevens* (New York, 1961); William York Tindall, *Wallace Stevens* (Minneapolis, 1961).

15. Roy Harvey Pearce, *The Continuity of American Poetry* (Princeton, 1961), p. 413.

16. Samuel French Morse, "The Native Element," in *The Achievement of Wallace Stevens*, pp. 193–210.

17. Clement Greenberg, untitled chapter in *Five Essays on Paul Klee*, ed., Merle Armitage (New York, 1950), pp. 29–33.

18. William Carlos Williams, "Wallace Stevens," *Poetry*, LXXXVII (January, 1956), 234.

19. William S. Lieberman, ed., *Max Ernst* (New York, 1961), pp. 11–12.

20. Frank Doggett, "Wallace Stevens' Later Poetry," *ELH*, XXV (June, 1958), 153.

21. Cf. note 18, Chapter 1.

INDEX

THIS LIST contains all titles of Stevens' poetry and prose mentioned in the text. It does not have references for short passages given principally to expand upon a point when another work is under discussion.

About One of Marianne Moore's Poems, 14–15

Academic Discourse at Havana, 108, 110

Adagia, 18, 143, 178, 209

Add This to Rhetoric, 136

Agenda, 132

American Sublime, The, 100–01

Anatomy of Monotony, 70

Anecdotal Revery, 55

Anecdote of Canna, 55

Anecdote of Men by the Thousand, 55, 68

Anecdote of the Abnormal, 55, 90–92

Anecdote of the Jar, 34–37, 55, 102

Anecdote of the Prince of Peacocks, 55, 184

Angel Surrounded by Paysans, 171

Another Weeping Woman, 54

Apostrophe to Vincentine, The, 54

Arcades of Philadelphia the Past, 29

Arrival at the Waldorf, 131, 141

Asides on the Oboe, 150

As You Leave the Room, 192

Auroras of Autumn, The [book], 45, 182, 183, 189

Auroras of Autumn, The [poem], 183–85

Ballade of the Pink Parasol, 18

Banal Sojourn, 67–68, 70

Bantams in Pine-Woods, 166, 168

Bed of Old John Zeller, The, 179

Bird with the Coppery, Keen Claws, The, 80–81, 118

Blue Buildings in the Summer Air, The, 102, 137

Botanist on Alp [No. 1 & 2], 104, 105

Bouquet, The, 188

Bouquet of Roses in Sunlight, 187–88

Bowl, Cat and Broomstick, 30

Brave Man, The, 98

Candle a Saint, The, 135, 173

Carlos among the Candles, 30, 54

Chocorua to Its Neighbor, 169–71, 241

Collected Poems, 44, 45, 46, 97, 132, 133, 147, 152, 209

Collect of Philosophy, A, 211

Comedian as the Letter C, The, 21, 31, 49, 84–92, 172

Common Life, The, 134

Completely New Set of Objects, A, 180

Connoisseur of Chaos, 136–37, 138

Constant Disquisition of the Wind, The, 20

Contrary Theses [1 & 2], 150

Cortège for Rosenbloom, 52–53

Creations of Sound, The, 159–60

Credences of Summer, 175–77, 183

Crude Foyer, 160

Cuisine Bourgeoise, 134

Dance of the Macabre Mice, 101–2, 137, 166

Death of a Soldier, The, 144, 146, 150

Debris of Life and Mind, 180

Delightful Evening, 100

Description without Place, 172–74, 178, 244

Desire to Make Love in a Pagoda, The, 241

Dish of Peaches in Russia, A, 29

Disillusionment of Ten O'Clock, 52

Domination of Black, 71–72, 189, 240

Drum-Majors in the Labor Day Parade, The, 102

Dry Loaf, 150

Dutch Graves in Bucks County, 177–78

Earthy Anecdote, 55

Emperor of Ice-Cream, The, 199–203

Esthétique du Mal [book], 45, 185

Esthétique du Mal [poem], 21, 160, 203–7, 221

Evening without Angels, 108, 110

Examination of the Hero in a Time of War, 151–55, 241

Extracts from Addresses to the Academy of Fine Ideas, 137–40, 143, 196

Fading of the Sun, A, 106

Farewell to Florida, 108, 131, 183

Figure of the Youth as Virile Poet, The, 212

Final Soliloquy of the Interior Paramour, 190–91

Fish-Scale Sunrise, A, 98

Five Grotesque Pieces, 103

Floral Decorations for bananas, 68–70

Forces, the Will & the Weather, 29

Four Characters, 201

Frogs Eat Butterflies. Snakes Eat Frogs. Hogs Eat Snakes. Men Eat Hogs, 98

From the Misery of Don Joost, 54

Ghosts as Cocoons, 103–4, 173

God Is Good. It Is a Beautiful Night, 158

Good Man Has No Shape, The, 178

Gray Stones and Gray Pigeons, 99

Green Plant, The, 190

Gubbinal, 69

Harmonium: 8, 44, 46–48, 54–59 *passim*, 69, 72, 76, 77, 78, 81–94 *passim*, 96, 97, 98, 100, 102, 108, 111–14 *passim*, 129, 130, 135, 140, 147, 149, 150, 151, 156, 158, 172, 177, 187, 189, 212, 236

Her First Escapade, 243

High-Toned Old Christian Woman, A, 75–76, 162

Homunculus et La Belle Étoile, 56–58, 72, 241

How to Live. What to Do, 98–99

Idea of Order at Key West, The, 108–11

Ideas of Order [Alcestis Press], 7, 44

Ideas of Order [Knopf], 7, 44, 93, 96, 97, 102–5, 108, 110, 113, 114, 122, 125

Idiom of the Hero, 134

In the Carolinas, 98

In the Clear Season of Grapes, 48

In the Dead of Night, 53

In the Northwest, 49

In the South, 49

Jasmine's Beautiful Thoughts underneath the Willow, 54

John Crowe Ransom: Tennessean, 36–37

Jouga, 160

Last Looks at the Lilacs, 54–55, 57

Latest Freed Man, The, 135

Lebensweisheitspielerei, 190

Lettres d'un Soldat, 146

Life Is Motion, 53

Life on a Battleship, 132–34, 138, 218, 241

Like Decorations in a Nigger Cemetery, 111–13, 114, 122, 134, 162, 240

Lions in Sweden, 104–5, 135

Load of Sugar-Cane, The, 48, 187

Loneliness in Jersey City, 25

Long and Sluggish Lines, 190

Lytton Strachey, Also, Enters into Heaven, 102

Man Carrying Thing, 159

Man on the Dump, The, 131–32

Man Whose Pharynx Was Bad, The, 69–70

Man with the Blue Guitar, The [book], 28, 44, 96–97, 103, 111, 112, 113, 120, 129

Man with the Blue Guitar, The [poem], 13, 31, 52, 74, 96, 97, 111, 113, 114, 121–30, 135, 138, 164, 169–70, 171, 186

Martial Cadenza, 150–51, 158, 170, 241

Mattino Domenicale, 123

Mechanical Optimist, The, 103

Meditation Celestial and Terrestrial, 98

Men Made Out of Words, 178

Men That Are Falling, The, 97, 129–30

Metamorphosis, 223–24

Metaphors of a Magnifico, 16–17, 20, 60, 111, 170, 174

Monocle de Mon Oncle, Le, 31, 81–85

Mozart, 1935, 106

Mrs. Alfred Uruguay, 137

Mud Master, 98

Mythology Reflects Its Region, A, 182

Necessary Angel, The, 45, 207–8, 211

New England Verses, 61

Noble Rider and the Sound of Words, The, 210–12, 215

No Possum, No Sop, No Taters, 158

Note on "Les Plus Belles Pages", A, 58–59

Note on Samuel French Morse, A, 42

Note on "The Emperor of Ice-Cream", A, 200–01

Notes toward a Supreme Fiction [book], 45, 147

Notes toward a Supreme Fiction [poem], 21, 155, 156, 161–69

Of Hartford in a Purple Light, 29

Of Ideal Time and Choice, 209–10

Old Lutheran Bells at Home, The, 180–81

On "Domination of Black," 70–71

On the Adequacy of Landscape, 135

On "The Emperor of Ice-Cream," 200

On the Manner of Addressing Clouds, 64–66, 73

On the Road Home, 136

Opus Posthumous, 45, 102, 114, 117, 123, 182, 211

Ordinary Evening in New Haven, An, 21, 181–82

Outside the Hospital, 18, 244

Owl in the Sarcophagus, The, 188

Owl's Clover [book], 44

Owl's Clover [poem], 28–29, 44, 66, 96, 97, 101, 113, 114–22, 123, 129, 130, 134, 137, 152, 153, 165, 183, 227

Palace of the Babies, 72

Parochial Theme, 131

Part of His Education, 6–7

Parts of a World, 44, 96, 97, 130–36 *passim,* 140, 143, 147, 148, 151, 152, 156

Pecksniffiana, 54

Peter Quince at the Clavier, 76–77

Phases, 19, 146

Pieces, 159

Place of Poetry—Inaccessible Utopia, The, 74

Plain Sense of Things, The, 187

Pleasures of Merely Circulating, The, 99–100

Ploughing on Sunday, 48

Plus Belles Pages, Les, 58

Poem that Took the Place of a Mountain, The, 170, 241

Poetry Is a Destructive Force, 135

Postcard from the Volcano, A, 107–8, 109, 130, 192

Prejudice against the Past, The, 22–24, 26–27

Primitive like an Orb, A [book], 45, 185

Primitive like an Orb, A [poem], 185–87

Primordia, 48–49, 53, 57, 111, 177

Prologues to What Is Possible, 230

Quatrain ["Go not, young cloud . . ."], 65

Reader, The, 99

Red Loves Kit, 83

Relations between Poetry and Painting, The, 231

Repetitions of a Young Captain, 156–57, 170

Re-statement of Romance, 99

Revolutionists Stop for Orangeade, The, 146–47

"Rock, The," [part of *Collected Poems*], 45, 183, 190, 191, 193, 236

Rock, The [poem], 191

Romance for a Demoiselle lying in the Grass, 54

Sad Strains of a Gay Waltz, 106

Sailing after Lunch, 105, 168

Sail of Ulysses, The, 193

Search for Sound Free from Motion, The, 178

Sea Surface Full of Clouds, 61–65, 72–73, 86, 108, 111, 113, 175, 178, 212

Silver Plough-Boy, The, 48

Six Significant Landscapes, 60

Snow Man, The, 67–68, 70, 158

So-And-So Reclining on Her Couch, 160

Some Friends from Pascagoula, 98

Someone Puts a Pineapple Together, 9–10, 209

Statement on jacket of *Ideas of Order*, 96

Statement on jacket of *The Man with the Blue Guitar*, 97

Statement on poetry and war in *Parts of a World*, 148

Sunday Morning, 59, 77–84 *passim*, 90, 108, 117, 118, 130, 138, 154, 163, 167, 182, 188, 206

Sun This March, The, 98–99, 130

Sur Ma Guzzla Gracile, 54

Tattoo, 69

Tea, 48

Tea at the Palaz of Hoon, 185

Theory, 66–67

Things of August, 189–90

Thinking of a Relation between the Images of Metaphors, 180

Thirteen Ways of Looking at a Blackbird, 9, 60, 185

Thought Revolved, A, 97, 103

Three Academic Pieces [book], 45

Three Academic Pieces [essay and poems], 209–10

Three Travelers Watch a Sunrise, 30, 50, 242–44

To an Old Philosopher in Rome, 31–32

To the One of Fictive Music, 72–75, 81

To the Roaring Wind, 57

Transport to Summer, 45, 143, 155–61 *passim*, 169, 172, 177

Two at Norfolk, 54

Two Figures in Dense Violet Night, 54

Two Illustrations That the World Is What You Made of It, 20

Two Prefaces, 26, 59

Two Versions of the Same Poem, 179

Variations on a Summer Day, 134–35

Waving Adieu, Adieu, Adieu, 105–6

What They Call Red Cherry Pie, 103

Wind Shifts, The, 48

Winter Bells, 99

Woman That Had More Babies than That, The, 133–34, 135

Woman Who Blamed Life on a Spaniard, The, 83–84

World as Meditation, The, 193

World Is Larger in Summer, The, 20

Worms at Heaven's Gate, The, 50–52